TWISTY LITTLE PASSAGES

TWISTY LITTLE PASSAGES

AN APPROACH TO INTERACTIVE FICTION

NICK MONTFORT

THE MIT PRESS
CAMBRIDGE, MASSACHUSETTS
LONDON, ENGLAND

First MIT Press paperback edition, 2005

This book was set in Bembo and Meta by The MIT Press and was printed and bound in the United States of America.

Library of Congress Cataloging-in-Publication Data

Montfort, Nick.
Twisty little passages : an approach to interactive fiction / Nick Montfort.
p. cm.
Includes bibliographical references and index.
ISBN 978-0-262-13436-1 (hc.: alk. paper), 978-0-262-63318-5 (pb)
1. Interactive multimedia. 2. Digital media. I. Title.
QA76.76.I59M66 2004
006.7—dc21   2003051374

The Shield—Riddle No. 5, taken from *The Exeter Book of Riddles* published by Penguin Books UK, Copyright © Kevin Crossley-Holland 1965 by kind permission of the author c/o Rogers, Coleridge & White Ltd., London, W11 1JN.

CONTENTS

Many different forms are usefully discussed as "computer literature" or "electronic literature": MUDs and MOOs, hypertext fiction, automatic story and poetry generators, and conversational programs (also called chatterbots), to name just a few. Many different sorts of cybertexts, electronic or not, present different texts to be read depending upon the actions of the reader: the Choose Your Own Adventure book, the systematic oracle, the box of pages that can be shuffled into any order and then read. This book is about one form, interactive fiction, which includes what has been called the "text game" or "text adventure" along with other works, some of them quite unusual, that cannot be easily classed as adventures or games. Such works are able to understand natural language input to some extent and, based on such input, to effect action in a systematic world that they simulate.

Specifically, the interactive fiction works considered here are those computer programs that display text, accept textual responses, and then display additional text in reaction to what has been typed (Jerz 2000a; Short 2001). The exchange between user and computer (textual, in the case considered here) continues until the person interacting terminates the program or reaches a conclusion.

For a work to be interactive fiction, as the term is understood by those who use it today, it must be able to react to input meaningfully. The component that analyzes natural language input in an interactive fiction work is called the *parser*. A program is not interactive fiction if it simply prints the same series of texts, or a random series of texts, in response to input, or if it outputs some transformation of the input string without understanding that string. A textual work that offers an interface that does not accept natural language at times (e.g., it sometimes presents menus, or once in a while asks a question that is to be answered with *y* or *n*) can still be an interactive fiction work, however, as long as natural language is used in the normal framework for interaction. This aspect was singled out by literary critics early on as important in defining the form: "In the development of interactive fiction, the original 'Adventure' with its legion of imitators and successors is important because, for the first time, the game let the reader answer with words instead of numbers" (Niesz and Holland 1984, 114).

The setting of an interactive fiction work—whether it exists purely for exploration, functions mostly as a metaphorical table holding jigsaw-like puzzle challenges, or serves as an obviously novel location in which meaningful events play out—is more than a setting. It is a simulated *world*, which in practice is represented computationally in some sort of data structure or collection of objects. It is this simulated world that distinguishes a work of interactive fiction from a conversational character or from an expert system that employs natural language understanding. Even if the conversational character is drawn with literary care, even if the expert system operates on some fictional or fantastic domain that suggests a bizarre world or situation, such programs are not interactive fiction, since they do not simulate worlds in a way that allows the interactor to act and see the results of simulated actions within those worlds.

Since interactive fiction works are not best understood as electronic documents, no one should expect them to be like Web pages or other sorts of linked constructions. But they also are not understood well in terms of certain systems that accept text input and generate text, such as relational databases—systems in which queries generate reports from tables. Similarly, they are difficult to understand in terms of video games, since the few elements that they share with video games function quite differently in interactive fiction. They are unique programs, best understood in terms of their two essential components, the world model and the parser, which implement the two essential features of interactive fiction.

The world model is typically implemented in the interactive fiction program as some type of graph or tree of structures of some sort (e.g., record, object, list) with associated procedures, methods, or functions (Graves 1987). It represents the physical environment of the interactive fiction and the things in that environment, including characters, any physical objects in the setting that can be manipulated or further examined in any way, and the player character. It also represents, and simulates, the physical laws of that "setting"—one reason this element is more appropriately called the interactive fiction world. The passage of time, the player character's possible ways of progressing through the required tasks, the levels of awareness of different characters, and such things as the presence or absence of light in different areas are all modeled by this component.

The parser is that part of the program that accepts natural language input from the interactor and analyzes it. ("Parser" is used as a term for all components of the program that handle natural language input, including some components that are distinguished from parsers in natural language processing.) In the case of *Adventure*'s "two-word" parser, which only accepts input of the form "verb" or "verb noun," determining the grammatical structure of the input is trivial. More complex sentences are accepted by other interactive fiction works. Such input can be compared to recognized structures by the parser, considering those objects that might possibly be referred to, and the likeliest match can then be accepted. Since the input text only needs to be interpreted in relation to the simulated world and the range of actions possible within that world, this analysis is tractable. Outside interactive fiction, even "go west" might mean any of several things (it could be, e.g., a suggestion that a young person explore new options, a cheer for an all-star team, or a euphemism for death), but in the specific domain of interactive fiction such input can be understood reliably and unambiguously.

The implementation of the world model and the parser can differ, and there is nothing about the definition of interactive fiction presented here that requires they actually be implemented as cleanly separated modules. It is still useful to distinguish these two "parts" of an interactive fiction program, however, corresponding as they do to the two major essential functions performed by an interactive fiction work. There are other ways to talk about the elements and functioning of an interactive fiction work, some of which I detail in the book's first two chapters; these two are mentioned here since they are so closely related to the definition of the form.

The overall organization of this book is roughly chronological, with most chapters considering a certain era of interactive fiction. The subjects of chapters do overlap in time, and the book's earliest topics are from long before the first actual interactive fiction work was created. Chapter 1 introduces the form in a bit more detail while discussing its current place in electronic literature scholarship, then provides a short annotated transcript and a discussion of the elements of the form from the perspective of narratology. Chapter 2 deals with the most important and oldest ancestor of interactive fiction, the riddle, describing that form's history and the way in which its workings can help us understand interactive fiction. Chapter 3 discusses *Adventure* after looking at important predecessors to interactive fiction, including literary machines, *Dungeons and Dragons,* computer games, conversational computer programs, and SHRDLU. Chapter 4 considers the mainframe era and those games developed at universities in reaction to *Adventure,* with a focus on the most widely distributed and influential interactive fiction work from that time, *Zork.* The beginning of commercial interactive fiction for the personal computer is the subject of chapter 5, which deals mainly with the popular interactive fiction works of Infocom. Competing companies who produced interactive fiction works during the commercial era, including those outside the United States, are considered in chapter 6. Chapter 7 steps back in time to describe how development of "homebrew" interactive fiction began and how such development, along with the beginnings of an online community, resulted in new sorts of creative results during the 1990s. Finally, the influence that interactive fiction works and the interactive fiction form has had on other forms of literary and gaming production, digital and otherwise, is discussed in chapter 8, where some possibilities for the future of interactive fiction are also considered.

While the decision to focus on textual interactive fiction was undertaken thoughtfully, some of the boundaries of this discussion come not from careful consideration but from my own background, the context of my experiences, and my own limitations. I have tried to consider works from other places in the world, but I am American and have the perspective on interactive fiction that comes from being in the United States during the commercial era. I have experienced interactive fiction almost exclusively in

English, and in this book I can do little more than admit that it is also written in other languages. As an interactive fiction author, I have used Inform to create works; for this reason or other reasons, I may have preferred Z-machine interactive fiction to that written in TADS or other systems when writing chapter 7, despite the existence of works of equal merit that have been developed using other systems. Nevertheless, one has to begin somewhere. This is the approach I can offer, one that I hope will be of use to scholars and teachers and also to today's community of interactive fiction authors and aficionados.

This book is not precisely an attempt at a survey (looking over the entire terrain), nor can it manage to be a comprehensive history (chronologically narrating every important event and explaining the causes of these events). It is intended instead as an approach, leading up to a richer experience of interactive fiction (for those familiar with the form already) or to a more enjoyable first experience of it (for those familiar with computing and literature but not yet aware of interactive fiction). The approach, in climbing terminology, is only the trail taken to reach the climb, which is what is really of interest. This book, then, has a rather anti-Platonic goal, in a certain sense: It seeks to provide a way into the cave and, for those who have been there already, to provide some new thoughts on how to better appreciate its exploration—in the hope that new types of wonder will be possible.

ACKNOWLEDGMENTS

I first offer my thanks to John Slatin and Michael Benedikt, the readers of my 1995 undergraduate thesis on computer literature and interactive fiction. Their help and encouragement as I began to look more seriously at this topic enabled me to move ahead toward the project of this book and to become a critic of interactive fiction as well as an interested interactor and author.

In pursuing interactive fiction during my studies at MIT I am thankful for the mentorship of Janet Murray, who taught a class on interactive narrative, the class she now teaches at Georgia Tech. Among other things this provided me with my first excuse to explore interactive fiction authorship in Inform. I appreciate, as well, the discussions I had and the work I did with Justine Cassell and Glorianna Davenport there.

I also thank Robert Pinsky, who spoke with me enthusiastically about interactive fiction soon after I came to MIT and contacted him. It was while hearing him speak at MIT's Bartos Theater about the relationship between poetry and the computer that I realized a different path would be best; after completing my master's degree at MIT, and then working independently as a writer and authoring some interactive fiction, I went to Boston University to study poetry. There, studying with Pinsky and other inspirational students and professors, I came to better understand the figures that have provided me the most effective new ways of thinking about interactive fiction.

My work on this book was facilitated by the research libraries of the New York Public Library, the MIT libraries, the Boston University libraries, the Library of Congress, the Johns Hopkins Eisenhower Library, and the University of Pennsylvania libraries; my thanks go to the staffs at these institutions. I consulted many online resources that have been painstakingly assembled by volunteers, many of which are noted in chapters 1 and 7. The work of these Web site authors and maintainers is a less official business than that of running a library, but it was just as essential to this project and is equally appreciated.

I offer thanks to the many people involved with interactive fiction whom I interviewed, particularly Tim Anderson and Adam Cadre, who set aside time to meet with me in person. Several people involved in the field reviewed portions of the manuscript at my request. I am very grateful to those who looked at one or more chapters in detail and provided comments: Adam Cadre, Dennis G. Jerz, Dave Lebling, my fellow participants in Katherine Hayles's Summer 2001 NEH Seminar, and particularly Stuart Moulthrop, whose support for this project and my other scholarly and creative work in interactive fiction has been essential. I am grateful to Espen Aarseth for discussing ideas about theoretical investigations into interactive fiction with me when this project was in the early stages, and to Will Hochman for his support and for discussing the topic of this book with me. At the University of Pennsylvania, I particularly wish to thank Mitch Marcus, for his discussions with me and for inviting me to speak to his class about the topic, and Gerald Prince, who looked at my attempts to apply narratology to interactive fiction and provided important guidance. I also thank my advisor, Michael Kearns, for his backing. I greatly appreciate the helpful comments from the anonymous reviewers that The MIT Press selected.

Thanks go to Emily Short and Duncan Stevens for helping me to better understand the Latin texts that I have translated here. The failures of these translations are of course entirely my own.

Without extending the list of names by too much—and while risking making a slew of specific omissions—I should mention that I appreciate the suggestions from and the company of my many colleagues and friends from IFNYC, the Digital Arts and Culture conference, Computers and Writing, ACM Hypertext, and Technology Platforms for Twenty-First

Century Literature. I particularly appreciate the help of Scott Rettberg, who worked to make the Boston T1 Party happen and also invited me to speak about one of the central topics of this book. I'm very grateful for the support of my erstwhile collaborator William Gillespie and for our many discussions about literature. This is a much better book because of my experience working with a capable co-editor, Noah Wardrip-Fruin, on our other MIT Press book on a related topic. I also appreciate the many conversations I have had about interactive fiction topics with friends from an enjoyable and topical online community, ifMUD.

This book exists in this form thanks to the efforts of many people at The MIT Press; I appreciate all of their help. It is hard to imagine that the project would have been possible at all without the backing, encouragement, and hard work of my editor at The MIT Press, Doug Sery.

In chapter 1, the section "The Elements of Interactive Fiction" is based on a longer article that has already been made available on the Web in draft and is to appear in the book *IF Theory* (Montfort 2002b). Several paragraphs of chapter 1 and two paragraphs of chapter 5 are based on material previously published in *ebr* (Montfort 2000-2001). Most of chapter 4—that part covering *Zork*—appeared in a much rougher form in *Text Technology* (Montfort 2002a).

ONE

THE PLEASURE OF THE TEXT ADVENTURE

It was strange enough that a reading of "electronic literature" was going on at the Boston Public Library that evening of April 25, 2001. About a hundred people were gathered in the main auditorium, lured by the publicity from sponsoring organizations—the Boston Cyberarts Festival and the Electronic Literature Organization—and clearly interested to see what new sorts of literary works people were creating for computers. The focus was not only on the author on stage, but also on the image being projected from a computer beside the author. But was something wrong with the screen as the first reader looked up to introduce his work? Instead of a Web browser or some sort of e-book interface, as one would expect from contemporary computers, there was an obsolete-looking command line. Was this going to be some homage to antiquated entertainment software of the 1980s? A nod to the influence of *Pac-Man,* or something, before the more serious stuff kicked in?

It may have been hard to tell what it was, for Adam Cadre had only a few minutes to start in on a reading of *Photopia,* a work of interactive fiction in different segments, each of which is told in a different voice. The work, winner of the 1998 Interactive Fiction Competition, used an interface that would be familiar to players of the famous early interactive fiction *Zork,* but *Photopia* was in many ways unlike anything that had been done in the 1980s or at any time before. The seemingly disparate segments of the work are revealed as coherent only after a person has gone through several of them. An interaction with *Photopia* reveals, among other things, the story of a young girl's death—hardly the material of typical computer entertainment, although this was also hardly the first time an interactive fiction work had treated such a serious subject. Many of the other pieces read that evening were Web-based or were hypertexts of some sort, striving to present configurations of words and experiences of interaction that were similarly affective and provoking. Readings of hypertext literature (although not wildly popular) weren't new. What was new was that interactive fiction, along with other interesting non-hypertextual forms, had finally been included in a reading of this sort. One effect may have been to connect interactive fiction authors and new sorts of people who might enjoy interactive fiction but wouldn't stumble upon it online. Perhaps it was also the beginning of a broader concept of what computer literature or electronic literature could be. Or perhaps there was still much to be done: afterward, many of the authors and some members of the audience went to a restaurant, but the scene was like a junior high dance, with interactive fiction on one side and hypertext on the other.

Interactive fiction, that type of computer program exemplified by the text adventure, was a significant part of the early computing experience and has been a major current in electronic literature. Works in this form became the first best-sellers on PCs during the early 1980s, and have clearly influenced software engineering, interface design, online communities such as MUDs and MOOs, and other forms of digital and nondigital media. Authors of interactive fiction include several important literary figures from the non-electronic realm. While the commercial heyday of interactive fiction is clearly over, the supposedly defunct form is still making advances. Today's authors, using free development systems, continue to innovate in the form, pleasing those nostalgic for the works of the 1980s and also attracting new devotees. The potential of interactive fiction is still being revealed—but clearly this potential is great, whether the form is considered only as a puzzling and challenging diversion or also as a new sort of literary art.

Not everyone will immediately agree with the assertion that a work with aspects of a game, and with a history so involved with the entertainment software market, should be thought of in literary terms. Isn't the pleasure of the text adventure purely a ludic pleasure, or a pleasure related to mastery—one that comes from overcoming mental challenges formed as the verbal equivalent of jigsaw puzzles, with only one set solution? There are in fact other aspects of interactive fiction that prevent an easy affirmative answer to this question.

For one thing, the puzzles in a work of interactive fiction function to control the revelation of the narrative; they are part of an interactive process that generates narrative. Roland Barthes offered, in *The Pleasure of the Text,* an erotic concept of the reading experience. The text reveals itself in a sort of striptease, according to Barthes (1975), and the reader who skips boring passages resembles "a spectator in a nightclub who climbs onto the stage and speeds up the dancer's striptease, tearing off her clothing, but in the same order" as the author would have (11). As Jean Baudrillard (1983) wondered, "What could be more seductive than the secret?" (64). (Perhaps there was something, but Baudrillard seductively chose to keep that a secret.) In interactive fiction, the secret is locked away and a different sort of effort—a puzzle solving that manifests itself as actual writing—is needed to unlock it. In text adventures, in part, the "pleasure is in solving them, in learning the secret" (J. Murray 1995, 137). Not only does the "reader" of a work of interactive fiction metaphorically climb up onto the stage and start ripping off clothing—this time in an order that he or she chooses—this person also figures out *how* to do so in order to proceed. The pleasure involved in interaction is not simply that of reading. Nor is it entirely alien from that of reading; if the component reading and writing processes are arranged using puzzles in such a way that the challenges of an interactive fiction world are hard enough and easy enough, the other elements can enhance, and be integral to, the reading pleasure that is involved. The person who reads and writes to interact is the "operator" of an interactive fiction in cybertextual terminology (Aarseth 1997); in general computing terms, this person is the "user." So as to emphasize that the actions of reading, writing, playing, and figuring out are all involved in such operation or use, the term "interactor" is used in this book to refer to a person in this role, following Joe Bates's Oz Project and other critics (J. Murray 1995, 161) who discuss interactive fiction specifically.

Even aside from the fact that narrative disclosure can be controlled by puzzles, the combination of an explicit challenge and a verbal literary work has a clear precedent. The most direct counterpart to interactive fiction in oral and written literature is seen in the riddle, in true literary riddles such as those of the Latin poet Symphosius and of the early English text *The Exeter Book*. By presenting a metaphorical system that the listener or reader must inhabit and figure out in order to fully experience, and in order to answer correctly, the riddle offers its way of thinking and engages its audience as no other work of literature does. Interactive fiction is related to the riddle because the interactor, in facing a puzzle-based interactive fiction, is in a situation similar to that of the riddlee. In an interactive fiction work, the interactor directs a character (the "player character") in the interactive fiction world to enact an understanding of that world. "Riddle" comes from the Anglo-Saxon "raedan"—to advise, guide, or explain; hence a riddle serves to teach by offering a new way of seeing. Here, for example, is a short riddle (the assiduous reader will find the answer in the next chapter) that offers a new way of thinking: "I am the greatest of all teachers, but unfortunately, I kill all my students."

There is also the sense of exploring a new world or space, independent of the events that transpire in that space and are narrated. The enjoyment related to this aspect is not tied to particular puzzles and their solutions, as one author describes: "In *Adventure,* much of the pleasure comes from the sense of going deeper and deeper into the cave and discovering unexpected passages. Monsters and treasures aside, it conveys the feeling of exploring a spectacular area" (McGath 1984, 21). Certainly this relates to the pleasures experienced in literary reading of other sorts.

The interactor, confronting the riddle of an interactive fiction work, is a reader—and also a writer. Perhaps the interactor's true writerly ability (an ability to literally write and contribute to the text, not to be confused with the form of reading that is *metaphorically* called "writerly" by Barthes in *S/Z*) is not great, in existing works, when the amount of text contributed is considered. The interactor's useful writing generally consists of contributions such as *go north, jump off the roof,* or *eat a peach.* But such texts are actually understood, within the specific domain of the interactive fiction world, by the work's parser. They are then translated, if possible, into actions. The interactor is not adding marginalia for later personal use or for some other reader's future reference, but is actually contributing writing that is part of the text and serves to operate the program, causing it to produce additional text that is interleaved with that of the interactor and meaningfully responds to it. At best, if we take the perspective of a unilinear narrative, the interactor can use such commands only to control how small-scale episodes play out; determining whole new plots not imagined at all by the author or designer is seldom possible in interactive fiction as it now exists. Even when taking this limited view of interactive fiction, the ability to vary certain episodes in this way is important. Different Greek tragedies that tell the same mythological story demonstrate this. Although the underlying stories are well known and what happens is fixed by convention, the episodic variation and the nuances and excellence of narration provided Greek dramatists with the ability to innovate within boundaries, even without control over what the important incidents of the drama would be. Determining the arrangement of the incidents was enough.

In the future, interactive fiction may provide even more appealing possibilities for the interactor. It may allow for a more co-authorial role, or it may provide, by serving as a riddle in the richest literary sense, a more profound and responsive type of systematic world. Already, in the short history of the form—a form that has progressed in fits and starts—many interesting works have been executed, and many suggest new courses that could lead to works of greater power.

Interactive fiction has been through about thirty years of history so far, although closely related forms go back centuries or even, in the case of the riddle, millennia. Interactive fiction began in an academic and research context, with early development seldom being part of any official research project. The form saw a commercial heyday when works were created in the context of game companies. It has been explored recently in new ways by individual authors participating in an active online community. A discussion of the form that explores the literary, gaming, and computing context in which it arose, and the influences on it and currents in it through these different stages of development, is timely. This book seeks to describe some of the intellectual history of the form and its relationship to other literary and gaming forms, and to computing and other computer programs, while critically examining a representative selection of important works and describing their interrelationships. It would be impossible in a book of this size to provide even capsule reviews of all the works of interactive fiction that are of some importance or merit. Work in the form is already far too rich to offer anything but a catalog if an attempt were made to put together a truly comprehensive list. Resources online such as *Adventureland* (Meier and Persson 2002) and *Baf's Guide to the Interactive Fiction Archive* (Muckenhoupt 2002) already provide sizable catalogs, anyway, with continuous updates as new works are released and as new details appear for old ones. This book instead considers trends and currents in interactive fiction and how particular innovations have expanded the conceptual range of the form.

THE TERMS "TEXT ADVENTURE" AND "INTERACTIVE FICTION"

Text adventure and *interactive fiction* do not mean exactly the same thing. Despite the use of the term in the title of this chapter to draw a connection between reading pleasure and the pleasures of interactive fiction, the text adventure, however widespread it may be, is not the only type of interactive fiction possible or realized so far. An adventure is some out-of-the-ordinary undertaking involving risk or danger. A text adventure can therefore be described as an interactive fiction work in which the interactor controls a player character who sets out on out-of-the-ordinary undertakings involving risk or danger. Whether the impulse is correct or not, the term text adventure suggests to some people a popular and less literary work, since adventures have been, in contemporary writing, the domain of popular fiction.

Not all interactive fiction works, and not even all classic works in the form, are text adventures. The third work from Infocom, Marc Blank's *Deadline*, is not a text adventure but a detective mystery, in contrast to the fantasy adventures of the *Zork* series and contemporary adventures such as *Infidel*. The setting is a house, and the entire plan of the house is provided in the documentation. Although interviewing murder suspects may be unusual for the interactor and may involve some danger to the protagonist, the situation is a very ordinary one for the main character, a detective. One could still argue that the intrigue involved qualifies *Deadline* for the "adventure" label, despite the ordinary setting. But it is difficult to make the case for other interactive fiction works, such as *Exhibition* by Ian Finley (a work without puzzles, based on observation through multiple perspectives and set in an art gallery) or *Galatea* by Emily Short (a conversation-based work set in a single room of a museum). It is true that most well-known interactive fiction works—including works of acknowledged literary quality, such as

Robert Pinsky's *Mindwheel* and Brian Moriarty's *Trinity*—are unambiguously text adventures, however. In referring to such a work, either "text adventure" or "interactive fiction" can be used. The term interactive fiction is usually abbreviated as "IF" by those who discuss it; this abbreviation is used at times in this book.

To those in the IF community today, it may seem exceedingly strange that others would object to the use of the term interactive fiction to refer to the type of work I've just defined. An aficionado of the form might react to such a challenge the way an author or bibliophile would if approached by someone and told, "I think the term 'book' doesn't seem very appropriate. We'd prefer that you refer to these things as 'bound sheaves.'" Yet, since some academics do look askance at the widely used and accepted term, the case for the term interactive fiction (which has been made before more briefly (Montfort 2000–2001)) is now presented.

In tracing the origins of the term interactive fiction, Aarseth (1997, 48) has correctly pointed out that "interactive" has been used as a commercial catchword, to promise vague technological enhancements and improvements. Hypertext author and critic Michael Joyce (1995, 132) also finds the term risible, stating that the only truly interactive system he can think of is a pacemaker. Historically, "interactive" has been used with precision to distinguish computer processes that respond to user input during execution (as interactive fiction does) from batch processes (such as print jobs or fully automatic programs to create stories) that are completely configured beforehand and run without any user intervention. In computing, "interactive" is as specific and meaningful a term as "kernel" or "compiler." Used in that sense, of course, the term interactive is very broad, but the phrase interactive fiction has its own history. It was apparently coined by Robert Lafore and popularized by Scott Adams of Adventure International more than twenty years ago (Liddil 1981; Lafore 2002), and was then used widely by Infocom to designate its canonical works and to refer to a work of exactly the sort discussed in this book. "Interactive fiction" is also used to designate the two Usenet newsgroups where these works are discussed: rec.games.int-fiction (where hint requests are fielded and announcements of new works are made) and rec.arts.int-fiction (for more theoretical discussion and requests for programming help). The annual Internet-wide competition for short works of this form is also called "The Interactive Fiction Competition."

Certainly, the term interactive fiction has been used in many contexts to mean many different things. For example, chapter 7 of Jay David Bolter's *Writing Space,* called "Interactive Fiction" in both editions of the book, deals mainly with works more often classified as hypertext fiction, as do several articles from the early 1990s that have "interactive fiction" in their titles (Howell and Douglas 1990; Moulthrop and Kaplan 1991). (An early article titled simply "Interactive Fiction," however, is about exactly the types of works discussed in this book, "works of fiction which *explicitly* call upon the reader to interact with them by means of queries or replies" (Niesz and Holland 1984, 111).) I have also used the term in a more expansive sense, employing it to designate certain print literature, hypertext fiction, and conversational characters along with the form that is the focus of this book, textual interactive fiction (Montfort 1995). The different meanings of the term in different contexts do not present a real problem, though. The words "program" and "poem" have also been used, after all, to mean many different things; used carefully they still serve well. Broader categories than interactive fiction (as it is discussed here) can be indicated by other good terms such as "computer literature," "electronic literature," "cybertext," and "digital art." When discussing works that have text adventure–like interfaces and simulated settings while allowing works without adventuring motifs to be included, as in this book, the best term still seems to be that used by those who create works in this form: interactive fiction.

FORGOTTEN HISTORY AND THE DIGITAL LITERARY DIVIDE

"The history of interactive fiction in the twentieth century has yet to be written," Graham Nelson, IF author and creator of the Inform development system, states in introducing the most comprehensive historical survey of the form so far, a twenty-two-page chapter in his *Inform Designer's Manual* (2001b, 342). Important individual works have, fortunately, had historical articles written about them, and *Adventure* and *Zork* get frequent mention in popular histories of computing. Parts of two books have been devoted to a detailed study of *Deadline* (Aarseth 1997; Sloane 2000), a Ph.D. dissertation has been written on *Adventure* (Buckles 1985), and *Zork* has been treated in sections of one book and one Ph.D. dissertation (J. Murray 1997;

Laurel 1986). Dennis Jerz's recent annotated bibliography (2001a), an invaluable resource, joins a wealth of online information about the details of interactive fiction's past. Discussion on newsgroups has also helped to clarify many aspects of early IF works and their development, and reviews of works have made it easier for interactors to select those of most interest without weeks of interactive effort. There have also been numerous books about programming interactive fiction on home computers. Yet a book or book-sized resource on interactive fiction's history and implications—one that considers how the form came into being and how it developed through the decades, with basic theoretical discussion of the nature of the form and at least an introductory critical discussion of important works—has never been published.

The more recent form of hypertext fiction has been either a major topic in, or the sole subject of, more than a dozen books. This bodes well; all those interested in the future of the word on the computer should applaud that this branch of electronic literature is beginning to be taken seriously, is the focus of criticism and analysis, and is progressing toward much-deserved acceptance within academic and literary communities. Hypertext fiction is still relatively neglected, and additional, thoughtful study should certainly be undertaken to investigate it and to call attention to its promises and merits. More important, authors should continue to create challenging and thoughtful works of hypertext fiction and should try to bring them to readers inside and outside the university.

It is unfortunate, however, that while hypertext fiction has gained some acceptance in academic and literary circles, interactive fiction has usually been dismissed as a triviality. Even worse is the fact that hypertext fiction authors and critics have often quickly joined in its dismissal, sometimes without ever experiencing interactive fiction or after only slight exposure to the form. To see one reason why a solid treatment of this form needs to be written, one need only consider this selection from the single page that mentions interactive fiction in Ilana Snyder's *Hypertext: The Electronic Labyrinth* (1996):

The precedent was Adventure, developed in the 1960s at Stanford University's Artificial Intelligence Laboratory (SAIL). The program was conceived of as an experimental game. A computerised version of role-playing games like Dungeons and Dragons, Adventure

comprises a series of descriptions of fictional locations inspired by
J. R. R. Tolkien's fantasy *The Lord of the Rings* (1954), and set in the
surrounding Californian mountains. (87)

These three sentences state six specific things about *Adventure*—when,
where, and why it was developed, that it is a computerized version of
Dungeons and Dragons, that its fictional locations are inspired by Tolkien, and
that it is set in California. At least four of these six statements are clearly
false, and the remaining two are misleading.

Adventure was not developed in the 1960s, but in 1975 and 1976; confusion on this point is extremely widespread, as is discussed in chapter 3. It
was not developed at SAIL, but was originated by one programmer and
author, Will Crowther, who worked at Bolt, Beranek and Newman (BBN)
in Cambridge, Massachusetts. With Crowther's permission, it was then augmented by another programmer and author, Don Woods, who used the
SAIL computer at Stanford. It is misleading to call the work "an experimental game" developed by an artificial intelligence laboratory, since it was
a program created originally by an individual for the enjoyment, as
Crowther said, of "non-computer people"; while it was later expanded by
another individual, it never existed as any sort of official academic project
or experiment. (Confusion on this point is also frequent; a book on adventure game programming makes the same mistake, e.g., characterizing
Adventure as "an exercise in problem solving, artificial intelligence, and simulation" as if it were created for research purposes (Vile 1984, viii).)
Adventure was influenced by *Dungeons and Dragons* and it is often referred to
as a "version" of that game (Crowther himself has called it that), but that
characterization is at best very limiting. Crowther was an accomplished
caver who said he created *Adventure* to be "a re-creation in fantasy of my
caving, and also . . . a game for the kids [his daughters], and perhaps [to have]
some aspects of the Dungeons and Dragons I had been playing" (Peterson
1983, 188). The locations bear the names and detailed descriptions of specific portions of the Flint Mammoth Cave System, near the Bedquilt
Entrance, in Kentucky, and were not fictional ones inspired by *The Lord of
the Rings;* the influence of Tolkien on *Adventure* is real but often overstated.
Needless to say, the Kentucky cave setting of *Adventure* is not situated
beneath simulated California mountains.

Unfortunately, the single inaccurate reference to *Adventure* in a book that purports to map the future of electronic literature is typical. Jane Douglas's more recent *The End of Books—Or Books Without End?: Reading Interactive Narratives* (2000) also mentions *Adventure* only in passing, defining the two types of "interactive narrative," hypertext and "image-based" works, so as to not even admit the existence of interactive fiction:

> To distinguish between different kinds of interactive narratives, we will call text-based narratives like "Twelve Blue" and Stuart Moulthrop's *Victory Garden* "hypertext fiction" and, following Janet Murray's lead, refer to image-based texts like *The Last Express* and Shannon Gilligan's Multimedia Murder series as "digital narratives." (6)

Douglas continues:

> Digital narratives primarily follow the trajectory of *Adventure,* a work considered venerable only by the techies who first played it in the 1970s, cybergaming geeks, and the writers, theorists, and practitioners who deal with interactivity. Hypertext fiction, on the other hand, follows and furthers the trajectory of hallowed touchstones of print culture, especially the avant-garde novel. (6–7)

In this view, *Adventure* clearly has no literary ancestry. There is also a suggestion that it should not be considered venerable—although one would suspect that Douglas, who deals with interactivity, would actually be one of the people who venerate it.

But this is almost all that is said about *Adventure* and interactive fiction in the whole book, although Douglas (2000) later discusses at great length how a certain class of "cybergaming geeks," game-playing boys, are too obsessed with their "joysticks" (161–163). From the way *Adventure* is portrayed in this book—a book that offers to cover the whole topic of "interactive narratives"—one would be forced to falsely conclude that *Adventure* is "image-based." There is also the strong suggestion that it was written solely for male computer geeks, although Crowther has stated that his non-computer-using daughters were the intended audience. But the main issue is that a whole category of work that is text-based and yet clearly is not hypertext in the accepted definition, a category that without doubt pertains to the study of "hypertext fiction" vis-à-vis "digital narratives" and to the overall issue of literature on the computer, was not only omitted but essentially defined out of existence. This oversight is hardly part of some conscious hypertextual plot to wipe out all consideration of interactive fiction. In fact, Douglas was one of the first professors to make the detailed study of interactive fiction part of a literature class.

Such inclusion of interactive fiction in the curriculum is, unfortunately, much less typical than is the omission of it from scholarship. Aarseth (1997) aptly describes the kind of reception interactive fiction often gets in the university: "Compared to all other literary formats, including hypertext novels, the adventure game's structure is too alien, too far removed from the genus of hegemonic literature to be recognized by any but a few xenophiles, who risk professional suspicion or ridicule" (109). Fortunately, some influential hypertext authors are now willing to recognize that interactive fiction is a valid and interesting form. Hopefully, others will also soon consider interactive fiction to be worthy of serious consideration, and that all the various forms of computer literature should be welcomed.

A hypertext fiction (as it is most commonly defined and discussed) is a system of fictional interconnected texts traversed using links. An interconnected text is referred to by George Landow (1992) and others as a *lexia,* a term borrowed from Barthes (1974), who applied it differently as a block of signification or unit of reading that was empirically determined, during a reading. Sometimes "hypertext" is defined more broadly than this. In some hypertext works, the reader may annotate the text or interact differently. There is, however, nothing in the nature of the lexia or the link, those fundamental elements of hypertext, that allows the reader to type and contribute text or provides the computer with the means to parse or understand natural language. Such understanding, used to react to typed text from the interactor, is essential to interactive fiction as discussed here. Hypertext fiction also does not maintain an intermediate, programmatic representation of the narrated world, as interactive fiction does. Although a hypertext novel may have a setting and may present a map that offers access to lexias, the space of texts is not the same as a programmatically simulated space, such as the IF world.

There is of course nothing to prevent a work from having both the defining characteristics of interactive fiction and also having those of a hypertext fiction. *Reagan Library* by Stuart Moulthrop, with its linked lexia and a few elements of a programmatically simulated world, does in fact have certain qualities of each, although it does not accept natural language input. *The Space Under the Window* by Andrew Plotkin was built with an interactive fiction development system but is actually a hypertext work; it could have been extended to have IF aspects as well. The HTML TADS development system allows works that are interactive fiction and output HTML to be developed, although HTML is employed in such works currently only for its formatting abilities and to provide command shortcuts. Obviously, the particular elements of a combination hypertext fiction/interactive fiction work can be examined using the techniques and terminology used by critics of both forms, and will likely call for new critical approaches, or for the application of critical approaches that are general enough to treat both forms. What new things may happen when these elements combine in different ways promises to be very interesting indeed, but since interactive fiction itself has not yet been thoroughly discussed at all in any book a detailed investigation of such combinations will have to wait.

PERSPECTIVES ON INTERACTIVE FICTION

A narrative film can be appreciated and critically examined both narratologically and in terms of the photographic and directorial techniques employed in it. Some of these directorial techniques may be used in ways that do not bear on the story—for instance, in non-narrative segments of the film. Thus, although they are all part of the experience of the film, the quality and impact of certain techniques may have little or nothing to do with the narrative per se. An IF work also has different elements, which are best illuminated by different sorts of analysis. Usually some of these are potential narrative elements: An interaction will result in a text that describes something about the IF world, and events will transpire to move a main character past obstacles along what could be seen as the arc of a plot. Often other characters will be depicted, too. IF works are often, among other things, games, with an optimal outcome that the interactor, acting as a player, tries to attain. The interactor can win such a game by solving puzzles. Although many IF works are games and do have puzzles, the game and puzzle elements involved can often be better understood in terms of a different concept, that of the riddle. Finally, an IF work is a computer program, with input, output, and internal representations that must be considered for critics and authors to fully comprehend the form. No doubt, interactive fiction can fruitfully be considered from other perspectives—a dramatic one, for instance, of the sort that Brenda Laurel has used to examine *Zork* and *Star Raiders* (Laurel 1986) and then has expanded to comment on all computer interaction (Laurel 1993). The earlier three aspects seem the best starting points, however, for a thorough analysis of works in this form in the context of their history. Thus this book considers works from the standpoint of the narratives they can generate, the way they function as riddles, and their nature as computer programs.

The narratives generated during an interaction are often more trivial and repetitive than even the bluntest folktale, but they can be essential to the experience of the interactor. Only through consideration of narrative aspects such as plot, episode, character, setting, atmosphere, and focalization—as they can be extended or applied to interactive fiction—can the interactive generation of narratives in this form be understood and improved upon. In examining this aspect, I rely on the usual tools for the formal analysis of stories (the narratology of Gérard Gennette, Gerald Prince, and others), with consideration of the nature of IF as potential narrative rather than narrative. It is the effect of the narrative *in the process of being generated* that is important, after all, not the quality of the text that is output when the session is over, and not the effect of any post hoc reading of that output text.

While it is assumed by most critics that IF works are games, few have gone on to consider the nature of "games" closely, or describe what sort of game IF works actually are. There has been little discussion of whether "game" and "puzzle" are truly essential to the form. Tension between game and narrative aspects of a work may explain certain problems inherent in the form, or these two aspects may be discernible elements of a unified work, as seen in some of the best examples of interactive fiction. Because it is misleading to categorize interactive fiction as only a game, the term *IF works* is used in this book to refer to specific computer programs that are interactive fiction. (Calling such a work an "interactive story" or "interactive narrative" has also been avoided here, because although those terms do have a meaningful interpretation, it is best to use a term that does not elide an IF work's nature as a *potential* narrative.) The qualities that pertain to the game and the puzzle, and particularly the most relevant associated form—the riddle—will be explored in depth. The riddle serves as the central figure for understanding the workings and poesis of interactive fiction within a tradition that is literary and also demands explicit engagement.

Finally, since an IF work is a computer program with a world model and parser, it is important to consider its nature as software. A particular work may have been developed using an object-oriented methodology or using a functional programming language. Works of interactive fiction are marked by choices made early in development. Code reuse can explain why different IF works may produce similar replies that are inappropriate in some works and appropriate in others, for instance. It is also the reason many works could be developed quickly by companies in the 1980s, when such a number of works would otherwise have been far too difficult and costly for a small business to create. Additionally, a relationship between interaction with an IF work and computer programming (and the pleasures thereof) has been noted by both IF authors and theorists (Levy 1984, 141; Crowther 1994, 2–3), but the implications of this relationship for IF aesthetics and poetics have not yet been explored.

THE BASICS OF INTERACTION

The best way to explain how one interacts with interactive fiction is by example. Contrived example transcripts appear in the documentation accompanying most IF works that were commercially published. Here, instead, is a transcript from an actual IF session with an enjoyable and illustrative work, Dan Schmidt's 1999 *For a Change*. As is the case with almost any discussion of the specifics of an IF work, reading this transcript (specifically, the last bit of it) will spoil some of the pleasure of interacting with *For a Change* later; this transcript describes how to solve one of several puzzles. Only those "spoilers" that are essential to the discussion have been included, however, as is the case elsewhere in the book.

Spoilers: To allow readers to skip sections of the book that contain such spoilers, passages that give away important information about a work are surrounded by boxes, like this.

The sun has gone. It must be brought. You have a rock.

FOR A CHANGE
For A Change, v1.02
Dan Schmidt <dfan@alum.mit.edu>
Release 1 / Serial number 990930 / Inform v6.21 Library 6/9

UNDER THE HIGH WALL (ON THE RESTING)
Sweetness fills the shade of the High Wall to your east. Under this
sweetness lies a small expanse of fod. A mobile releases mildly to the
west; far in that direction a tower proudly plants itself, while the
ground rises more slowly to the south and relaxes to the north.

Spread on the resting is a guidebook.

Sleep gradually departs from your eyes. A small stone has been
insinuated into your hand.

This text contains the *prologue*, the description of the IF world given before
there is any opportunity for the interactor to give a command. When actually running *For a Change*, a ">" prompt is printed after this text and the
program waits for input. Text that was typed by the interactor during this
session is printed in italics after this prompt.

>*look at the stone*
It is a small smooth stone, the size of a small gland, a size to roll
between your fingertips, nothing more than a pebble.

>*pick up the guidebook*
Taken.

The interactor can command the player character to sense things in the IF
world or to take some action that will affect that world. Commands to pick
up objects are typical, as are commands to look at things. Notice that very
little has been mentioned about the player character up to this point. All that
has been stated is that this character has recently awakened and is supposed

to bring the sun back to this world, presumably using the pebble that has been provided. The player character could be the "nameless adventurer" of *Adventure, Zork,* and many other text adventures, with gender, age, race, and personal history all left unspecified. But some later narration that is produced might reveal more information about who this character is.

>*go west*
The resting must first be departed.

>*consult the guidebook about the resting*
'The RESTING is a device made for that selfsame purpose.'

>*stand up*
The resting sighs at your departure.

>*examine the resting*
The resting sits on five wooden legs and slopes gradually.

The nature of the IF world is not always ordinary. Here, a piece of furniture is called a "resting" and a "mobile" (as one can guess from the description Under the High Wall, or one can learn by consulting the guidebook) is the term for a road. The resting also seems to be unusually expressive. The precedent, as Schmidt has explained, is the unusual book *The Age of Wire and String* by Ben Marcus.

>*w*

IN THE SHADE
The land increases towards your head to the south, and decreases away from your feet to the north. Mobiles lead accordingly in both directions. The High Wall may also be approached to the east. A long walk to the west is a tower, dwarfing your form, and dwarfed in turn by the wall.

It is clear, after a time, that all things are shaded, everywhere. Thus the Wall.

Inscribed on the brown grass is a toolman.

The toolman jingles in the breeze.

The letter *w* is an abbreviation for *go west*, one of several abbreviations commonly used by interactors and recognized by works. Commands to move in one of the compass directions can be abbreviated to the first letters of that direction, which is convenient, because moving around to different locations is done very frequently. The player character here has moved into a different area, also called a *room*. Even outdoor locations can be called "rooms" in interactive fiction; the term just refers to a discrete location of any sort where a different set of actions is possible than was before. The names of rooms, printed in bold in the original session, are set in a different typeface here.

> *>examine the toolman*
> The toolman is bright and misty. Thoughts and uses hang from his
> shoulders like birds.

> *>look up toolman in the guidebook*
> 'The TOOLMAN is the grower and keeper of tools. He takes with
> a hand and likewise provides.'

Although the toolman's purpose may not yet be clear, seeing him "inscribed upon the grass," and yet like a living creature in some ways, can help the interactor understand more about the unusual nature of this IF world.

> *>s*

> OUTSIDE CAVE
> The mobile from the north ends as the land's slope increases too
> greatly. Dirt glistens blue. To the south, amid the land, a way opens
> into darkness, while more ground lies to the east.

> *>s*

INSIDE THE CAVE

A dark volume, curried from the surrounding stone, fills your eyes and ears. To the north a passing opens into dimness; from further inside, to the east, a slight glow weakly straggles into the room.

>*e*

LANTERN ROOM

This subsection of the inset brightens and flickers. The shadows belong to the air more than you do, it seems. They walk the cord-stone walls; they move and excite. The shadows look to a wall, to bars in the wall, and the songlantern behind them. Further in is east, further out is west, and a slope obtains up to the south.

>*examine the songlantern*
The songlantern hums and burbles, circled by brightening words, evading the bars and piercing the silence and darkness.

>*take it*
The bars divide any possible touch between you and the lantern.

>*move the bars*
One bar is loose, and looser, and then free.

>*inventory*
In hand:
    an iron bar (forthright and content)
    a guidebook (loquacious and proud)
    a small stone (humble and true)

>*take the songlantern*
The songlantern is wider than the gap.

The songlantern murmurs and sings.

The player character has acquired an iron bar, but is still unable to get the caged songlantern, which is almost certain to be of use where there are caves to explore. The command *inventory* (which can be abbreviated *i*) instructs the player character to take stock of what he or she currently holds.

>*consult the guidebook about the songlantern*
'The SONGLANTERN brightens without intervention; its tones enlighten its words, as all tones do.'

>*s*

SLOPING PASSAGE
The walls and light contract as this space leads up and westward. The light and song from the north weaken with distance.

>*w*

WITHOUT LIGHT
You are surrounded by the lack of thought and light.

The song of the lantern dances in and out of your hearing, faint with distance.

The stereotypical adventure-game puzzle would involve acquiring the lantern, which doesn't seem possible, as things stand. If the interactor couldn't figure out what to do here, it could also be useful to explore the parts of the IF world that are, as yet, unseen, to see if they holds objects that can be directly used to solve this dilemma—or if they hold clues that help reveal the nature of the IF world in a way that leads to a solution to this puzzle.

In fact, what has been learned about the world so far provides enough information to allow the player character to light the way, even without the songlantern.

>*sing*
Words tumble and float from you, and brighten your eyes.

DEAD END

The passage ends without foreshadowing, as if the end came without warning.

A worn anchisel rests on the roughened floor.

>*take the anchisel*
Taken.

The song of the lantern dances in and out of your hearing, faint with distance.

>*save*
Enter a file name.
Default is "change.sav": anchisel.sav
Ok.

>*quit*
Are you sure you want to quit? yes
[Hit any key to exit.]

For a Change is not typical in all ways, but it functions the same way most interactive fiction does: it simulates a world that the interactor is supposed to figure out (see figure 1.1). In this case, understanding an aspect of the IF world (that it is singing, not a particular object, that produces light) allows an additional room to be explored and a new object to be discovered.

At the end of this session, the interactor typed *save* so that this particular situation could be restored in a later session, and then typed *quit,* terminating the program. The commands given here do a good job of suggesting what actions are usually possible for a player character in an IF work, although they certainly do not exhaust the possibilities. This transcript also explains how some of these commands can be communicated effectively to a typical parser. With this introduction out of the way, it is helpful to describe the nature of these commands and other sorts of inputs, and how exactly the IF world relates to a transcript like this.

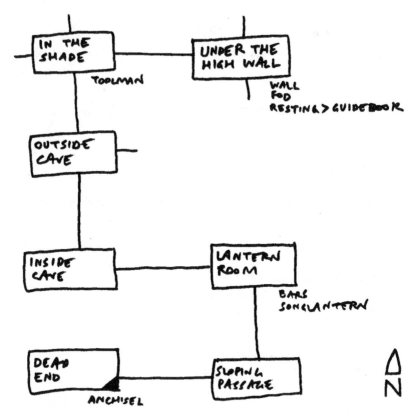

FIGURE 1.1

A hand-drawn, partial map of *For a Change*. This map, drawn by an interactor, represents the part of the world that is discovered during this session.

THE ELEMENTS OF INTERACTIVE FICTION

Later in this book, I examine many IF works; some, such as *Zork,* are discussed extensively. It would have been a hopeless task to try, at this point, to treat any work of interactive fiction as thoroughly as is conventionally done in a book about a single literary work, for example, as thoroughly as the *Odyssey* was treated in Erwin Cook's *The Odyssey in Athens.* Cook was able to assume that his readers had at least read the *Odyssey* in translation, whereas many who are interested in computer literature have not spent much time with interactive fiction. Furthermore, literary theory existed before that work of scholarship was written, and a new approach to the *Odyssey* could build upon or overturn what had been written before.

Simply put, there is no theory to help us understand works in the interactive fiction form directly. Several applicable theories and concepts exist, such as Espen Aarseth's formulation of ergodic literature and the Oulipo's concept of potential literature, both of which help to explain how narratology can be used to understand these objects that are not, in fact, narratives, but that produce narratives when a person interacts with them. But there is still much to do to develop a strong theory that is specific to the form of interactive fiction.

In this section a possible starting point for such a theory is sketched. This discussion is adapted from a more detailed article on the topic that is intended for a readership conversant with many different IF works (Montfort 2002b). The theory envisioned is sensitive to the nature of an interactive fiction work as

- a text-accepting, text-generating computer program;
- a potential narrative, that is, a system that produces narrative during interaction;
- a simulation of an environment or world; and
- a structure of rules within which an outcome is sought, also known as a game.

It is useful to begin with form in trying to understand interactive fiction. In this unfamiliar territory, matters of interpretation and questions of how an interactor learns to interact will be much harder to address without a basic understanding of form. Since an IF work can be implemented in different ways and function identically, definitions of the formal elements of an IF work from a theoretical perspective should be done without making reference to a program's specific data structures, functions, objects, and so forth, considering the program instead (for the purposes of this analysis) as a black box that accepts input and generates output. The clearest justification for this is seen in cases where two programs that are the identical IF work, from the standpoint of the interactor, are implemented in radically different ways—for instance, first using a functional programming language and then using a procedural one. Different objects can of course also be used in two different object-oriented implementations. It may happen that sensible programmers developing IF works have found it convenient to encapsulate certain fundamental elements as discrete entities in code. Those studying interactive fiction formally should not need to rely on or refer to the internals of a program in order to describe the important elements of interactive fiction as experienced in interaction, however.

In any consideration of the elements of interactive fiction, the nature of works in this form as *programs, potential narratives, worlds,* and *games* are important to attend to. This discussion also describes how the perspective of the person interacting can be distinguished from what is computed and displayed by the program.

How does the transcript presented earlier relate to the actual work of interactive fiction *For a Change*? It is a transcript of a *session,* which is what happens during the execution of an IF program. The session begins when an IF program starts running. It ends when the program terminates. The text that results (both text typed by the interactor and text produced by the program) can be called a transcript or (to emphasize that it corresponds to a single session) a *session text*.

An *interaction* describes a series of continuous exchanges of texts between the program and the interactor. "Continuous" does not have a formal meaning, nor is it a property of the text or program. The interactor's sense of continuity and unity is what makes a certain experience a single interaction, and different interactors may have different opinions of what an interaction is. The text (from both interactor and program) that corresponds to an interaction is an *interaction text*.

The experience of interaction belongs to the interactor (or interactors), while the session is a property of the program and its execution. Still, interactions and sessions often correspond, as we can easily imagine they did in this case. If the interactor had left on vacation halfway through the session, then returned after a week away to interact further, it would probably be more appropriate to consider that this single session spanned two interactions.

The astute reader will notice that the last two things typed by the interactor at the prompt are different from the others. They control how the program works but do not influence the IF world. The different types of input that can be provided, and the different outputs that the program generates, are discussed next.

CYCLES, EXCHANGES, AND THE IF WORLD

Anything the interactor contributed, from a press of the space bar to a long typed text, is an *input*. Whatever texts are produced by the program are *output*, even if these include things previously typed by the interactor. A *cycle* is one input and all the output that follows it until the next input. The *initial output* is whatever output is produced before the first opportunity for input; this is before the first cycle. All of this is defined formally with regard to an IF work's nature as a computer program, without regard to how important or unimportant such inputs and outputs are. Pressing the space bar in response to "[MORE]" is an input, for instance, even though it normally provides the interactor no opportunity to influence the course of the narrative that is being produced.

A work of IF is not itself a narrative; it is an interactive computer program. A *narrative* is "the representation of real or fictive events and situations in a time sequence" (Prince 1980, 180); this can result from an interactive session but does not describe any IF work itself. Similarly, interactive fiction is not a *story* in the sense of the things that happen in a narrative, or more precisely, "the content plane of narrative as opposed to its expression or discourse; the 'what' of a narrative as opposed to its 'how'" (Prince 1987, 91). In everyday speech, of course, "story" also refers to a particular genre, the type of thing people expect to hear when they say in conversation "so, tell me the story" or that which a child expects to hear after asking to be read a story. Interactive fiction is not precisely this sort of story, either, although there may be a "frame story" provided in the documentation or there may be a certain type of story that is always generated in successfully traversing the work. An IF work is always related to story and narrative since these terms are used together in narratology, even if a particular work does not have a "story" in this ordinary sense.

A distinction between story and narrative has been noted in various ways since Aristotle, who distinguished the argument, or *logos*, and how it was arranged into plot, or *mythos*; the Russian formalists also distinguished the material of the story or *fabula* from how it was told in the *sjuzet* (Chatman 1975, 295). Interactive fiction has the potential to produce narratives, usually as a result of the interactor typing things to effect action in the IF world. In fact IF works are *potential literature* in the sense of the Ouvroir de Littérature Potentielle (Workshop for Potential Literature, abbreviated Oulipo) (Mathews and Brotchie 1998; Motte 1986), and specifically they are potential narratives.

Works of interactive fiction also present simulated worlds: These are not merely the setting of the literature that is realized; they also, among other things, serve to constrain and define the operation of the narrative-generating program. IF worlds are reflected in, but not equivalent to, maps, object trees, and descriptive texts. The IF world is no less than the content plane of interactive fiction, just as story is the content plane of a narrative.

An input that refers to an action in the IF world is a *command;* this input is *diegetic* (Genette 1980, 227-234; Cadre 2002b). This command is usually in the form of an imperative to the player character and does not have to refer to a physical action. Commands include *think,* any input directing the player character to speak, and any input directing the player character to examine something or otherwise sense something about the IF world. Commands that do not succeed but that are understood by the parser are still considered commands. The input given to clarify a command (e.g., *kill the troll* What do you want to kill the troll with? *the sword*) is considered part of the command being clarified. An input that refers to several actions (e.g., *take all*) consists of the several commands into which it is decomposed by the parser.

All other inputs, such as those that save, restore, quit, restart, change the level of detail in the room descriptions, or address some entity that is not part of the IF world—for instance, to ask for hints—are *directives*. A directive is *extradiegetic* (Genette 1980, 227-231). Commands and directives are two distinct sets; all inputs are one or the other. Directives include what Graham Nelson (2001b) refers to as "meta" actions in Inform (90). Based on this, the term *meta-command* has been previously suggested to refer to such inputs that are outside the IF world (Olsson 1997), but it confuses the matter somewhat that "meta" has already been used by Genette in the opposite direction—to refer to narratives within narratives rather than to refer to the level of narration itself. To avoid confusion "meta-command" is left for its specific meaning within Inform programming; "directive" is used, instead, for all inputs that do not refer to the IF world. (Also, the level that is within the diegetic is called "hypodiegetic" in this book.) There are actually certain directives that are not meta-commands; any input that is unrecognized—a typo, or the use of a word not in the work's vocabulary—provides an example. It may seem surprising, at first, that a typo is considered a directive, but this follows directly from the definition of a directive as any input that is not a command. In fact, all inputs, not just text that is entered at the prompt, can be easily classified into directives and commands. Pressing the space bar when "[MORE]" is displayed is a directive, for instance, while typing a number to select one of several conversation options is a command. Some borderline cases from a famous IF work, *Zork,* illustrate this distinction. *What is a grue?* appears to be a directive, since there is no one within the IF world to whom this question is addressed; the information is apparently related to the interactor outside the IF world. On the other hand, *plugh* is a command, because it refers to the player character speaking the word "plugh"; it results in a hollow voice within the IF world saying "Cretin" in reply.

Outputs that follow input from the interactor and describe anything about the IF world and events in it (including the inability of the player character to enact a particular action as commanded) are *replies.* Whether the text is a direct result of what the interactor typed or whether the event it describes occurred because of a timed or random event, it is considered a reply, as long as it describes the IF world. All other outputs—that is, all outputs that do not describe the IF world—are *reports.* "[MORE]" and "[Press space to continue]" as they usually appear are reports, as are "Are you sure you want to quit?" "Your score is 0 out of a possible 100, in 2 moves," and "Brief descriptions." The two types of inputs and outputs, and the relationship between them and the roles of interactor and player character, are described in table 1.1.

An *exchange* is one command and the reply that follows it; the reply in this case includes all references to the IF world in all the output, up until the next command is entered. As command and reply correspond to input and output, so exchange corresponds to cycle. The session text from *For a Change* consists of an initial output (which contains the prologue as well as some text, like the author's name and email address, which is not descriptive of the IF world) followed by twenty-two exchanges; at the very end the interactor provided five inputs that were directives: *save,* the filename

TABLE 1.1

The two simplest levels of diegesis and their relationship to input and output in interactive fiction

	Extradiegetic	Diegetic
	Interactor	Player character
Input	Directive	Command
e.g.	quit	pick up the phone booth
Output	Report	Reply
e.g.	Are you sure you want to quit?	You find nothing of interest there

anchisel.sav, quit, the word yes to confirm quitting the program, and a press of the space bar (not shown) to end the program after "[Hit any key to exit.]" was output.

The following excerpt from a session text of Zork presents two exchanges, in bold:

>*open the mailbox*
Opening the small mailbox reveals:
    A leaflet.

>ear the leaflet
I don't know the word "ear".

>*eat the leaflet*
Taken.
I don't think that the leaflet would agree with you.

In the first exchange, the player character is ordered to open a mailbox. This is accomplished and the result, that a leaflet is now visible, is narrated. Next is an input that is not a command, since it is not understood to refer to the IF world. This is a directive that produces a report, "I don't know the word 'ear'"—revealing the limited vocabulary and brittle nature of interaction in early interactive fiction, problems that have only been mitigated in part. That cycle does not constitute an exchange. Finally there is a command for the player character to eat the leaflet. This results in the player character taking possession of it but not actually eating it. The reply seems bizarre in context; an understanding of the distinction between the diegetic and the extradiegetic, and between the command and directive, helps to explain why. "I don't think that the leaflet would agree with you," coming at this point in this session text, makes it seem as if the extradiegetic "I" in the previous report (the "I" who cannot understand certain words and translate them into actions) is now somehow within the IF world, counseling the player character not to eat a piece of direct mail.

DIEGESIS, HYPODIEGESIS, AND EXTRADIEGESIS

Up to now "IF world" has been used as if there were a single world for each IF work. Actually, there may be many worlds in a given IF work, just as there may be several stories told in a single text. (E.g., the "frame story" of the *1001 Nights* is diegetic, while the stories Scheherazade tells are hypodiegetic.) IF worlds, like the stories in a text, may be linked in certain ways. In Steven Meretzky's 1985 *A Mind Forever Voyaging,* discussed in more detail in chapter 5, there are six simulated future worlds in which Perry Simm is the player character; these occur in a framework in which PRISM, a sentient computer, is the player character. The world with PRISM is *diegetic,* while the worlds with Perry Simm are *hypodiegetic.* Commands that refer to action in such a world can be called *hypodiegetic commands.* In *A Mind Forever Voyaging,* a hypodiegetic world can be reached by putting the player character into Simulation Mode, one of several modes that are available. As Perry Simm, the player character then walks around a simulated version of the city Rockvil. Typing *north* in this mode provides a hypodiegetic command (it is an instruction for the simulated human being Perry Simm to go north), while *record on* is a command of the usual sort (it is an instruction for the computer PRISM, in the frame world, to begin recording what Perry Simm is seeing).

Michael Berlyn's 1983 *Suspended,* also discussed further in chapter 5, presents an interesting case in which the player character is in partial suspended animation in a cylinder, and only a few commands (e.g., *wait*) refer directly to actions of the PC. Most commands are hypodiegetic commands issued to robots, who, although they are described by the generated narratives as being in the same physical space, an underground complex, are really in a different IF world. The robots, unlike the immobile human player character, can be told to go to different parts of the complex, can sense things, and can manipulate the environment to effect repairs. They exist and act in the IF world of this underground complex. The human "controller," fixed in the canister in the middle of a large room in the complex and unable to take any physical action at all, is most clearly seen as being part of a different (but linked) IF world. Rather than seeing the robots (who are under the complete command of the interactor) as non-player characters, it makes sense to see them as player characters in a hypodiegetic world, similar to Perry Simm in one of the simulated futures of Rockvil. That the top-level world can be breached by a robot in the second-level world, who can be commanded to open the cylinder, ripping wires from and killing the player character in the frame world, can be seen as an instance of fatal *metalepsis* (Genette 1980, 234–237), a transgression between different levels of story or between story and narration.

One clear and memorable instance of metalepsis, early on in the history of the form, is in Steven Meretzky's 1983 *Planetfall*. The robot Floyd (within the IF world) comments amusingly on the use of the *save* directive, which is extradiegetic and which Floyd should not know about. In *Planetfall,* the awareness of metalepsis allowed humorous use of it; the unintentional metalepsis shown in the *Zork* session text is, instead, awkward.

Understanding the basics of diegesis, hypodiegesis, and extradiegesis allows one to make more sense of the seeming polyphony of voices in which statements are made in the computer-generated text of interactive fiction. According to Nelson (2001b), "There are at least three identities involved in play: the person typing and reading ('player'), the main character within the story ('protagonist'), and the voice speaking about what this character sees and feels ('narrator')" (368). Nelson states that this narrator speaks the prologue, but notes that "in some games it might be said that the parser, who asks questions like 'Which do you mean . . . ?' and in some games speaks only in square brackets, is a fourth character, quite different from the narrator" (373). These different speakers in the computer-generated text are what have led others to identify the narrative voice not "as a singular speaker but, rather, as a composite, mechanical chorus coming from both inside and outside the intrigue envelope" (Aarseth 1997, 120).

Just as a work of interactive fiction can have many worlds, it can have many different narrators—which need not all correspond neatly to each of the worlds. For instance, at different times, different narrators might report the events that transpire in a single world. The voice of the parser (and of other parts of the program, such as those responsible for the ability to *save* and *restore* a particular situation) is extranarrative, and need not correspond to any of these narrators. Similarly, the voice that reports on hypodiegetic events (those that happen in a world within the main IF world) is hyponarrative. The numerous voices evident in even a simple work of interactive fiction are not an undifferentiated confusion or chorus, but typically correspond to different functions in interactive fiction that can be separated. Even in those cases where different voices are confused (as with the earlier example from *Zork*) the particular voices which are being confused, intentionally or unintentionally, can be identified.

COURSES AND TRAVERSALS

The state of the IF world after the prologue and the other initial output, when the first opportunity to enter a command is presented, is the *initial situation*. The initial situation refers to the state of the IF world, not to how that state is described. A work of interactive fiction may begin immediately with a prompt, describing nothing about the IF world. Jon Ingold's 2001 *All Roads* begins with a quotation and a menu but does not state anything about the IF world or the player character's situation. Thus, it has a *null prologue,* as does the 1998 *Bad Machine* by Dan Shiovitz. Nevertheless, like all IF works, these have an initial situation—this situation is simply not described before the first prompt for input. As commands are provided by the interactor, the replies reveal what this initial situation was.

The *final reply* is that reply after which the narration of events in the IF world cannot be continued. The state of the world at this point is a *final situation,* which might be a state of victory or a state in which the player character is dead, for instance. After the final reply either the program terminates or the only option is to input a directive, such as *quit, restore,* and *restart*—none of which allow the current narration to continue. A final reply is not required for a work to be interactive fiction, and some works, by design, do not produce a final reply. An unfinished or bug-ridden work might also not produce a final reply at all; it might instead, unintentionally, only manage to produce a final report that is an extradiegetic error message, explaining what caused the program to crash.

A series of exchanges that are part of the same narration, and that are presented along with all the embedded directives and reports, constitutes a *course*. The earlier excerpt from a *Zork* session text describes a course, for instance, as does the transcript from *For a Change*. Typing *restore* and restoring an earlier situation brings one to the end of an earlier course, where the *save* directive had been issued. This allows a single course to extend across several sessions. A course can also extend across several interactions.

Can the same situation recur within a course? This depends on the nature of the IF world. In a world in which time always progresses, one cannot return to the same situation within a course; it will be later, so at least one aspect of the situation will have changed. But if time does not exist or if its laws are different, it may be possible. In fact, it is only impossible for a situation to occur twice in a course if an irreversible event occurs after every command. The progression of time is a special case of this. Note that keeping count of how many "moves" have been made may or may not pertain to the IF world. If events always occur in the IF world after a certain number of moves have been made, this is relevant to that IF world, but the number of moves made may just be provided (in a report) for the interactor's information. The interactor, of course, may not be stepping in the same stream twice when a situation recurs, since she may have a different level of knowledge the second time. But "situation" refers only to the state of the IF world, not to that of the interactor.

A *traversal* of an IF work is a course extending from a prologue to a final reply, and from an initial situation to a final situation. The term traversal, which essentially means "crossing," has conveniently already been used in graph theory and would also be familiar to cavers, since it is used in rock climbing. A *successful traversal* ends with a final situation that corresponds to winning.

PLAYER CHARACTERS AND NON-PLAYER CHARACTERS

A *character* in interactive fiction is a person in the IF world who is simulated within the IF world. A good indication of this is that a character's actions as narrated can differ, depending upon the input provided. The term as it pertains to interactive fiction derives not only from dramatic use and from discussion of the novel, but also from the specific use of the terms *player character* and *non-player character* in the prototypical fantasy role-playing game,

Dungeons and Dragons, discussed in chapter 3. These terms have a similar special meaning in interactive fiction.

A *player character,* or PC, is a character directly commanded by the interactor. Any other character is a *non-player character,* or NPC. The interactor may request that an NPC do something, or even command an NPC to do something, but such a request or command will always be done via the PC, who is directly commanded. NPCs certainly include entities that can take actions within the IF world like the PC can—called *actors* (Lebling, Blank, and Anderson 1979)—but they may appear in other forms, as long as they are simulated within the world and not under direct command of the interactor.

There are also *other persons* who are mentioned but who are neither PCs nor NPCs. (Since the terms player character and non-player character seem to complete the set of characters, these other persons are better not called characters; besides, in the study of narratives the term "characters" only refers to those people who actually exist within the story, not those who are simply mentioned.) Marshall Robner, the man whose death sets up the initial situation in Marc Blank's 1982 *Deadline,* is not a character in that work of interactive fiction. In Brian Moriarty's 1985 *Wishbringer,* the dragon Thermofax appears alive (albeit in a daydream) in the prologue, but it is not possible at any other point during an interaction for Thermofax to be mentioned again in a reply, and thus no input causes his actions to vary and he is not simulated. Thermofax is a person, but not a character.

The idea of a *character* (including player characters and non-player characters) in interactive fiction is analogous to the idea of a character in a narrative, defined as "an EXISTENT endowed with anthropomorphic traits and engaged in anthropomorphic actions; an ACTOR with anthropomorphic attributes" (Prince 1987, 12). The difference is that a character in interactive fiction must be an existent who acts within the IF world. Being a part of the simulation, rather than being a part of the story that the generated narrative tells, is what is essential for a character in interactive fiction. Since people may disagree about what traits are sufficiently anthropomorphic to allow an entity to be a character in a story, there are sure to be some similar disagreements about whether something is a character (or indeed, whether it is even in the broader anthropomorphic category "person") in interactive fiction. But the category "character" in interactive fiction is similar to that category in narrative, and should be as useful. The presence of entities that cannot easily be seen as anthropomorphic or not, as seen in the *For a Change* session text, has an interesting effect, in part, because it tends to defy the easy categorization that readers and interactors would like to make when thinking about characters.

INTERACTIVE FICTION AS GAME

Although IF works are always called games, and almost all of them are games, their nature as games is seldom discussed very explicitly. For instance, many people assume in casual discussion that the computer program is one player and the interactor is another, or that the author of an interactive fiction work is playing against the interactor. But neither the computer nor the author is literally the opponent in interactive fiction, any more than is the case in a computer version of solitare. Instead, the program usually serves as a referee; if the program provides hints it may be also acting in a different role, that of a second (Solomon 1984, 20).

As discussed in chapter 3 in the specific case of *Adventure*, interactive fiction is a cooperative game. If several people play, they work together to solve puzzles. From the standpoint of game theory, the typical interactive fiction game differs from a game like chess not only because the players in chess oppose one another but because in that game total information about the situation is always available to players. Not only is the state of the game (i.e., the situation of the IF world) known only in part in interactive fiction, but the workings of this world (and of the interface to it) are at first also only partly known, so even card games without total information may not be good points of comparison. Learning to operate the text, and discovering what language is accepted and understood, is part of the pleasure of interactive fiction. According to Menick (1984), "The first step for the player is figuring out what language the game speaks.... One of the joys of adventuring is that discovery of the extents and limitations of the game's vocabulary" (56). It is "the discovery of the rules, through trial and error, [that] is one of the principal attractions of the game. The mark of a well-designed game of this type is that the rules reveal a consistent style, and are not merely arbitrary" (Solomon 1984, 20).

The nature of interactive fiction as game is too complex a topic to explore further in this discussion, but clearly it is necessary here as well to recognize what type of game it is and what aspects of that sort of game help to make it interesting. It is worth noting that the perspective of game theory does support the figure of the riddle as a way of understanding interactive fiction, although the riddle may not formally be the same type of game. The text of a riddle itself is completely known to a riddlee (the person to whom a riddle is posed), but solving a riddle requires that the workings of the riddle's world be explored and understood and that its rules be discovered.

This discussion has not even broached the more difficult topic of the puzzle. As an element of interactive fiction, the puzzle should certainly be considered in formal terms and in terms of the interactor's interpretive activity. Some in-depth discussion of the puzzle is beginning as well (Carbol 2001; Short 2001; Montfort 2002b). The formal nature of the puzzle is but one piece of the overall question of how interactive fiction operates, one of many pieces that can only be mentioned in the current discussion. This narratological perspective on the form is offered as one starting point for further investigation that concerns the relationship between simulation and narrative. Another starting point of a different sort is offered in chapter 2, which considers a different form that is both an early ancestor of interactive fiction and a powerful figure for understanding how it works. This form is the literary riddle.

TWO

RIDDLES

The riddle is not only the most important early ancestor of interactive fiction but also an extremely valuable figure for understanding it, perhaps the most directly useful figure in considering the aesthetics and poetics of the form today. One obvious way of understanding something new is to see it in terms of something older and better understood, while keeping in mind the limitations of the particular comparison and what particular new types of understanding it can afford. But consideration of this new form in terms of game, story, novel, or puzzle—although each manages to highlight certain interesting aspects of the form—fails to illuminate interactive fiction completely (Montfort 2003). The riddle, almost never invoked in discussions about interactive fiction until now, has more explanatory power than any of those other often referenced figures. The workings of the riddle are so closely tied to those of interactive fiction that the early history of the form should properly begin not with sessions of *Dungeons and Dragons* or with twentieth-century literary experiments but with ancient exchanges of riddles.

The connection between poetry and the computer has been noted before (Novak 1991; Pinsky 1995, 1997); one London newspaper has even declared that "interactive fiction is computer gaming's best parallel with poetry: complex, subtle, and these days absolutely unsaleable" (Guest 2002). Perhaps the most striking statement about the importance of poetry to computing is by architect Marcos Novak (1991), who begins an article with a description of Federico Garcia Lorca's concept of poetic logic and goes on to declare that cyberspace is "poetry inhabited":

> What is the technology of magic? For the answer we must turn not only to computer science but to the most ancient of arts, perhaps the only art: poetry. It is in poetry that we find a developed understanding of the workings of magic, and not only that, but a wise and powerful knowledge of its purposes and potentials. (228–229)

But rather than discuss the relationship between poetry and the computer in general, or the relationship between poetry and cyberspace—although these relationships are important ones—here it is most productive to focus on one species of poetry: the riddle, a form that corresponds in a rather direct and useful way to the specific new media form under consideration, interactive fiction.

Although the riddle is a literary form of great antiquity, it is often dismissed as nothing more than a diversion for children; "riddle" may not even be commonly understood in the sense that scholars of folk and literary riddles use it. In some ways, then, it may be even more difficult to draw a connection between the riddle and interactive fiction than between Lorca's idea of poetry and the concept of cyberspace. But the riddle is certainly accepted by many as poetry. One dictionary of poetic forms states: "The riddle is a short lyric poem that poses a question, the answer to which lies hidden in hints" (Turco 1986, 134). The true riddle is not merely enigmatic; it actually poses a question (a real one, although it need not be explicit) that is to be answered by the reader or listener—the riddlee. This description of the riddle as a poem is in harmony with a structural definition that has been offered, one that includes folk riddles as well: "A riddle is a traditional verbal expression which contains one or more descriptive elements, a pair of which may be in opposition; the referent of the elements is to be guessed" (Georges and Dundes 1963, 113). (The taxonomy of the riddle offered following this definition distinguishes those that have elements in opposition, such as "covered with eyes, but it can't see—*a potato*" from those that do not.) Defining the riddle this way admits a range of literary and folk texts and utterances:

I tremble at each breath of air
And yet can heaviest burdens bear.
[A riddle does not have to explicitly ask a question. This one describes something, as required, and implicitly asks *who am I?*, to which the answer is, in this case, *water* (Wilbur 1989, 333).]

What lives in a river?
[The answer to this literal riddle, which is part of oral tradition and was recorded by a folklorist, is *a fish* (Georges and Dundes 1963). Riddles need not be clever to meet the previous definition.]

Out of the eater came forth meat, and out of the strong came forth sweetness.
[Judges 14:14. This is a type of "neck-riddle," the sort of exceedingly difficult riddle often used by the condemned to win pardon (Abrahams 1980; Dorst 1983). This one is used by Samson to place a wager, not in an attempt to save his life, but it is certainly of the neck-riddle type. The answer is *a honeycomb in a lion's carcass*. As is the case with most neck-riddles, the answer can only be guessed with detailed knowledge of Samson's life. He slew a lion and when later returning across the same field saw the lion's carcass with a honey-comb in it.]

Here are a few non-riddles, according to the definition provided:

How many Freudians does it take to change a light bulb?
[Response-format jokes are not riddles since they do not describe something that is genuinely to be guessed but rather provide the set-up for a punch line.]

What's that thing on top of the engine that controls the mix of fuel and air?
[If someone can't think of the term *carburetor* and simply asks this in order the find out what that term is, the descriptive phrases are not offered to be guessed but rather in the hopes of learning the answer.]

What profit hath a man of all his labor which he taketh under the sun?

[Ecclesiastes 1:3. Perhaps this question could be interpreted as a rhetorical question, with the implied answer to it being *none*. Another interpretation is that while the question is not rhetorical, it has no one answer that can be guessed, but is in the category one riddle scholar has described as "eternal puzzles that torment the human consciousness" (Amit 1996, 285). In either case, this is not a riddle.]

Such a distinction is a good start, but there are problems with this and any structural definition of the riddle. It is ultimately the riddling *context* that makes an expression with descriptive elements into the question part of a riddle. In fact, "to be guessed" in the preceding definition already brings the notion of the riddling context into that supposedly structural definition. In chapter 5 of *The Hobbit,* "What have I got in my pocket?" becomes a riddle accidentally, illustrating the importance of a good definition of a riddle but also showing that the context in which a question is offered can be very important. Bilbo mutters this question out loud, not intending for Gollum to guess it, and then decides to enter it—a poor riddle by most standards but typical of neck-riddles in that it is essentially impossible to solve without special knowledge—into the ongoing riddling contest. Some scholars specify the literary riddle so as to require such a context of competition or challenge: "Every proper riddle must fulfill two conditions: the first is its social function as a competition between the riddler and riddlees; the second is its literary form, which must be difficult and enigmatic, yet containing the clues necessary to decipher it" (Pagis 1996, 81). The second condition would disallow Bilbo's question and would probably also disallow literal riddles, which are not "difficult and enigmatic" yet are actually posed as riddles in oral discourse situations and in literature. (It is possible, of course, that their literal nature makes them hard to guess—people are *expecting* a hard riddle and are thrown off guard by an easy one—and so literal riddles actually could be allowed under this definition.) At any rate, as far as literary riddles are concerned, this seems a sensible criterion.

It seems reasonable to distinguish mathematical problems from riddles, as scholars have done (Amit 1996, 284). Some riddles (including ancient ones, such as riddle 46 from *The Exeter Book* and the riddle about Diophantus's age in the *Palatine Anthology*) rely on counting and arithmetic or other mathematical operations. Generally the literary riddle relies on description and metaphor, however, and thus different versions of the same riddle may be seen to vary in quality depending on how well they are written; clarity is usually the only aspect of language valued in mathematical problems, on the other hand.

One other form, the situational puzzle, seems to be closely related to the riddle and may bear a close relationship to interactive fiction. Such a puzzle describes a situation and challenges the listener to give the full context of the description. For instance: "A man walks into a bar and asks for a drink. The bartender pulls out a gun and points it at him. The man says, 'Thank you,' and walks out" (Hartman 1999). Once such a situation is described the one who gave the description will reply to *yes* or *no* questions asked by the others. "Irrelevant" is also sometimes given as an answer. For this situation (originally given in Agnes 1953) others might ask, "Did he want a drink?" "Yes." "Was he trying to rob the bar?" "No." "Was the man really thankful?" "Yes." etc. After a while those trying to figure out the situation might hit upon the answer, *the man had the hiccups and the bartender cured them by scaring him.*

The situational puzzle is certainly not as old as the riddle, and no real consideration has been given to these puzzles as literature. They do not seem to have been presented in their current form until the twentieth century; the classic collection of situational puzzles appeared in 1953 (Agnes). They are an active part of folk culture and are known by many names; one puzzle aficionado lists some of these as "mystery questions, story riddles, . . . mini-mysteries, minute mysteries, missing links, how come?, situational puzzles, law school puzzles, quistels (in the Netherlands and other parts of Europe), mystery puzzles, and so on" (Hartman 1993). "Situation puzzles" and "story games" are other terms used. They are quite frequently known as "lateral thinking puzzles" today (although some distinguish the two (Hartman 1998)) but were only formulated as an exercise for "lateral thinking" when that term was coined in 1967 (de Bono). Situational puzzles are related to interactive fiction in ways that usual riddles are not, particularly in the way that they allow further interrogation using a set of rules, but they are not as helpful as riddles are in relating the literary aspects of interactive fiction with those ways in which the form explicitly calls for a solution.

For purposes of comparison to interactive fiction the riddles considered are ones meant to challenge the listener but to be soluble, rather than those meant to be insoluble (such as neck-riddles) or those not intended to challenge (such as literal riddles). Excellent riddles will therefore have to be both enjoyably challenging yet soluble with the information provided. Neck-riddles can make for interesting stories and might demonstrate the resourcefulness of a character, but they are seldom profound. The neck-riddle itself may reveal little about the world beyond what is in Bilbo's pocket. Literal riddles are interesting phenomena from certain perspectives and can provide insight into the nature of riddling, human discourse, and culture, but the fact that a fish lives in a river also does not, by itself, provide much of a new perspective on the world. Whatever the merits of such riddles, they simply do not relate to interactive fiction very strongly.

The focus here is on *literary riddles* rather than folk riddles, not out of some simple desire to privilege written production but because of certain correspondences that exist only between interactive fiction and the literary riddle. Such riddles are generally of the type described earlier—challenging but soluble. Additionally, since the IF work is a program, its code has a fixity more like that of a printed literary riddle than an orally transmitted one. In all but the case of the very first IF work, *Adventure,* which is often mentioned without reference to its authors, there is a relationship to the way in which, as Dan Pagis writes, "in the literary, 'learned' realm, the riddler is the author himself, who reserves the same rights over his own riddles as over his other works" (1996, 81). The description Pagis (1996) gives of the literary riddling situation also relates to interactive fiction:

> The archetypal riddling situation . . . is in private, where the individual reader contends with riddles transmitted in writing; but here as well—again, contrary to common belief—the public riddling situation was quite popular, and in some eras even predominant. (83)

Although the stereotype is for IF works to be encountered in the solitary, "private" situation, "public" interaction with interactive fiction, in which multiple interactors try to make progress using a single computer, is actually quite common. Finally, the length and intricacy of the literary riddle, when compared to the folk riddle (Taylor 1948, 3), make it more like an IF work and suggest that a comparison focusing on literary riddles can be more useful.

Having selected riddles of this type—literary riddles that are challenging and yet solvable—what remains is to demonstrate that such riddles relate to interactive fiction in an interesting way, and that they shed some additional light on a form that has been characterized by reference to many different genres of literature and activity but has not yet been well understood. For the purposes of this chapter, the focus is on interactive fiction works that are structured with puzzles (or challenges, or obstacles) rather than those that are "puzzleless." The insights gleaned should actually apply to puzzleless IF works as well, but the comparison to those more common IF works with puzzles is more straightforward and makes for a better starting point. Literary riddles and this type of interactive fiction are related in four important ways: Both have a *systematic world,* are *something to be solved,* present *challenge and appropriate difficulty,* and join *the literary and the puzzling.*

A SYSTEMATIC WORLD

THE RIDDLE CREATES ONE THROUGH METAPHOR
Beyond simply having a literary setting, the riddle offers what can be understood as a "world" in which things relate to each other and are endowed with special abilities or attributes systematically. This world has its own nomenclature that reflects a different sort of ordering and a different conception of the world we live in. Hence it is common for scholarship on the riddle to refer to the world of particular riddles: "The riddle can reveal in a brief flash an excluded cosmos, a non-world or topsy-turvy world lurking just beneath or within our properly ordered and familiar one" (Hasan-Rokem and Shulman 1996, 4). This concept of the world also describes the relationship between the riddler (who creates this world) and the riddlee (who must explore it to figure out how it works):

> Riddlers, like poets, imitate God by creating their own cosmos; they re-create through words, making familiar objects into something completely new, re-arranging the parts of pieces of things to produce creatures with strange combinations of arms, legs, eyes and mouths. In this transformed world, a distorted mirror of the real

world, the riddler is in control, but the reader has the ability to break the code and solve the mystery. (Wehlau 1997, 99–100)

Of course plays, novels, stories, and poems that are not riddles all can be said to have their own "worlds"—settings, laws governing events, or Lorca's poetic logic governing the progression of images—but the concept of the world as it relates to the riddle is applicable to interactive fiction in a way that these other worlds are not, since the systematic but unusual nature of the riddle's world is presented for explicit understanding and solution by the riddlee. If the workings of the world of a story are obscure to a reader, the reader can still finish the story and often even understand some important things about it. Without understanding the workings of the riddle's world, however, the solution cannot be reached and the experience of the riddle remains incomplete. It has been suggested that the "making strange" described by the Russian Formalists can be used as a test of an interactive fiction work's literary nature (Randall 1988), but the specific way in which the literary riddle makes strange—and then invites the riddlee to figure its strangeness—may offer an even better way to understand interactive fiction.

INTERACTIVE FICTION CREATES ONE THROUGH COMPUTER SIMULATION

As described in the preface, the world model is an essential component of any IF work. Interactive fiction is distinguished from many other forms (such as the novel) in that it does not just have a setting that is described but actually simulates a world in which places, objects, and characters are modeled and obey programmed rules describing how they interact. There are certainly things to be learned about interactive fiction from considering the role of setting in other literature, but in many ways the systematic world of an IF work is more like the "cosmos" created by the riddler than like a novel's setting. Interactive fiction, as one reviewer of works in the form wrote, "should fit together as a self-consistent world. This means that the puzzles should play fair, but it includes much more. Elements that are foreign to the game's milieu shouldn't intrude" (McGath 1984, 21).

While the setting may be one aspect considered in the aesthetics of the novel, the consistency of the world in interactive fiction is important not only to the appreciation of the generated text but also to the interactor's ability to interact. Considering an IF work as a cybertextual machine (Aarseth 1997), one can see that the construction of the world influences not just the textual output of the machine but also the operation of the machine. Similarly, the riddlee can find it more or less difficult to solve a riddle depending on how well-constructed and self-consistent the world or "cosmos" of the riddle is.

SOMETHING TO BE EXPLICITLY SOLVED

THE RIDDLE IS PRESENTED FOR SOLUTION

As one scholar of the riddle writes:

> The unique quality of the riddle as communication is that it engages the attention of the riddlee in particular ways and it contains a test for its success in this area. Its basic structure emphasizes the importance of the two parties to this communication: the riddle would not exist if it were not for one subject who created it and another subject who could enter the communication and solve it, or be deceived by it. (Cohen 1996, 311)

Mystery novels may be written so as to encourage readers to guess who the murderer is, but they do not ask to be *explicitly* solved the way that a riddle (posed in a true riddling situation) does. Similarly, as enigmatic as *Finnegans Wake* may be, there is no way for readers to reply to the book itself or to James Joyce with some answer and to then learn that they are right or wrong. However involved with riddles certain of Jorge Luis Borges's fictions may be (and certainly "La Casa de Asterion" (The House of Asterion) and "El Hacedor" (The Maker) seem about as close to riddles as one can get in a narrative prose form), there is also no explicit way to "solve" or "answer" them. Neither of these stories contains "a test for its success"; in fact, they instead contain their answers at the end. (Borges himself, in "El Jardin de Senderos que se Bifurcan" (The Garden of Forking Paths), has one of his characters explain that a true riddle may not contain its own answer.) So while certain other literary works invite the reader's engagement in a riddle-like way, the riddle is special in requiring it. This process of solving is not incidental; as Cohen (1996) states, rather,

> the riddlee's involvement in the riddle-work is essential. The rid-
> dlee is the one who has to carry out the task of turning the
> unknown and unfamiliar into the familiar. It seems that the process
> of perceiving and solving a riddle, while at times dangerous, is a
> path toward new achievements in the development of experience
> and awareness and in constructing new relations to objects that are
> perceived as containing an inner life independent of one's own
> experience. (301)

INTERACTIVE FICTION IS PRESENTED FOR SOLUTION

In the strict computational sense of "interactive," an IF work relies on user input during execution. If nothing is typed, nothing happens. (There are a few exceptions: in certain IF works, such as the Synapse Electronic Novels and Marc Blank's *Border Zone*, timed events occur even if nothing is typed; the interactor still has to type, however, in order to make other events happen and to successfully traverse the work.) In the usual sort of IF work discussed here, the interactor is required not simply to type but to solve puzzles and explicitly report the solutions before making progress.

When one considers this process of explicit solution in detail, the limitations of comparing interactive fiction to mystery novels or other difficult pieces of writing become clear. Because solving, not just reading, is involved, theories of reader response that have been invoked at times (Randall 1988; O'Brian 1993; Montfort 1995, sec. 3) have, at the very least, severe limitations when it comes to explaining the *new* features of interactive fiction and the way in which the interactor operates the text. The interactor is indeed engaged in literary appreciation and interpretation of the text that is generated, and thus the approaches used for understanding the response of the reader to a text can be brought to bear at the level of the generated text in the usual way (Niesz and Holland 1984, 124). But this "reader" is also trying to find the solution to puzzles and to explore and understand the world so as to successfully traverse the IF work. Instead of assigning these two tasks to the incompatible categories of "reading" and "game playing," it makes the most sense to see them as similar to the unified activity of the riddlee. Only when the riddlee's interpretation is aligned with that of the riddler as represented in the riddle—and when this interpretation explains all of the descriptions consistently—will it work to solve the riddle. The riddle lays down boundaries on interpretation because it has an answer, just as most IF works must be understood explicitly in certain ways so that the correct actions can be indicated by the interactor and completed within the IF world.

EXCELLENCE REQUIRES CHALLENGE AND APPROPRIATE DIFFICULTY

RIDDLES SHOULD PROVIDE APPROPRIATE CHALLENGE

Despite the riddle contest between Bilbo and Gollum, and the riddle posed by Samson, the situation of literary riddling generally requires fair riddles, as Pagis (1996) explains:

> The riddling situation of the literary riddle is thus founded on an agreement between riddler and riddlee. The author is obliged to pose a riddle tantalizing in its opacity, yet fair in the clues it provides. The riddlee is obliged to solve the riddle, to announce the solution and to explain the author's intent with reference to the clues. (84)

Merely stating the answer to the riddle is not enough for a solution—this is worth emphasizing. The riddlee who has truly reached a solution should be able to completely explain the riddle-question and how each of the metaphorical clues operates.

INTERACTIVE FICTION SHOULD PROVIDE APPROPRIATE CHALLENGE

In most interactive fiction, puzzles (sorts of challenges or obstacles) are part of the world the player character moves through. In order to complete the IF work, the interactor must figure out how to meet these challenges. The solutions may be arrived at through the player character's senses or by having the player character manipulate things in the surroundings and then observe the results to determine the workings of the world. In terms of appropriate difficulty, the comparison between literary riddles and IF works is much more direct than one could find by considering traditional, precomputer games, as Marc Blank of Infocom did:

> We like to judge ourselves by the classic games, the really good ones like Monopoly or Risk. A game should be interesting and fair; it should have feedback, so you have a way of knowing whether you are doing well. It should have replay value, so it is fun the second, third, and tenth time that you play it. Our games should serve the same function as any entertainment does—provide diversion for people that could use some. I think our games are good entertainment because they are not mindless; they are mind-exercising entertainment. They are not intended to be educational or spiritually uplifting; they are intended to be fun. (qtd. in Dyer 1984)

Blank's statements clearly made sense from a marketing perspective, since Monopoly and Risk sell better than riddles do and since it was important to distinguish Infocom's products from educational software, which people almost never buy of their own volition.

But how can one look at the arrangement of rules that make Monopoly and Risk "interesting" and apply lessons learned from these games to interactive fiction? These rules are established to make play fair between some small number of players, each working individually toward the same goal on a game board, speaking to each other in a competitive social situation, and moving tokens about. Infocom's interactive fiction, like most interactive fiction, is generally held by players to not have replay value in the usual sense, much as one cannot simply "replay" a riddle to which one knows the answer (although one can pose it to another, think about it again once the answer has been forgotten, or appreciate it in new ways with knowledge of the solution). Critics have noted that "once this kind of finite interactive fiction has been mastered, it generally ceases to hold the reader's interest, save for demonstrating prowess or ingenuity to the uninitiated. A finite interactive text is like pop fiction, read once and no more" (Niesz and Holland 1984, 122).

Once one learns to play a board game, on the other hand, the knowledge gained from one game hardly ruins the experience of the next one. Adjusting the difficulty of a riddle by describing things more clearly or providing more hints, unlike changing the rules of a game, is very directly related to making an IF work, or individual challenges within it, more or less difficult. The situation of the written literary riddle and the riddlee or riddlees attempting to solve it—so different than four people sitting around a Risk board forming and breaking alliances in the course of play—is very similar to that of one or more interactors attempting to solve a work of interactive fiction. The riddle can also help one understand how a work may not need to be made infinite in order to deal with the problem of "replay value." One does not need a book that is too large to read in a lifetime to hold one's interest, after all. An IF work can be solvable and finite on one level (in terms of how long it takes to move from initial state to final state through its world) and endlessly profound on other levels.

As for whether or not interactive fiction can be "spiritually uplifting," although Blank stated this was not Infocom's goal (the year before *A Mind Forever Voyaging* and *Trinity* were released, ironically) the relationship to the riddle should by itself suggest that IF works of this sort are at least possible. Without diminishing the cultural importance of games, players would not expect Monopoly, Risk, or other board games, considered as objects that one contemplates, to be profound or affecting. Literary riddles, with the new view of the world that they offer, can be.

Considering a few of the items in "A Bill of Player's Rights" (Nelson 1993) should make the relationship between riddling and IF poetics even clearer. Nelson states in this influential document that one right is "not to be given horribly unclear hints," which has no parallel at all to board gaming (almost none of these rights do) but a clear parallel to riddling. Another of the player's rights, "not to need to do unlikely things," also relates to the object of a riddle being something widely known; the actions required to solve an IF work should similarly not be bizarre or obscure. Even "not to have to type exactly the right verb" and "to be allowed reasonable synonyms" relate to riddling, since a riddler who did not accept reasonable synonyms, but required the exact word being thought of to be guessed, would be unfair in the same way. "Not to be given too many red herrings" relates to the requirement that the parts of a riddle's description all describe important and necessary features of whatever is the answer. Even the after-the-fact understanding that should exist when a successful riddling session has concluded is represented in the list by the right "to be able to understand a problem once it is solved."

LANGUAGE, STRUCTURE, AND MEANING

RIDDLES ARE LITERARY AND PUZZLING

The literary riddle is a poem and therefore the poetics of that form applies directly to it. This is quite different than is the case with the language in which a mathematical problem is couched or with which the rules of a game are presented. A metrical riddle can have stresses arranged within its metrical framework well or poorly, as is the case with any other metrical poem. A riddle, like a poem, can also be distinguished by its diction.

The arrangement of the riddle's statements—the order in which the qualities of the unknown object are described—can also be better or worse, as the poet Richard Wilbur (1989) describes:

> Aristotle speaks in his *Rhetoric* of this pattern of surprise, delay, and excited recognition, observing that metaphor enlivens language by deceiving expectations . . . If poetry deals in surprise and delayed apprehensions, then the riddle exaggerates an essential characteristic of poetry. (347)

Swift's long riddles become more and more obvious in order to bring the riddlee along and achieve the intended effect. If they were rearranged with their "easiest" part at the beginning (some of Swenson's riddles are constructed like this) a completely different effect would be achieved because the awareness of the answer would be immediate instead of gradual.

Finally, a riddle has a subject (often, but not always, its answer) and it can treat it with consideration of broader questions or themes. The way in which the riddlee arrives at the riddle's answer involves understanding the relationship of the parts of the riddle and grasping a new ordering of things, and along with it the meaning of the riddle. The reason literal riddles and neck-riddles disappoint is not only because they are too easy or too hard, but because they usually do not present a reordered world that is very interesting—what they mean is not compelling.

INTERACTIVE FICTION IS LITERARY AND PUZZLING

The "same" puzzles can be implemented well or poorly in different IF works—and many have been implemented in better or worse ways—

depending upon the working of the parser and world model but also as a result of better or worse writing. The writing in an IF work is not some surface feature to be applied at the last moment any more than the choice of words in a riddle can be done "last." Although structure as well as writing is important, the writing is intimately related to the workings of an IF world. The arrangement of challenges and the way in which the IF world can be experienced can be discussed with reference to the riddle. (An art such as architecture, which considers that people may take different courses through a space, also has advantages in considering this aspect.) To understand how language functions in interactive fiction and what the literary aspects of interactive fiction are, the best comparison seems to be not to the novel but to the form of poetry considered here, the riddle. The riddle, like an IF work, must express itself clearly enough to be solved, obliquely enough to be challenging, and beautifully enough to be compelling. These are all different aspects of the same goal; they are not in competition. An excellent interactive fiction work is no more "a crossword at war with a narrative" (Nelson 1995a) than a poem is sound at war with sense.

THE RIDDLE THROUGH HISTORY

Not everyone shares Wilbur's (1989) view that the riddle "is a poem, not a mere verbal trick, and one might wish to hear a good one many times, even if one knows the answer" (339), or his view that the riddle

> was never a trivial puzzle. To make a riddle, or to answer one, was to see the peculiar qualities of an object or creature, to discern its resemblance to other forms and forces, and to have an insight into the relatedness of all phenomena, the reticulum of the world. (334)

Even those who study the riddle have slighted the form, as seen in one early-twentieth-century article that mentions riddles as "intellectual fencing," "an exercise of the wits," and "mental gymnastics" (Schevill 1911). Although Andrew Welsh (1978) devoted a chapter to understanding lyric poetry through the riddle, he considered that "riddles are now just a game and even to folklorists a minor form of folk literature" (26). There is a risk, then, in associating interactive fiction—a denigrated form—with another form often held in slight esteem. Consideration of the history of the riddle as literature should help to demonstrate that it has been and remains a form of some real importance. Because the nature of the riddle is so related to that of its computer descendant, interactive fiction, it is also in the history of the riddle that the earliest origins of interactive fiction are found.

The riddle is older than history, but writing does record much of the development of the literary riddle as distinct from the folk riddle. Folk riddles were not only transmitted as oral poems with didactic and entertainment purposes, but also had important roles in marriage and funeral ceremonies. Their role persists today in certain cultures and suggests some of the ways riddles may have worked centuries ago. According to Hasan-Rokem and Shulman (1996),

> The Gonds of central India perform a ritual when a member of their tribe is dying: at night, the adult men divide into two groups and gather at the boundary of the village; one group chants riddles to the beat of a drum, and the other group searches for the answers. No riddle can go unanswered, and each answer has to reproduce a text sanctified by tradition. (3)

Early oral riddles of course played different roles in different cultures, although many cross-cultural riddles, or *world riddles,* are known. The earliest written riddles that survive are from a Babylonian schoolbook, appearing there in both Assyrian and Sumerian. Like many early riddles that exist in the written record, they are best classified as folk riddles that have been written down; they lack the more elaborate development that literary riddles usually have. "My knees hasten, my feet do not rest, a shepherd without pity drives me to pasture" is one of these; an answer that has been suggested is *river.* Another is: "Who becomes pregnant without conceiving, who becomes fat without eating?" Scholars agree that *rain cloud* is the answer (Taylor 1948, 12–13).

Riddles appear in early sacred texts as well. According to Archer Taylor (1948), "Some very old Sanskrit riddles that are in part literary and in part popular have been dressed up for use in ritual. The oldest of them are in the Rigveda." These deal with cosmological themes; units of time are the answers to some of them (13–15). Taylor exempts biblical riddles from his consideration of the Hebrew literary riddle, considering neither the neck-riddle Samson offers nor the riddle-like description of old age in Ecclesiastes to be true literary riddles (31–32). Although they do not contain riddles set off as clearly as those in the Rigveda, both the Bible and the Koran refer to riddling. It is generally thought that riddles with abstract answers (e.g., units of time) are part of literary rather than folk traditions (Taylor 1948, 13; Welsh 1978, 34); religious riddles are some of the earliest of this sort.

Riddles, well regarded in ancient Greece, were an important part of rhetorical and literary tradition there. One legend, reported in fragment 56 of Heraclitus, is that Homer was confounded by a riddle and died of frustration:

> Men deceive themselves in their knowledge of the obvious, even Homer the [blind] astronomer, considered wisest of all Greeks. For he [died of grief over a riddle when he] was fooled by boys killing lice who said: what we see and catch we leave behind; and what we neither see nor catch we carry away. (Crowe 1996; emendments are by the translator)

W. S. Merwin used the answer to this riddle as the title of his sixth book of poems. This riddle presents a compelling figure for how those aspects of literature that are most understandable are "left behind," while those that are difficult remain to pester readers. Aristotle held that "well-constructed riddles are attractive . . . a new idea is conveyed, and there is metaphorical expression" (1961, 3:11). Pindar and Theocritus wrote riddles, and other riddles are found in the *Palatine Anthology,* which includes an algebraic word problem that encodes the age of Diophantus, Greek father of Algebra. The most famous riddle from an ancient Greek source is no doubt the riddle of the Sphinx in the legend of Oedipus, a legend that may be of Egyptian origin. One version of it is, "What is that which has one voice and yet becomes four-footed and two-footed and three-footed?" The answer he gave was *man,* "for as a babe he is four-footed, going on four limbs, as an adult he is two-footed, and as an old man he gets besides a third support in a staff" (Apollodorus 3.5.7). Over time, the Sphinx became emblematic of riddles; several English anthologies of riddles from the past two centuries have titles that mention the Sphinx.

Post-classical literary riddling began about the fifth century C.E. Taylor (1948) explains that "in western Europe, literary riddling began with the hundred Latin riddles of Symphosius. For more than a thousand years Symphosius has been a model for writers of riddles, as Martial has been for writers of epigrams" (52). Called "the father of the riddles of our era" (Tupper 1910, xvii), his riddles, each of which is written in three hexameter lines, became the best-known of any single author's. Although they are not nearly as long as many later literary riddles would be, they are written as poems and incorporate nuanced description of detail; they share certain themes and language with other Latin poetry. One scholar and translator of Symphosius writes: "The Latinity is excellent, there being virtually no departures from the classical norm. . . . His meter is of equal excellence" (Ohl 1928, 16). Riddle 16 is a good example:

Littera me pavit, nec quid sit littera novi.
In libris vixi, nec sum studiosior inde.
Exedi Musas, nec adhuc tamen ipsa profeci. (Ohl 1928, 48)
[Letters have fed me, letters I'm ignorant of.
I've lived in books but am no sort of scholar.
Nourished by Muses, I still don't get very far.]

This is the first of many *bookworm* riddles known from the past fifteen hundred years, in Latin and vernacular languages. Not all of Symphosius's riddles were imitated as directly as this one was in later riddling, but different versions and translations of his riddles appear in many later collections. One sign of his influence is that many riddlers imitated him by writing books of a hundred riddles.

The next known Latin riddler was the author of the sixty-two seventh-century Berne Riddles, whom Taylor (1948) calls "the first medieval riddle-master in Italy" (59). Of the English riddlers who wrote in Latin, all of whom were strongly influenced by Symphosius and many of whom knew these Berne riddles as well, one was Aldhelm, who wrote a collection of one hundred riddles around 700 C.E. Forty riddles, some about religion, were written by Archbishop Tatwine of Canterbury, who died in 734 C.E. He introduced them with a couplet:

Sub deno quater haec diverse enigmata torques
Stamine metrorum exstructor consera retexit. (Taylor 1948, 62)
[Beneath—a necklace: forty different riddles
the builder planted, meter-strung, disclosed.]

This highly constrained writing shows one of the ways masterful riddlers could fit language together. Taylor (1948) describes how "the first line of this couplet contains the initial letters of the forty riddles, and the second line contains, in reverse order, the initial letters of the last word in the first lines" (62). The contemporary Eusebius wrote sixty more riddles to add to these. Taylor (1948) noted that "the themes begin with God, an angel, man, the sky, and the letters of the alphabet" (62–63). The other notable riddler of this era was Boniface, who wrote riddles on ten virtues and ten vices (Taylor 1948, 63).

The most important document in English riddling is *The Exeter Book,* one of the four existing collections of Anglo-Saxon poetry. It was bequeathed to the Exeter Cathedral Library by Leofric in 1072 C.E. The book, of unknown authorship, contains one hundred riddles, some of which are translations from Symphosius; others reflect the Christian background of the riddler. It contains some short, recorded folk riddles and some that are more elaborate and literary in form. Here is riddle 5, in Kevin Crossley-Holland's (1993) translation:

I'm by nature solitary, scarred by iron
and wounded by sword, weary of battle.
I often see the face of war, and fight
hateful enemies; yet I hold no hope
of help being brought to me in battle
before I'm cut to pieces and perish.
At the city wall sharp-edged swords,
skillfully forged in flame by smiths,
bite deeply into me. I must await
a more fearsome encounter; it is not for me
to find a physician on the battlefield,
one of those men who heals wounds with herbs.
My sword wounds gape wider and wider;
death blows are dealt me by day and by night. (9)

This presents an interesting personification of the *shield* as constantly wounded and standing alone in battle. Not only does the shield bear scars and suffer constant battering, it cannot even hope for medical aid during the battle. This personification of the shield obliquely indicates the importance of such aid to the warrior, and the importance of fellowship in battle. The riddle is not actually *about* a shield, although that is the answer; it is about what the warrior values most during the desperate moments of battle.

One way that the influence of riddles on Anglo-Saxon writing can be seen is in how "the entire body of Old English poetry is packed out with mini-riddles; they are known as 'kennings,' and are in fact condensed metaphors" (Crossley-Holland 1993, x). Of course kennings are not strictly riddles in that they are not posed in order to be solved, but they reveal the influence of enigmatic writing in the typical texture of poetry of the time (Welsh 1978, 36–37).

In the sixteenth century riddling progressed apace throughout Europe, much of it still in Latin. According to Taylor (1948), "For reasons which are quite obscure, Protestant German scholars, especially those resident in western Germany, showed a great liking for riddles" (79). The 1540 riddle book by Johannes Lorichius Secundus of Hadamer contained this riddle:

> Qui manibus compinget opus, non indiget illo,
> Quique emit, hoc uti non vult, quique utitur ipso,
> Ignorat, quamvis habeat, tu solve, quid hoc sit. (Taylor 1948, 80)
> [Whose hands have framed this work does not require it,
> the buyer does not wish to use it. The user,
> though he possess it, does not know what it is.]

This is an early riddle—there are many later, similar ones—with the *coffin* as its answer. Other German Protestant riddlers of the time included Ludovicus Helmbold, who published a book of a hundred riddles; Nicolaus Reusner, who wrote longer riddles less related to folk traditions; and Johannes Pincier. In Spain, the literary riddle developed as distinct from the folk riddle after the appearances of folk riddles in fifteenth-century anthologies. Cervantes included several riddles in his 1585 *Galatea*. Taylor writes that the first French riddle collection to appear in print was issued during this time, in

1557: *Odes, ènigmes et èpigrammes* by Charles Fontaine (Taylor 1948, 109). An earlier French riddle collection, *Proverbes en rimes,* had been put together around 1480 C.E. and was, as a museum catalog describes it, "the earliest known example of a form of secular text made to appeal to middle-class tastes and pockets" (Johnston 1997, 117). In 1551 C.E. a treatise on riddles by Lilio Gregorio Giraldi compiled what was known about classical riddles; this book drew attention to the form and gained further popularity for the riddle in Italy. During this century Italian handbooks of poetics first discussed riddles in depth and many Italian riddles were written (Taylor 1948, 72). Italy's tradition of literary riddling would grow to become the most vital in Europe; there is a three-volume history of the literary riddle in Italy through 1800 C.E. (de Filippis 1948, 1953, 1967).

In the English Renaissance many notable literary figures wrote at least a few riddles. One of these, by Thomas Wyatt, is as follows:

> Vvulcane begat me: Minerua me taught:
> Nature, my mother: Craft nourisht me yere by yere:
> Three bodyes are my foode: my strength is in naught:
> Angre, wrath, wast, and noyce are my children dere.
> Gesse, frend, what I am: and how I am wraught:
> Monster of sea, or of land, or of els where.
> Know me, and vse me: and I may thee defend:
> And if I be thine enmy, I may thy life end. (Tottel 1557, K4v)

This "Discripcion of a gonne" provides a genealogy of the *gun* and portrays it as both defender and killer, and as indifferent to which side it is on. The gun's food, gunpowder, is literally made of three components (saltpeter, charcoal, and sulfur) while its strength is not in "zero," but is in "naught" in its other meaning from that time: wickedness. Even without drawing a connection between this poem and another by Wyatt from the same volume—the one beginning "The furious goonne, in his most ragyng yre," which compares the speaker's heart to a gun that "Crakes in sunder"—there is a compelling play between the abstract and concrete: the answer to this riddle could *almost* be "war," but a few details demand an object that is born of Vulcan, can literally be wraught, is fed with something made from three components, and can be known and used for defense. Riddles would remain of some interest to writers in England; later Shakespeare would incorporate riddling into the gravediggers' banter in *Hamlet*.

Wilbur (1989) writes, "By the latter part of the seventeenth century, the making and guessing of riddles had become a sophisticated amusement in the salons of Paris" (338). Most riddles during this time were circulated anonymously in France; the Abbé Cotin was unusual in taking credit for his (*Cornhill Magazine* 1891). By the early eighteenth century, this renewed interest in riddles had spread to England. Wilbur (1989) called Jonathan Swift "the chief figure in this English 'riddlemania,'" noting that his voice as a riddler was "that of a clever party guest who is entertaining us with a guessing game" (338). Swift wrote riddles that, unlike their serious forebears, were not mysteriously deep and cosmological. Consider this example:

> I with borrowed silver shine,
> What you see is none of mine.
> First I show you but a quarter,
> like the bow that guards the Tartar;
> Then the half, and then the whole,
> Ever dancing round the pole;
> And true it is, I chiefly owe
> My beauty to the shades below. (*Cornhill Magazine* 1891)

Many of Swift's riddles were longer and more elaborate than this one (whose answer is the *moon*), offering more and more information until the solution is made evident. Wilbur (1989) finds a reason for the renewed interest in the riddle at this time in England—and for this interest being less serious than at other times:

> It is not surprising that the riddle turned into a parlor diversion just at the time when Cartesian philosophy and the scientific worldview were conquering men's minds. In an age when the objects and creatures of the physical world were more and more generally conceived of as mere mechanisms, partaking not at all of mind or spirit, and truly describable only by mathematics, how could one take at all seriously a poetic mode in which clouds and clams pretend to speak, or are treated as fellow beings? (339)

As Wilbur (1989) noted, "when the eighteenth-century riddle craze petered out . . . riddles were consigned on the whole to the nursery" (339), but there have been many interesting English literary riddles written since that time, despite the lack of any new riddle craze among English-speaking literati. Emily Dickinson wrote many riddles that remain well known; here is the beginning of her poem 311:

> It lifts from Leaden Sieves —
> It powders all the Wood.
> It fills with Alabaster Wool
> The Wrinkles of the Road — (1960, 146)

The answer to this poem of five stanzas is *snow*. Some of Dickinson's riddles are among her most frequently studied poems. One example is 986 ("A narrow Fellow in the Grass"), a riddle with the answer *snake*. Her riddles have been anthologized separately and a book of criticism has been devoted to them (Lucas 1969). For some of these riddles, such as 297 ("It's like the Light —"), many answers have been proposed and there is still not complete critical agreement about which is the right one.

The most notable book of literary riddles published in the United States in the past century is by May Swenson. Sold as a children's book, *Poems to Solve* (Swenson 1966) contains many riddles that are rather easy, some even obvious, and yet please both as poems and more specifically as riddles. (Her 1971 *More Poems to Solve* contained five riddles along with other poems.) One riddle from *Poems to Solve* that has *cars* as its answer is titled "Southbound on the Freeway." It begins "A tourist came in from Orbitville, / parked in the air, and said . . ." and continues with a description of cars as bizarre creatures, ending with the amusing but profound question "Those soft shapes, / shadowy inside // the hard bodies—are they / their guts or their brains?" If Swenson's book was not an inspiration for the Martian Poetry movement, beginning in the 1970s and with Craig Raine and Christopher Reid as its main poets, it certainly prefigured that riddle-influenced school. Other notable poets of the twentieth century composed riddles; Richard Wilbur (1989) quotes riddles from Robert Frost, Howard Nemerov, and Donald Justice in his case for the riddle in *The Yale Review*.

Although riddling has not occupied the place in English literary tradition that it held in other cultures, the literary riddle is of importance in world literature and has made its mark in English as well. Riddles are particularly helpful in understanding the nature of interactive fiction. They will certainly also remain of interest not only to folklorists and anthropologists but to poets and critics of literature as well. With respect to literary riddles as well as folk riddles, the remarks of two scholars of the riddle are apt: Riddles, "far from being no more than an amusing bit of entertainment, are inextricably bound to those most sophisticated of human systems: language, culture, and art" (Pepicello and Green 1984, 144).

THE POETICS OF THE RIDDLE

The riddle can accomplish certain things by inviting the riddlee to awaken to a new vision of the world. It is not a form well suited to all sorts of discourse, however. According to Cohen (1996),

> It is clear that the riddle is not the best way of communicating about unknown things. If we want to learn from another person about something that he knows and we do not, a genuine question would serve us better than any riddle. On the other hand, if we want to communicate our experiences and our ideas, we may use any of many possible expressions, from the prosaic and literal to the elaborate and artistic, without having to be confined to the riddle format. (311)

So the riddle is best at giving a new perspective on something already familiar in certain ways, in reorganizing our perception or thinking. "The process involved is inherently enigmatic and also transformative: the transition effected leaves reality changed, restructured, its basic categories restated, recognized, affirmed" (Hasan-Rokem and Shulman 1996, 4). The riddle thus excels at recategorization and transformation—both of the external world and the world of our consciousness. Certain IF works, including *Wishbringer*, *A Mind Forever Voyaging*, and *Shade*, present IF worlds that change during the course of the narrated events and relate to this aspect of the riddle in a particularly interesting way that I consider later.

There are interesting points made in these anonymous comments about the riddle:

> For a good enigma we must have a perfectly true description of a thing: every term used must be as scrupulously appropriate as in a logical definition; but it must be so ingeniously phrased and worded that the sense is not obvious, and the interpreter is baffled. There is vast room for the development of skill in this art, to make an enigma such that it shall be not merely obscure, but at the same time stimulating to the curiosity. A further step is to give it the charm of poetic beauty. This is quite germane to the nature of the enigma, which has a natural affinity with the epigrammatic form of poetry. (*Cornhill Magazine* 1891)

How a riddle's description can be "perfectly true" in some "logical" sense probably needs further elaboration; the "logic" mentioned here seems to be of a more prosaic sort than Lorca's poetic logic. Also, the "charm of poetic beauty" is probably better considered as being integrated with the riddle's purpose instead of being mentioned as a "further step." But an essential point is made here: that an excellent riddle should be "not merely obscure, but at the same time stimulating to the curiosity." This principle suggests that a work of interactive fiction should motivate the interactor to continue to figure out its world just as the riddle should compel further thought and further work toward a solution, which is consistent with Adam Cadre's (2002a) advice to authors: "The player should always have a pretty compelling reason to type something other than QUIT."

There are some more recent and more interesting poetry principles to consider, inspired by the riddle and offered by Howard Nemerov:

> it came to me to write five riddles in verse; whence arose a probably impossible ideal for poetry, thus:
> 1. a poem must seem very mysterious.
> 2. but it must have an answer (= a meaning) which is precise, literal, and total; that is, which accounts for every item in the poem.
> 3. it must remain very mysterious, or even become more so, when you know the answer. (qtd. in Wilbur 1989, 350)

These have rather direct application when interactive fiction is considered in terms of the riddle. The first principle suggests that a work of interactive fiction should invite the interactor to solve it, by being enigmatic in a certain way or by presenting something to be solved that is alluring. This is similar to the earlier point that riddles, and thus interactive fiction, should be "stimulating to the curiosity" and is related to the allure of the secret as discussed in the previous chapter. Principle 2 also provides for the economy of objects in the world. If there are "red herrings" provided in an excellent work, they must be part of the *meaning* of the work even if they are not involved in the explicit answer or solution; there is no room for things that are extraneous in every sense. Or, as has been suggested with regared to interactive fiction authorship: "The pieces of text you write are the player's reward for thinking of the command that calls them up. So make them rewarding. Every diegetic piece of text should have something to recommend it" (Cadre 2002a). What is poorly formulated as "replay value" can be better considered in light of principle 3. When the explicit mysteries of an interactive fiction are solved, a work that becomes more profoundly mysterious can be experienced again with interest even when the solution is known.

This is the case even with a simple riddle such as the one related in the last chapter, "I am the greatest of all teachers, but unfortunately, I kill all my students." It certainly is not the case that arriving at the answer *time* leaves the riddlee comfortable, everything important having been settled. To solve this riddle is to uncover the disturbing nature of the world, leaving one with other worries and plenty to think about. Even when the answer is not an abstraction, the literary riddle resonates beyond its answer. Northrop Frye (1976) makes this point in his discussion of riddle 33 from *The Exeter Book,* the answer to which is *iceberg*:

> The real answer to the question implied in a riddle is not a "thing" outside it, but that which is both word and thing, and is both inside and outside the poem. This is the universal of which the poem is the manifestation, the order of words that tells us of battles and shipwrecks, of the intimate connection of beauty and terror, of cycles of life and death, of mutability and apocalypse, of the echoes of Leviathan and Virgil's Juno and Demeter and Kali and Circe and

Tiamat and Midgard and the mermaids and the Valkyries, all of which is focused on and stirred up by this "iceberg." (147)

The riddle, venerable ancestor of interactive fiction that it is, also goes a long way toward explaining how the literary and puzzling aspects of the form are hardly inherently antagonistic, but rather must work together for the effect of certain IF works to be achieved. Of course the riddle does not explain everything about interactive fiction, despite the many ways in which the poetics of the riddle relate closely to those of the IF form. Interactive fiction also has other ancestors, both on and off the computer, which are considered in the next chapter.

THREE

ADVENTURE AND ITS ANCESTORS

While interactive fiction has a special relationship to the riddle, the nature of interactive fiction as computer program, simulated world, generator of narrative, and game means that it has many other ancestors. The idea that devices could generate texts using procedures was realized many centuries earlier. Such devices have been classed as *ergodic literature* (Aarseth 1997, 9–13) but here it is reasonable to appropriate an earlier and simpler term, *literary machines,* to describe them. This reflects their literary nature and also calls attention to some of the concepts of cybertext theory. Another often-mentioned (but seldom examined) forebear is the fantasy role-playing game *Dungeons and Dragons,* a framework for a theatrical interaction, for the exploration of simulated spaces, and for puzzle solving. Within computing, three earlier types of systems were particularly influential in the development of interactive fiction: computer games, early conversational systems such as ELIZA/DOCTOR, and more sophisticated artificial intelligence systems, exemplified by the natural language processing program SHRDLU. After looking briefly at these progenitors and their histories through the early 1970s, this chapter describes how *Adventure* came about—and thus how interactive fiction as a form and ideal began.

LITERARY MACHINES

The literary machines that precede *Adventure* are not always physical machines. They could be considered as such, from one perspective: any set of procedures can be taken as a description of the action of a physical machine, if one allows the human being who carries out the operations of text manipulation to be considered a mechanical component (Aarseth 1997, 21). The phrase *literary machine* serves nicely to indicate text-generating machines, physical or conceptual, created for literary purposes. "Literary machines" was used by Theodor Nelson (1981) as the title of one of his books and was employed to refer to a more general sense of "literature" and to advance a concept of hypertext, albeit one much more sophisticated and complex than is seen in the link and node model popularized by the Web. The term is appropriated here to unite two ideas, that of an assembled text as literary and that of the computer as a machine that manipulates symbols. The *I Ching* is a formal system for generating different literary texts, for instance. It incorporates chance and provides explicit procedures for how to assemble fragments into a final text; it is thus a machine in the sense of the mathematical formulation of the general-purpose computer, the Turing machine (Dewdney 1989; Lewis and Papadimitriou 1981).

Translator Richard Wilhelm (1950) writes that "the Book of Changes—*I Ching* in Chinese—is unquestionably one of the most important books in the world's literature" (xxvii); it is this book, and machine, that will serve to begin the short history of literary machines here. The *I Ching* does not offer a unilinear text; it is actually a literary machine, a set of procedures for generating texts. It may be the earliest one known. Aarseth (1997) writes that "like the origin of *Adventure,* the origin of the *I Ching* . . . is not easy to establish" (177), although legends and scholarship provide some insight into its very early origins:

> In Chinese literature four holy men are cited as the authors of the Book of Changes, namely, Fu Hsi, King Wên, the Duke of Chou, and Confucius. Fu Hsi is a legendary figure representing the era of hunting and fishing and of the invention of cooking. The fact that he is designated as the inventor of the linear signs of the Book of Changes means that they ... antedate historical memory. (Wilhelm 1950, xxxviii)

The *I Ching* began, Wilhelm explains, as "a collection of linear signs to be used as oracles" (xxix), corresponding at least loosely to ancient Greek oracles such as the one at Delphi. These Western oracles almost certainly had some established systems for generating different texts under different circumstances. Such systems may have involved composition by male intermediaries (Parke 1939, 39) or direct address of the petitioner by the prophetess in a trance (Fontenrose 1978, 212); there is some evidence that the inhalation of intoxicating gases by those providing the oracle's reply was involved (de Boer, Hale, and Chanton 2001). Whatever procedures were used were esoteric. Thus, they did not remain to influence future Western providers of oracular wisdom, such as those participating in today's Internet Oracle (Kinzler et al. 1989–2002). (If Internet Oracle replies are written under the influence of intoxicants, presumably this is not due to the ancient oracular traditions of Greece.) Internet versions of the *I Ching,* on the other hand, directly encode the traditional procedures of divination.

The *I Ching* also grew to become more than just a means of fortune telling, earning it an even more important place in Chinese and world literature:

> [T]he book of divination had to become a book of wisdom.
>
> It was reserved for King Wên, who lived about 1150 B.C., and his son, the Duke of Chow, to bring about this change. They endowed the hitherto mute hexagrams and lines, from which the future had to be divined as an individual matter in each case, with definite counsels for correct conduct. (Wilhelm 1950, xxxiii)

The *I Ching* became more important still with the additions made by or because of Confucius. His influence is seen in both The Commentary on the Decision (which he may have written) and The Commentary on the Images (Wilhelm 1950, xxxix-xxx).

The literary machine in Western culture—as a physical machine, as well as a procedural way of generating texts—seems to have been devised in 1274 C.E. by the Catholic alchemist, mystic, and philosopher Ramon Llull (1232–1316). Although his system is too elaborate to explain fully here, he related nine letters of the alphabet each to a quality, a relation, a question, a subject, a virtue, and a vice, and then created a system to, as Llull scholar

Andrew Bonner (1997) writes, "combine these theological, scientific and moral components to produce arguments." One page of his *Ars Generalis Ultima* and the shortened version of that work, the *Ars Breva,* as they were circulated in Llull's time, typically included a physical text–generating machine that allowed three-letter combinations to be devised. There were three circles, each with the letters of the alphabet drawn along the circumference at even intervals. Bonner describes the way these parts were made into a machine: "In medieval manuscripts, the outside circle is normally drawn on the page, and the two inner ones are separate pieces of parchment or paper held in place on top of it by a little piece of string, permitting them to rotate in relation to each other and to the larger circle."

Although the *I Ching* is more widely known in the West today than is Llull's machine, the latter was also quite influential. Llull, known as "Doctor Illuminatus," had a tremendous following. He wrote approximately three hundred books, with the ones detailing his text-generating machine becoming some of the most important and influential. Chairs were established in universities in Barcelona and Valencia after his death to further his studies. When Gottfried Wilhelm Leibniz attempted to create the first mechanical calculator, his work was informed by Llull's writing and the description of his machine (Bonner 1997). Despite being beatified (usually the first step toward sainthood), Llull was not canonized. His ideas—which, as an article in *The Catholic Encyclopedia* explains, threatened "breaking down the distinction between natural and supernatural truth"—were condemned by the Church (Turner 1911).

The next important literary machine that was formulated in Western history was described only in satire, by a riddler who has been mentioned already. It appeared in *Gulliver's Travels.* A computer historian writes: "In 1726 Johnathan Swift published a description of a wonderful machine, made of equal parts of irony, sarcasm, and mockery, that would automatically write books on all the arts and sciences" (Weiss 1985, 164). Swift described Gulliver visiting Balnibarbi on his third voyage and surveying a range of absurd academic endeavors in the Grand Academy of Lagado. On meeting the first professor Gulliver sees

> a Frame . . . twenty Foot square, placed in the middle of the Room. The Superficies was composed of several Bits of Wood, about the

bigness of a Die, but some larger than others. They were all linked
together by slender Wires. These bits of Wood were covered on every
Square with Paper pasted on them, and on these Papers were written all the Words of their Language, in their several Moods, Tenses,
and Declensions, but without any Order. (Swift [1726] 1735, pt. 3,
chap. 4)

By turning iron handles at the edge, the professor's forty students bring different words into view. Then, as most of them look over the results and report
any series of words that might make a sentence, a few serving as scribes write
down these generated texts. Although offered in jest, Swift's hypothetical literary machine has been remembered and invoked in the information age.
Weiss (1985) explains that the machine's "purpose, the claims of its illustri-
ous professor-inventor, his call for public funding, and the operation of the
device by students clearly classify it as an early attempt at artificial intelligence
and have caused it to be cited often as typical of this discipline" (164).

The generation of secular texts by procedure was done early in the last
century to interesting effect, as William Burroughs tells it. He wrote that at a
"rally in the 1920's Tristan Tzara the man from nowhere proposed to create
a poem on the spot by pulling words out of a hat. A riot ensued wrecked the
theatre" (Burroughs 2003, 90). Romanian-born Tzara, who was a founder of
Dada and who went on to become an important part of another French
movement, surrealism, around 1930, is credited with being the originator of
the "cut-up" technique of random recombination of text. Tzara's perspective
on the production of language could not have been more different than that
of Llull, who sought to systematically establish important religious and philosophical truths. "Everything one looks at is false," Tzara wrote in the "Dada
Manifesto," the first of seven that he wrote. "I do not consider the relative
result more important than the choice between cake and cherries after dinner" (Tzara 1951).

Brion Gysin (1982) followed in that anti-tradition three decades later,
without at first realizing it:

While cutting a mount for a drawing in room 25, I sliced through a
pile of newspapers with my Stanley blade and thought of what I had
said to Burroughs some six months earlier about the necessity for

turning painters' techniques directly onto writing. I picked up the
raw words and began to piece together texts. (51)

The technique, developed in the summer of 1959, was used to write *Minutes to Go* (Burroughs 2003, 90). (Another interesting connection between computing and literature is that Burroughs was the grandson of the inventor of the Burroughs Adding Machine, who was also named William S. Burroughs; the novelist was heir to the fortune created by this early computer.) Burroughs felt this cut-up technique was a step toward the more complete automation of language. Burroughs wrote that the "cut-ups, permutations and tape recorder experiments carried out by Brion Gysin are aimed . . . toward making words talk on their own" (qtd. in Gysin 1982, xi).

France was the site of another important event in the history of the literary machine. On 24 November 1960 the Oulipo was founded by François Le Lionnais and Raymond Queneau. The group was dedicated not to the creation of literature, but to the creation of methods or ways of creating literature—hence the word "potential" in the name. The literary machine, a form of potential literature, was certainly a proper object of Oulipian study. The group's formulations included algorithms to be applied to an existing text (e.g., Jean Lescure's N + 7 rule for replacing each noun with the seventh noun after it in a dictionary (Mathews and Brotchie 1998, 198)) and constraints on the authorship of a text (e.g., the text must be a palindrome; letters and numbers must read the same forward and backward). The most succinct definition of the group was provided at a 5 April 1961 meeting by Queneau: "rats who construct the labyrinth from which they propose to escape" (Lescure 1986, 37; Mathews and Brotchie 1998, 201).

One physical device for generating texts was Queneau's 1961 *Cent mille milliard de poèmes* (*100,000,000,000,000 Poems*), which took the form of a book with ten sonnets (each of the usual fourteen lines) bound one in front of the other and with each line cut so that it could be "turned," like a page, separately. Any one of ten lines could thus be selected for each position. An entry in *Oulipo Compendium* explains: "The rhyme scheme of the sonnets is uniform; grammatical correctness is assured no matter what sequence of lines occurs" (Mathews and Brotchie 1998, 14). Hence there are 10^{14} possible poems in the book, which would take (by Queneau's calculation) more than 190 million years to read. This potential sonnet has, amazingly, been

translated into English twice—by Stanley Chapman and by John Crombie—
and it has been implemented both on computers and as a more stereotypical machine, with gears and rollers (Mathews and Brotchie 1998, 177–178).
Queneau also devised the first Choose Your Own Adventure type of story,
his 1967 "Un conte à votre façon" (which has been translated as "A story as
you like it" and "Yours for the telling"). This short work has twenty-one possible text segments; the reader is asked to make a choice after the first one is
read, and after each subsequent one, up to one of the possible endings.
Warren Motte explains that it was "inspired by the presentation of the
instructions given to computers, and by programmed teaching" (1997, 156).
The juvenile fiction series named Choose Your Own Adventure, of similar
inspiration, began in 1979 with Edward Packard's *The Cave of Time*—too late
to influence the early stages of interactive fiction, and in fact likely to have
been at least vaguely inspired by actual computer programs, including very
early interactive fiction. It was one of several series of childrens' books (in
many languages) that asked readers to choose the next step to take after each
page or so of text. There were more than two hundred such books published
in the two main Bantam series, Choose Your Own Adventure and Choose
Your Own Adventure for Younger Readers. *The Cave of Time* was itself made
into a graphical adventure game by Bantam Software and published in 1985.

One book-length antecedent to the Choose Your Own Adventure
was Julio Cortázar's 1963 *Rayuela* (translated as *Hopscotch,* 1966), a novel that
has "expendable chapters" and offers instructions for how to read along two
different paths. In one reading sequence, a scene with a very different
emotional tone (such as one depicting a rape, narrated by a rapist) is placed
between two others; in the others this scene is omitted and the reading is
quite different.

Another earlier antecedent was the even more reconfigurable
Composition no. 1 by Marc Saporta, published in France in 1961 and translated into English by Richard Howard in 1963. This book—not a codex but
150 loose, unnumbered pages in a box—invites the reader to shuffle the
pages and read them in any order. According to the text printed on the box,
the 149 texts on the loose pages (one is a title page) tell the story of X, who
has an affair, has a disastrous marriage, gambles, serves in the French army
during the occupation of Germany, rapes a girl, and is in an auto accident—
though not necessarily in that order. Each text describes something coherent

about a particular moment in X's life, providing enough context (often repeated in other, similar texts) to make the moment intelligible. Some of these events are fixed as having happened when X was a child or an adult, but there is ambiguity as to the exact sequence of some events; causation, in several cases, is also unclear, as is the exact nature of some events. A theft that X committed may have involved his stealing an envelope of money from his workplace, or it may have been an envelope of names that, as a member of the Resistance, he stole from the Germans.

The text on the box suggests that a particular reading of the pages, in a particular order, will resolve the events of the story into an order, and it suggests that this order of events will change depending upon how the pages are sorted. It does not seem as though a particular shuffling of the deck will actually render any the ambiguities of the potential story certain, however. A particular reading will allow the reader to ponder the elements of the story in a different order and to *try* to resolve them along the way. During the process, a different set of post hoc, propter hoc fallacies will inevitably be imagined by the reader, and these will suggest different connections among events, but by the time the reading is finished it will be hard to still believe in any of them. As J. David Bolter (2001) writes, while "Saporta's experiment . . . seems to position his work as an inevitable, final step in the exhaustion of printed literature," it seems, even if it is indeed offered as that, to also serve as "a bridge to the electronic medium" where the author constructs narrative possibility rather than narrative itself (150). It is in fact left to the reader of *Composition no. 1* to assemble the pages into a particular telling, and to realize a narrative from the deck of texts provided; although the ordering of events may never be certain, this hardly prevents the reader from associating meaning with and investing emotion in the events that did take place and the characters who took part in them.

Certain literary machines were implemented on computers in the United States before *Adventure*. Dale Peterson (1983) writes that "Louis Milic, an English professor at Cleveland State University, may have created the first computer poetry. In 1963, Milic programmed a computer to generate absurd English sentences" (138). Milic then refined his program to allow different poems to be generated with the same syntax. This effort had been anticipated by an attempt in England to generate (amusing and nonsensical) physics essays in the 1950s (141). Brion Gysin (1982) himself experimented with computer-generated texts with the help of a mathematician. The computer's use in the generation of poems and stories has its own interesting history. These are only few of the experiments that preceded the first work of interactive fiction; some of what followed included attempts at machine generation of stories (Meehan 1980), a thread of computational and literary endeavor that differs from the creation of interactive systems.

An important early literary machine of another sort was Theodor Nelson's 1970 *Labyrinth,* which Nelson has said was the first publicly accessible hypertext. *Labyrinth* was a hypertext catalog of the 1970 *Software* exhibition at the Jewish Museum. The exhibition, which proved controversial, included conceptual art and unusual applications of technology. The catalog was installed there on a PDP-8 with some difficulty, and it ran for the last month of the exhibition (Shanken 1998). Although this work was nonfiction, and although it was never as widely known as Nelson's influential books were, *Labyrinth* was pioneering in offering a reconfigurable text on a topic outside the usual sphere of mainframe computing.

Looking back from twentieth-century text-generating experiments to Llull and the *I Ching,* it is important to recognize that, as Peterson (1983) reminds us,

> When computer programmers and a few poets first produced machine poems based on much the same principle as that of Tristan Tzara . . . they did not see themselves as the odious speculators in Swift's Academy of Lagado, nor as poets in the Dada tradition. Mostly, they were light-hearted experimenters, trying to discover the word-manipulation possibilities of a new machine. (137)

Nevertheless, those working with computers were, and continue to be, influenced by early work on literary machines. Versions of early literary machines that have been implemented on digital computers, citations of these machines in computing literature, and presentations about these early innovations at computer-oriented conferences demonstrate such influence rather directly. In any case, this brief history should indicate something about the possibilities of computer literature, since it shows the wide range of purposes to which literary machines had already been put, before interactive fiction was devised: prophetic, theological, satirical, nihilistic, and playful.

DUNGEONS AND DRAGONS

The first successful fantasy role-playing game was formulated in the early 1970s in Lake Geneva, Wisconsin, and first published in 1974. Gary Gygax published a precursor to *Dungeons and Dragons* in a magazine he ran for the Castle and Crusade Society, part of the International Federation of Wargaming. Gaming of this sort involved 1:20 scale figurines and maps. With Dave Arenson, Gygax then developed a new sort of campaign incorporating character classes ("Heroes or Wizards"), experience points, and a dungeon maze. Spells and monsters were incorporated into this first *Dungeons and Dragons* campaign, Greyhawk (Gygax 1980). In summary,

> D&D is an open-ended game in which the players assume the roles of characters in a story and can have those characters attempt any action whatsoever. The game is controlled by a gamesmaster, who uses tables, dice, and personal judgment to decide on the effect of a character's efforts. (McGath 1984, 6)

This "gamesmaster" is called the dungeon master. The players say what their characters, the "player characters," do within the "world" of the campaign. Dice are rolled to assign ability points to player characters initially, and dice are employed to help determine the outcome of combat and other encounters. Over the course of many adventures, the members of a party advance in level and become more powerful—and the dungeon master devises new challenges for them.

Figurines and dice are not as central to *Dungeons and Dragons* as is sometimes thought. Miniatures, although important to certain war games that preceded *Dungeons and Dragons,* are seldom used in playing *Dungeons and Dragons*. For the most part they are simply merchandise, and are even advertised as "collectibles" rather than as essential components of the game. Dice, on the other hand, are frequently used in a typical game. The twenty-sided die and other dice of unusual shape have become iconic. Dice are used to introduce unpredictability; based on the roll of a die, events may transpire that were not anticipated, foiling even the dungeon master's plans. It is not unheard of for people to play without dice, however. Chance occurrences are simply one element within a framework of problem solving, role playing, and exploration of an imagined, fantastic world. Consider this player's perspective, printed in *Dragon* magazine:

> The dreamer's art, the ability to cut loose from the restraints of reality and touch new shores and lives, is the essence and lure of D + D. It is the challenge of pitting one's skills and common sense against a strange and sometimes hostile universe where death awaits with open arms. (Filmore 1980)

The extent to which *Dungeons and Dragons* is inspired by J. R. R. Tolkien's work has frequently been misunderstood and overstated. Although Tolkien's books are obviously important to the fantasy genre and were influential on many particular *Dungeons and Dragons* campaigns undertaken by groups of players, Tolkien can sometimes seem the single straw that those unfamiliar with fantasy and adventure writing grasp at when trying to understand where this game came from and how to situate it vis-à-vis literature. Recent film releases have not helped correct this misperception. Many writers have assumed that Tolkien's books are the basis for the game—for instance, Christian opponents of the game have assumed this (Weldon and Bjornstad 1984, 49). This confusion is not restricted to outside observers. Some players of *Dungeons and Dragons* have similarly thought that the game was Tolkien-inspired and Tolkien-centered. The official statement from TSR, the makers of the game, in response to letters from such players is that "*D&D* was not written to recreate or in any collective way simulate Professor Tolkien's world or beings . . . this system works with the worlds of R. E. Howard, Fritz Leiber and L. S. de Camp and Fletcher Pratt much better than that of Tolkien" (Kuntz 1980). Middle Earth was created for the sake of a single adventure, as TSR saw it, while other fantasy literature, more closely related to *Dungeons and Dragons,* has been set in a world rich with continual adventure.

There were other precedents for *Dungeons and Dragons* besides wargaming. Although fantasy sports leagues did not evolve into today's popular form until around 1980, an earlier type of game, called dice baseball, provided its own platform for fantasy and determined the outcome of events much as *Dungeons and Dragons* later would. In his 1968 novel, *The Universal Baseball Association, Inc.: J. Henry Waugh, Prop.,* Robert Coover memorably described how this sort of game, in which a roll of the dice would determine chance events, could even allow a player to imagine an entirely different world.

The original *Dungeons and Dragons* rules were intentionally left incomplete so that different groups of people could adopt different styles of play. In a rare moment of lucidity, one Christian critic of the game noted that "Dungeon Masters play the game differently. Some dislike situations in which characters get killed. Others feel a game is successful only when half the players die in battle" (Robie 1991, 47). The extent to which chance, theater, or puzzle solving is involved depends on the particular group playing *Dungeons and Dragons.* Yet the general framework of the game (not just its particular setting and fantasy theme) was clearly important to what would follow. Aarseth (1997) writes that the "*Dungeons and Dragons* genre might be regarded as an oral cybertext, the oral predecessor to computerized, written, adventure games" (98).

EARLY COMPUTER GAMES

In 1912 Leonardo Torres Quevedo (1852–1936), a Spanish engineer, devised the first computer game. He constructed the first true chess-playing automaton—one that operated without a human concealed inside. This caused a stir when first demonstrated publicly in Paris in 1914 (Perera Domínguez 1997). The automaton was an electromechanical device with a vertical chessboard; the pieces were pegs. The machine played a KRK chess endgame, playing rook and king against a person playing a lone king. The machine did not just signal its move: It physically moved its pieces with a mechanical arm. An illegal move was indicated by the illumination of a light bulb. Although the automaton would sometimes exceed fifty moves (thus giving the player a draw), it would always be able to eventually mate the human opponent's king on the first rank. This first machine had a fairly easy-to-use interface, but that was improved upon in 1920 when Torres built a second automaton with an ordinary chessboard. This one moved its pieces using electromagnets, and, hooked to a gramophone, it employed speech synthesis: It verbally announced check ("jaque al rey") and checkmate ("mate"). This second automaton is now housed in Madrid at the Colegio de Ingenieros de Caminos, Canales y Puertos and still functions perfectly (*Scientific American Supplement* 1915; Lopez 1998; Randell 1982; Atkinson 1993, 22).

There were certainly limitations to Torres's machine. It was not developed to work generally, even for the reduced problem of the KRK endgame. According to Atkinson (1993),

> Torres swiftly discovered that programming is not an easy task. . . . he decided to force the lone King to the first rank for the mate . . . he simplified the problem further by assuming that the two Kings were already on opposite sides of the rank controlled by the Rook. His final algorithm assumed a fixed starting position for the automaton's King and Rook, but allowed the human opponent's King to be placed on any unchecked square in the first six ranks. (21)

With these restrictions on the setup (defining a subset of possible KRK chess endgames, and allowing for 61 rather than 50 moves without the capture of a piece) Torres's algorithm guarantees a win. It does so without, requiring that the machine's king be moved diagonally—allowing for the device to be mechanically simpler (Atkinson 1993, 21).

Perhaps Torres's invention of the first computer game is overlooked because it seems a minor achievement of this important figure, who, in addition to devising a new type of semi-rigid airship and a remote-control boat, did pioneering work in the development of the modern computer by making advances in cybernetics and by developing calculating machines (Randell 1982). It may instead be that this device, coming so far before *general-purpose* digital computing was invented, is not considered a computer game. More likely, it has been overlooked by the English-speaking world because Torres himself has been overlooked in English-language scholarship on science and invention. Despite the neglect this father of the computer game has been shown, Torres's invention has had some influence: Many researchers working in chess automation, for instance, have been aware of the two automata Torres created and how they worked, and a photograph shows Torres's son demonstrating the second machine to pioneering cyberneticist Norbert Wiener in 1951 (Eames and Eames 1973). Contemporaries recognized these chess-playing automata as early steps toward artificial intelligence: "the automatons of Torres . . . attempt the accomplishment of things that have hitherto been reserved entirely for the human mind" (*Scientific American Supplement* 1915, 298).

After this spectacular beginning, there was little work done in computer game development until after World War II. With the arrival of the general-purpose computer came many opportunities for game making. During the early 1950s, before the advent of batch processing, Eric Solomon (1984) explains that though "machines of this period were slow, their immediacy made it possible for the adventurous to program the odd game," which might take the form of "reaction testing" (2–3). There were official and more elaborate efforts at computer games, too. In 1951 a computer game was displayed by Ferranti at the Festival of Britain. It was a special-purpose system that played Nim, in which the players alternately take one or more matches from different piles, and the one forced to take the last match loses (Bennett 1990, 283–284). The first academic paper on computer chess (Shannon 1950) led to the first new developments in that field since Torres. A remarkable checkers program was devised by Arthur Samuel at IBM that learned from the games it played and, by 1962, was able not only to defeat its creator (Spencer 1968, 14) but also to best a human champion (Samuel 1963, 103–104). The checkers programs even learned more rapidly than human players did, making greater progress over the same number of games (Williams 1972, 72). Beginning around 1950 computer war games were also developed in the United States, serving, as one early writer on computer games explained, "to simulate activity ranging from ... tactical action to a large full-scale war." One was the 1955 HUTSPIEL, which ran on an analog computer and was for two players, Red and Blue, representing the USSR and NATO; this may have been the first two-player computer game. Other programs included the tactical simulator CARMONETTE and the theater-level war game THEATER-SPIEL, both running on Univac computers (Spencer 1968, 12).

The batch-processing era was not as productive. Solomon (1984) writes: "The programmer found his access to the machine barred by a high counter, air-conditioning doors, and personnel in white coats. . . . These were the 'dark ages' for computer gaming" (3). When timesharing was introduced in the middle of the 1960s, working on games became easier. Still, those who were billed for computer time could not afford the activity. A few institutions where resources for game making were available would lead the way during this time. *Star Trek* was developed around 1967, offering a universe grid to explore, but the canonical version was written later, in 1972, by Mike Mayfield. That was also the year Gregory Yob wrote *Hunt the Wumpus*

(Nelson 2001b, 344), notable for having a world that was not a simple grid but a dodecahedron. This feature of *Hunt the Wumpus* inspired the irregular worlds of interactive fiction; different rooms, from the very beginning, could be interconnected by the designer in any way.

One center of early computer game development—and one that would become important to the history of interactive fiction—was MIT. The playful approach to computing pioneered by the self-proclaimed "hackers" of the Tech Model Railroad Club (or TMRC, founded in 1947) gave rise to many early games and other computer recreations (Levy 1984, 17–38). One early development on the TX-0, a prototype computer to which the group was given access, was *Mouse Maze,* which animated a mouse's traversal of a maze; the mouse ate cheese (and, in a later version, drank martinis that caused it to perform more poorly) along the way (Oberg 2001; Levy 1984). Games were also used as testbeds for artificial intelligence research and in other types of work. As one of the creators of *Zork* said, "MIT was a place where you could tell your boss 'I'm going to spend some time writing a game,' and that was okay" (Anderson 2001).

A notable computer game developed at MIT by Steve Russell and others was *Spacewar!* (Levy 1984, 59–69; Graetz 1981). In the 1962 *Spacewar!,* the ancestor of all modern video games, two players used special controls to manipulate their spaceships in a battle that was depicted on a CRT display. Although video games later became an important industry, spawning arcades and home game consoles, the influence of these graphics-based, action-oriented computer games on interactive fiction actually turned out to be rather slight, in the long run. Video games showed themselves to be a different branch of recreational computing.

Other sorts of games were developed and played at MIT, however. The Artificial Intelligence Lab and the Dynamic Modeling Group were both active gaming spots around 1970. The Dynamic Modeling Group (DM) got its start, one DM member explained, "writing libraries of reusable software that would dynamically link together as needed when the client program ran" (Lebling 2002). "DM was in a very good spot for computer gaming," Tim Anderson (2001) said, with Imlac terminals capable of graphics instead of the standard text-only VT-52s used elsewhere on campus. These terminals had green-on-black vector graphics, not the raster displays that are ubiquitous today. The Imlacs had their own processors and 8k of memory. There were stand-alone versions of *Hunt the Wumpus* and of a game like *Pong* that ran on them without using any of the resources of the PDP-10 to which they were connected; there was even an Imlac implementation of *Spacewar!* (Lebling 2002). Anderson (2001) said, "At DM, because the terminals were so expensive, we didn't have terminals in the offices. There was a terminal room with four or five Imlacs and some cubicle-like areas that were partitioned off."

According to Anderson (2001), "The most interesting thing was a game called *Maze*—which was later seen as *Mazewars* on the Altos." *Maze* was a video game—a multiplayer video game, and in fact it was the first first-person shooter, ancestor of *Doom, Quake, Unreal,* and their brethren. Dave Lebling (2002), who programmed the *Maze* server in PDP-10 assembly and who had also coded the Imlac versions of *Wumpus* and *Spacewar,* called *Maze* "a computer version of kids running around shooting each other with toy guns." Players' avatars (which simply appeared as their login names) were situated in a maze; the screen displayed a three-dimensional view of this maze from the avatar's perspective. Over opponents' "heads" were arrows showing which way they were facing—"or a pair of dots indicating eyes if they were facing directly at you," Lebling (2002) said. Greg Thompson, an undergraduate, programmed the Imlac client in assembly. Up to eight people could play, and the computer could take the place of some players if there were fewer than eight who wanted to play: Lebling also implemented the behaviors of the robot opponents. Anderson (2001) described *Maze* as "all about speed and reflexes," noting that "DM was the only place where you could play it."

A less visually spectacular MIT game—but one that was available on the ARPANet and became quite popular—was a text-only quiz game, *Trivia*. Tak To (who had also coded some additions to *Maze*) wrote the first version of *Trivia*, which Anderson said was an "utter kludge." Around 1975 or 1976 Marc Blank built a type of database system, a message store, as part of his work on a DM project. As a test of this, he created a new version of *Trivia*. Those who played *Trivia* on MIT's ARPANet host 80 would be the first ones outside MIT to discover a new game on that computer in 1977. In that year, four programmers and writers from the DM—Tim Anderson, *Trivia* programmer Marc Blank, Bruce Daniels, and *Maze* programmer David Lebling—would install a work of interactive fiction called *Zork*. That work is the subject of most of chapter 4.

ELIZA/DOCTOR AND COMPUTER CONVERSATION

The idea of computer conversation was developed along with the general-purpose digital computer; Turing (1950) presented it quite clearly in his influential paper "Computing Machinery and Intelligence," in which he established the well-known, if sometimes misapplied, "Turing Test." He gave the example of a parlor game in which a person of one gender tries to imitate a person of the other, and then suggested a similar game in which a computer would imitate a human in conversation. The question "Can machines think?" could then be replaced by one that was easier to answer: "Are there imaginable digital computers which would do well in the imitation game?" (Turing 1950, 54–55). In formulating this test, Turing highlighted the importance of conversational ability to our perception of intelligence, at a time when computers almost exclusively processed numbers rather than language.

There was not a lot of good human/computer conversation early in the 1950s, but by the start of the next decade several interesting systems were being developed. One of many important early conversational programs was Baseball, which could answer questions like "Who did the Red Sox lose to on July 5?" and "How many games did the Yankees play in July?" by searching through a store of this information, represented in English (Green et al. 1963, 211). A more sophisticated system was SIR (Semantic Information Retrieval), which was "capable of 'understanding' statements dealing with set relations, part-whole relations, ownership, and certain special relations" and which maintained a dynamic model of its knowledge in a special format, using word associations (Raphael 1968, 33–44). While SIR worked well, Terry Winograd (1972) noted that "the types of complex information it could use were highly limited, and could not be easily expanded" (37).

The next section discusses how the further development of knowledge representations, and attempts to understand sentences based on syntax, led to dramatic general advances in the understanding of language by computers. The most interesting development of the mid-1960s was no doubt that a researcher taking an entirely different approach—using a very unsophisticated representation of knowledge and a technique that could not be applied very generally—created a conversational system that has nevertheless been recognized as "astonishingly persuasive" (J. Murray 1997, 69).

That system was ELIZA. It was programmed in MAD-SLIP (a language similar to LISP) during 1964–1966 by Joseph Weizenbaum at MIT's Project MAC. ELIZA is a language analysis program that can run many different scripts and have different sorts of conversations; the most famous script by far was called DOCTOR, which Weizenbaum (1976) explained was "designed to permit it to play (I should really say parody) the role of a Rogerian psychotherapist engaged in an initial interview with a patient" (2–3). The system, running this script, became known as the first computer conversationalist, the first chatterbot. To simplify ELIZA's procedure—but not to simplify very much—the program would first search for keywords in input. If some were found, the program would transform the input according to a rule and print out the transformed sentence. If none were found, it would provide a default (usually noncommittal) output. Here is a bit of a conversation with ELIZA/DOCTOR, with the computer's reply in all capital letters:

Men are all alike.
IN WHAT WAY?
They're always bugging us about something or other.
CAN YOU THINK OF A SPECIFIC EXAMPLE?
Well, my boyfriend made me come here.
YOUR BOYFRIEND MADE YOU COME HERE
He says I'm depressed much of the time.
I AM SORRY TO HEAR YOU ARE DEPRESSED
(Weizenbaum 1966)

Although ELIZA was later used to do more sophisticated types of natural language understanding (Weizenbaum 1967; Winograd 1972, 38), Weizenbaum (1976) made it clear that it in no way offered a general solution to the problem of natural language understanding. Nevertheless, users were quite affected by it. Weizenbaum wrote that he "was startled to see how quickly and how very deeply people conversing with DOCTOR became emotionally involved with the computer" (6). Janet Murray (1997) described him as being "so disconcerted by his achievement that he wrote a book warning of the dangers of attributing human thought to machines" (71).

While other sorts of literary machines had been devised previously, ELIZA/DOCTOR may have been the first piece of interactive software to exhibit literary qualities. Certainly, there is no similar early program that is so widely known. One historian of the chatterbot writes that "anecdotes about Eliza instantly became part of computer science's folklore" (Leonard 1998, 42). Some psychiatrists thought ELIZA/DOCTOR should be used in therapy; people took contradictory positions on big questions in artificial intelligence based on ELIZA/DOCTOR; and the program inspired its own branch of computer literature based on conversation with fictional characters (J. Murray 1997, 214–247; Leonard 1998). ELIZA/DOCTOR has been widely distributed and implemented on different systems. While it was not immediately embraced as literary, by referring to it as "parody" Weizenbaum himself suggested it may have an element of literary art in it. As early as 1984 there was a suggestion that the system be considered by literary theorists (Neisz and Holland 1984, 118–119). It has no doubt been an inspiration to interactive fiction creators throughout the history of the form, and Janet Murray (1997) has spoken of the system's influence even more strongly: "Weizenbaum stands as the earliest, and still perhaps the premier, literary artist in the computer medium" (72).

SHRDLU: THE FIRST WORK OF INTERACTIVE FICTION?

It is well established that the first work of interactive fiction is *Adventure*. However, when considering the formal definition of interactive fiction that has already been advanced, one realizes that another computer program should actually be assigned this honor: Terry Winograd's SHRDLU, which he programmed in LISP at the MIT Artificial Intelligence Laboratory during 1968–1970 (Winograd 1972, 5). Although SHRDLU has been mentioned in online discussions and given as an example of a predecessor to interactive fiction in a book (McGath 1984, 11–14) and in Nelson's "Short History of Interactive Fiction" (2001, 334), no one has yet assigned it such importance.

This program (named after the second row of keys on a Linotype machine; see Winograd 1999)) carried on a dialog with the user via teletype, also displaying an image of a tabletop with blocks on it. It could respond to natural language commands in real time, in five to twenty seconds

(Winograd 1972, 7–8). It would move the simulated blocks around if asked to; it could also answer questions about them. According to Winograd,

> [T]he program is given a detailed model of a particular domain. In addition, the system has a simple model of its own mentality. It can remember and discuss its plans and actions as well as carrying them out. It enters into a dialog with a person, responding to English sentences with actions and English replies, asking for clarification when its heuristic programs cannot understand a sentence. (1)

SHRDLU used its knowledge of the simulated world to help it parse input. It represented its knowledge as procedures. SHRDLU had eleven different components. There was a module for generating replies to the user, for instance, and one for simulating the blocks world (Winograd 1972). Here is a short excerpt from a much longer SHRDLU sample transcript:

Person: WHAT DID THE RED CUBE SUPPORT BEFORE YOU STARTED TO CLEAN IT OFF?
Computer: THE GREEN PYRAMID.
Person: THERE WERE FIVE BLOCKS TO THE LEFT OF THE BOX THEN.
Computer: NO, ONLY FOUR OF THEM: THE RED CUBE, TWO LARGE GREEN CUBES AND A LARGE RED BLOCK.
Person: PUT THE BLUE PYRAMID ON THE BLOCK IN THE BOX.
Computer: OK. (does it)
Person: IS THERE ANYTHING WHICH IS BIGGER THAN EVERY PYRAMID BUT IS NOT AS WIDE AS THE THING THAT SUPPORTS IT?
Computer: YES, THE BLUE BLOCK. (Winograd 1999)

The great sophistication of SHRDLU should be evident from this brief exchange. SHRDLU was able to understand almost any input—just about anything that a human could understand—as long as it pertained to the blocks world. SHRDLU remembered everything that it had previously done to the blocks and all that had transpired in the conversation. Winograd's

Ph.D. thesis describing the system is widely recognized as a landmark. It was published in its entirety in 1972 in *Cognitive Psychology,* occupying a whole volume, and it was also published as a book that year.

Although it seems strange to classify it as such, SHRDLU is clearly a work of interactive fiction—formally. It is text-based (although graphics are part of the system), and it implements both natural language understanding and a simulated world. Considered as interactive fiction, SHRDLU is not at all impressive, since it does not provide the interactor with a compelling experience. Not only did SHRDLU lack the sort of challenge that makes a riddle work, it had no goal at all, not even an immediate one. The only reason for a user to interact was to see that the simulated robot could indeed understand and act upon natural language input. Being offered a conversation with a block-manipulating robot was not nearly as interesting as was the situation set up by SHRDLU's less intelligent cousin, ELIZA/DOCTOR.

Of course, SHRDLU was not created to be a work of interactive fiction or to be an interesting literary experience. It was supposed to be, and was, an extremely important advance (or series of advances) in artificial intelligence and natural language understanding. Interacting with it—even without having any motivation provided by the scenario—was quite impressive for researchers at the time. As the first work with all the formal elements of interactive fiction, SHRDLU not only achieved its research goals but also allowed for more interesting potential narratives, simulated spaces, and challenges to later be integrated with the sort of structure it exemplified. By augmenting SHRDLU's parser and world model (actually, a far simplified version of these) in this way, interactive fiction could be fully realized.

ADVENTURE: WE HAVE CAVE

In 1975 Sandy and Laura explored a cave by having a conversation with a PDP-10 computer, almost certainly by means of a remote ASR33 Teletype (Adams 2002). The girls would have been about five and seven years old then (Brucker and Watson 1987, 71). They ventured into the Flint Mammoth Cave System through the Bedquilt Entrance in Kentucky, opening a steel grate beside a dry stream bed and finding a place underground that was full of turns and wonders. The computer program that took them there was able to communicate in plain English. It had some of ELIZA/DOCTOR's charm—at least offering them a spectacular environment to explore and a motivation to interact—but like SHRDLU it could also understand them well enough to have their caver "player character" take action within the world. This new program, which these two early interactors are said to have enjoyed, was called *Adventure*. It was the first work of interactive fiction (certainly, the first created as such, with an intriguing world), and they were among the first to experience it—if not the very first—because it was written for them by their father, Will Crowther.

It was in 1975 that Crowther completed *Adventure*—his version of *Adventure*, the original, with the file name ADVENT. He made it available to his daughters and to any programmers on ARPANet-connected computers. Crowther, who worked at Bolt, Beranek and Newman (BBN) in Cambridge, Massachusetts, was one of the programmers who had developed the ARPANet, the basis for the Internet, a few years earlier. He had played *Dungeons and Dragons* regularly with a local group, started by a fellow employee at BBN. One of the players in that group, who joined after Crowther left, describes it as follows:

> Eric Roberts . . . started running a *D&D* group a year or so before *Adventure* was written. Eric had his own ideas about how *D&D* should be done, emphasizing story-telling and de-emphasizing the mechanical aspects of the game such as die-rolling (though there was still a lot of that). He tried to create a Tolkien-inspired world that was fun and consistent with Middle Earth. . . . I think one strong component of his *D&D* philosophy that carried over into *Zork* was to try to keep the mechanical workings of the game (the rules, or the implementation) as hidden as possible, which to me enhanced the fun and immersiveness of the experience. (Lebling 2002)

This report comes from one of the authors of *Zork*, who may have replaced Crowther in the group. He, like Crowther, played a thief. Their game sessions were, indeed, Tolkien-inspired, despite what TSR had to say about Tolkien and *Dungeons and Dragons*. Characters were killed off regularly, but usually not permanently.

Although Crowther was a player of these Tolkien-inspired *Dungeons and Dragons* games, when he described the underground setting of *Adventure* it wasn't fantasy writing. Crowther was also an experienced caver, and he had explored and mapped many parts of the cave system that *Adventure* simulates. In 1972 he had found a way to apply computing to caving by plotting maps of that cave system based on survey data, working with his wife Pat Crowther, who was also a BBN employee. The two had met at MIT, and she was also a caver (Brucker and Watson 1987, 167–177).

Will had been along with Pat on an unsuccessful 26 May 1972 expedition to try to find a connection from the Flint Ridge Cave System to Mammoth Cave, for instance. Later, on July 15, Pat managed to squeeze through the appropriately named Tight Spot in the Flint Ridge Cave System to explore, announcing to the others when she returned, "We have cave!" (Brucker and Watson 1987, 192). Then, on September 9, 1972, Pat was part of the first party to make it through the Tight Spot and find a connection from the Flint Ridge Cave System to Mammoth Cave. As a result of that expedition, more than 144 contiguous miles of cave were then surveyed. The two cave systems were joined to one, the Flint Mammoth Cave System, making it the longest in the world (Brucker and Watson 1987, 233–248).

Crowther explains that things were different later, when he began work on *Adventure:* "I got involved in a divorce, and that left me a bit pulled apart in various ways. In particular I was missing my kids" (qtd. in Peterson 1983, 187–188). He had stopped caving at that time as well, but decided, he said, to "write a program that was a re-creation in fantasy of my caving, and also would be a game for the kids, and perhaps [have] some aspects of the Dungeons and Dragons that I had been playing" (qtd. Peterson 1983, 188). Crowther explained that BBN fortunately was, like MIT, openminded about programmers developing games on their expensive computer hardware: "The idea was that you did your work and if the machines were sitting idle and you had something else that you wanted to do, why not?" (Crowther 1994, 8). He developed *Adventure* while working there, in FORTRAN on BBN's PDP-10. FORTRAN, which some regard as the first high-level programming language, was developed at IBM and used widely in mathematical, scientific, and engineering applications. It came to be used in business, too, but although many hackers knew it, most in the artificial intelligence community eschewed this procedural language for the functional language LISP or one of its variants.

Some versions of *Adventure* (dozens of commercial and free implementations have been made available) are called *Colossal Cave*. The work simulates an area known as Bedquilt Cave (Adams 2002) or the Bedquilt Entrance, which was connected to Colossal Cave in 1896 (Brucker and Watson 1987, 294). (Bedquilt and Colossal are both entrances to the Flint Mammoth Cave System.) One caver, Mel Park, relates that in the actual cave system, just as in *Adventure,* "there is a Hall of the Mountain King and a Two-Pit Room. The entrance is indeed a strong steel grate at the bottom of a twenty-foot depression" (qtd. in Adams 2002). A small outdoor area leads, through this grating, to the main part of *Adventure's* simulated underground world. This world is described much as one would expect a caver to describe it: succinctly, but using the same terminology and with the same attention to essential details. "Staircase," "dome," "room," and "hall" are used to indicate natural formations, and the emphasis is on where there is access for further travel. Here is one description of a location in *Adventure:*

YOU ARE AT A COMPLEX JUNCTION. A LOW HANDS AND KNEES PASSAGE FROM THE NORTH JOINS A HIGHER CRAWL FROM THE EAST TO MAKE A WALKING PASSAGE GOING WEST. THERE IS ALSO A LARGE ROOM ABOVE. THE AIR IS DAMP HERE.

Crowther, departing from the realistic simulation of caving, placed five treasures within as an incentive to explore the cave. The interactor also has to figure out how to get past a snake to have the player character move deeper into the cave. The player character is harassed at times by attacking dwarves and by a pirate who pilfers treasure. There was a single maze in this first version, one that was essentially impossible to get through without making a map. The lantern in *Adventure* had limited battery life, too, adding some time pressure—or turn pressure, since time in the simulated world only passed in response to input (Nelson 2001b, 344). Some of these were the aspects that made *Adventure* a "computer version" of *Dungeons and Dragons* (Crowther 1994, 1). It imitated that role-playing game not by having dice-driven combat based on ability and experience points, or by allowing the interactor to take the role of a particular fantasy character, but by providing opportunities for creative problem solving and by providing a challenge that could be definitively met. Like *Dungeons and Dragons, Adventure,* as Solomon (1984) explained, was a cooperative game: "If there are many players, as is often the case, they function as a team" (21). It seems likely that it was played cooperatively from the very beginning, by Crowther's daughters and by programmers working together. Another way in which it was more related to the riddle and to *Dungeons and Dragons* than to other types of gaming was that while it could be solved, Crowther's original *Adventure* did not keep score (Peterson 1983, 188).

But in 1975 *Adventure* had only begun. "Working at SAIL, the Stanford Artificial Intelligence Laboratory, in the Spring of 1976, Don Woods discovered Crowther's game among a number to be played across the burgeoning (110-computer) ARPANET" (Nelson 2001b, 345). Woods describes his impression of it and what happened next:

> I thought it was a neat idea for a game, but there wasn't a lot to it, and it was full of bugs. . . . I sent mail to crowther@xxx for every xxx on the net. I got back lots of error messages, but eventually did hear from Crowther . . . He sent me the source in return for a promise that I would send him any changes. (qtd. in Aarseth 1997, 99)

While *Adventure* was related to well-known artificial intelligence projects in some ways, and Woods was working in that field when he made his modifications to the program, he explained:

> It was certainly never an official project. SAIL was simply the computer system where I had my primary account while at Stanford. So when I found *Adventure* (which was actually on SUMEX, the Stanford Medical School's computer) and got the source from Crowther, I did all my development on it on the SAIL computer. I've certainly never claimed *Adventure* used any sort of AI (such as understanding natural language). To the contrary, I usually take care to emphasise that *Adventure*'s language parser was extremely primitive even for the state of the art at the time. (2002)

It is the Crowther and Woods version of *Adventure,* with its primitive but effective way of understanding language, that endures and that became widespread. It also became the archetype of the text adventure and of interactive fiction. Crowther's original, which may have been lost, is not publicly available today. Woods fixed bugs in the original, for instance, repairing one location that for no apparent reason lacked exits (Woods 2002). Nelson (2001b) recalls that "Woods reworked the caves and stocked them with magical items and puzzles, liberally ignoring the original style from time to time" (345). The new additions included a maze with a vending machine from which one could buy batteries for the lamp. This would allow the adventurer to stay in the cave longer. Woods introduced more magic, and placed some of it close to the surface; in the original work, what magic there was was deeply buried (Jerz 2001b). An intriguing addition was an "endgame" segment that referred to *Adventure* being a computer program: The cave closed after all the treasures were collected, and the player character was moved to a place where the various creatures of the IF world were sleeping like uninitalized variables. Woods (2002) wrote in an email, "I realise it was a bit off, because it 'broke the fourth wall' and referred to the game." Yet this segment of *Adventure* was "off" in a very interesting way. The canonical first work of interactive fiction concludes by violating levels of narrative and simulation, using metalepsis of the sort that makes many twentieth-century fiction works so intriguing. The new version was distributed widely, made available via the ARPANet and also handed out on tape by DECUS, a user group (Nelson 2001b, 345).

The two mazes provide one of the most popular expressions to originate with *Adventure*. (The magic word "XYZZY," with its frequent mention in computing culture (Rothstein 1998) is the other.)

The pirate's maze offers rooms that are all uniformly described as "a maze of twisty little passages, all alike." To figure out which room is which, the player character must drop objects to mark the different rooms. The rooms, once all alike, can then be differentiated based on their contents and mapping of the usual sort is possible. In the other maze, the interactor reads in one room that the location is "a maze of twisty little passages, all different" and may imagine being similarly stymied; but the next room will be something like "a maze of little twisty passages, all different" and there is a reward for close reading.

From the perspective of the interactor, a work of interactive fiction can itself be seen as a maze of twisty little textual passages—some alike, some different; some produced by the computer, some typed by the interactor—that is to be traversed. But of course it is also a maze of simulated passages through an IF world; this is what distinguishes works in this form from hypertext fiction, chatterbots, and random poetry generators.

Sarah Sloane (2000) noted that "from this one early game, Adventure . . . came a variety of digital fiction conventions in how to move through the story space" (58), such as abbreviations for different compass directions. Not only did it establish interface conventions and provide the default (underground) environment, the revised *Adventure* of Crowther and Woods also drew together a simulation of cave exploration, magic, and problem solving to create a work that had the archetypal texture of a text adventure.

Many different dates are given for Crowther's creation of the original *Adventure* and for the canonical version as augmented by Woods. The specific dates given range at least from 1967 (Herz 1997, 10) to 1978 (de Geus, Jongean, and Koelmans 1985, 1). Oddly, the one Ph.D. dissertation that has been written about this work (Buckles 1985) does not mention when *Adventure* was completed. Crowther himself has not given an exact date but says it was written within a year of 1975 (Jerz 2001b). The question of the date is so involved that a paper has been written about establishing the date of *Adventure*'s creation from existing sources (Wille 1999). (It concludes that 1975 is most likely.) Given that *Dungeons and Dragons* was not published until 1974 (McGath 1984, 6) and that Don Woods named April 1976 as the month of release of the substantially modified version he created (Aarseth 1997, 99), it is very likely, if not certain, that, as one famous computer scientist has concluded, "Adventure . . . was originally written by Will Crowther in 1975" (Knuth 1998, 1).

Adventure may not have been much of an artificial intelligence system, but it was, as Crowther (1994) described it, "a thing that gave you the illusion anyway that you'd typed in English commands and it did what you said" (2). Understanding the interactor and doing what was specified within a simulated world made the program SHRDLU-like; the part that was an illusion of understanding—and was convincing—was following the tradition of ELIZA/DOCTOR. These two programs were its most direct predecessors on the computer (McGath 1984, 11–14), though they did not directly give birth to interactive fiction. While *Adventure* used natural language (or at least a subset of English, as far as input was concered) and was intended for people who were not programmers, its pleasures were in some ways similar to those of programming, according to Crowther (1994): "People enjoy it . . . Because it's exactly the kind of thing that computer programmers do. They're struggling with an obstinate system that can do what you want but only if you can figure out the right thing to say to it" (2–3). Indeed, many programmers found that they did enjoy *Adventure,* which Steven Levy (1984) described as "a metaphor for computer programming itself—the deep recesses you explored in the Adventure world were akin to the basic, most obscure levels of the machine" (141). Whether the cave was a metaphor for the machine or not (and the final sequence that Woods added to *Adventure* certainly suggests that it is) the work presented a compelling challenge, to figure out both what to do and how to do it.

By 1981 *Adventure* was widely known among programmers and, as described in the next chapter, it was also widely imitated by them. Tracy Kidder's Pulitzer Prize–winning *Soul of a New Machine* brought it to the attention of the general reader that year. The book described, probably better than any academic article or piece of journalism since then, how a particular interactor actually approached a work of interactive fiction:

> Carl Asling's cluttered little area made a small rectangle of light. Strewn before me across the surface of his desk, like relics from a party, lay dozens of roughly drawn maps. They consisted of circles, inside of which were scrawled names such as Dirty Passage, Hall of Mists, Hall of the Mountain King . . . Webs of lines connected the circles, and each line was labeled, some with points of the compass, some with the words *up* and *down.* Here and there on the maps were notations—"water here," "oil here," and "damn that pirate!" (Kidder 1981, 86)

Making such maps was an essential part of solving *Adventure* and would remain essential to interacting with most other works of interactive fiction. Kidder also described how, during an after-hours introduction to *Adventure,* more than one person was involved in interacting. In this case, Kidder typed while Asling looked at what he was doing and commented. This was one observation of people, playing this cooperative game, who did not interact in solitude.

Adventure has been the topic of a good deal of discussion and analysis, even if many important questions about it remain. This short section has treated only the most important aspects of the history and creation of *Adventure*. Despite the uncertainties that remain about exact dates and about the differences between the original and expanded works, a great deal is known about the influences on *Adventure*, the contexts in which it was created, and the authors themselves. While Crowther's original program is not available as of this writing, the canonical *Adventure* as expanded by Woods is one of the most universally available computer programs in existence, running on hundreds of platforms.

As important as *Adventure* is, however, it is impossible to learn about the course of interactive fiction's development by looking in detail at only this first work; the development of the form must be seen in how later works differ from *Adventure*. The next chapter undertakes a detailed comparison of *Zork* and *Adventure*, with a focus on the former work. Aarseth (1997) complains, with justification, that *Zork* "is often, and undeservingly, claimed as the paradigmatic adventure game" (108). (For instance, *Hamlet on the Holodeck*, the first scholarly book to discuss *Zork* at length, does not mention *Adventure* (J. Murray 1997).) In this book *Zork* is treated in more detail than *Adventure* to illuminate the form's history, not to set up *Zork* as the paradigm for the form. *Zork* was certainly important and popular, however; it and the other mainframe works that followed would serve to show that *Adventure* was not a dead end.

FOUR

ZORK AND OTHER MAINFRAME WORKS

For those who had access to mainframe computer time, writing one's own *Adventure*-like program seems to have been almost as popular an activity as was playing *Adventure*. Thus, *Adventure* became the model for computing gaming overall; Nelson (2001b) writes that "for the five years to 1982 almost every game created was another 'Advent'" (347). At Stanford, where Don Woods had augmented Will Crowther's original work to create the canonical *Adventure*, at least two follow-ups were written on different systems during this time: *FisK* and *Lugi* (Meier 2002). The authors of these two works are not recorded online, and the source code has not been made available. At the University of Waterloo in Canada, Marc Niemiec created a language called F (for Fantasy) for the development of interactive fiction on the Honeywell Level 66, using it to write *New Adventure*. Brad Templeton and Kieran Carroll wrote *Martian Adventure* in F, incorporating at least one puzzle that was somewhat "Martian" in the sense of the Martian Poetry movement, and shows the relationship between the riddle and early interactive fiction: the player character encounters "keys" that cannot be picked up. It turns out these are not the sort of keys one expects in an adventure; to deal with them one is supposed to type (Meier and Persson 2002). For the Hewlett Packard 1000, two IF works were programmed and made freely available: *Mystery Mansion* by Bill Wolpert and *Warp*. An incomplete adaptation of *The Lord of the Rings* entitled *Lord,* created at the University of

Helsinki by Olli J. Paavola, has been called, by Nelson (2001b), "the first book adaptation in interactive fiction" (347). Nelson noted that *Lord,* influenced by *Zork* as well as *Adventure,* was particularly authentic in the way it created a world with the sort of detail Tolkien would appreciate.

At Carnegie Mellon University, during 1979–1982, John Laird (1997) wrote the *Adventure* follow-up *Haunt,* which he has described as "over-the-top," "quirky" and also "a bit buggy." Nelson calls it "not inspired" but notes that it is the first non-cave work of interactive fiction (2001b, 353). The outrageous prologue is worth quoting from extensively. It merely introduced the sort of treasure-hunt situation that quickly became stereotypical, but it is a great departure from *Adventure* and *Zork,* which simply begin with the player character in the woods.

> Along [sic] time ago, a young couple was picnicing [sic] near the woods on the outskirts of town. They were celebrating the birth of their first child. Unfortunately, a crazed moose inhabited that area and attacked them. The child and husband were unharmed, but the wife was gored to death by the moose.
>
> After the funeral, the man bought the land where the incident occurred and constructed a large mansion: CHEZ MOOSE. He filled it with the treasures of his family and claimed that his wife's soul was still in the area. He vowed to remain in the mansion until he had returned her soul to human flesh. He tried to bridge the gap between life and death to reclaim her. . . . Several people have entered the mansion looking for him but none of them have ever returned. There were rumors that he and his wife now haunt the house.
>
> That would be the end of the story except that the house still stands and is filled with priceless treasures. The house and all its contents are willed to his only descendant. . . . The terms of the Will say you get to keep any treasure you get to the lawn, but of course you must also get off the premises alive. . . . If you are insane enough to try, your adventure starts at a bus stop.

Laird (1997) himself wrote that "the puzzles were way too obscure (many based on Saturday morning cartoons from my youth)" but admitted they were certainly creative, suggesting a different, even wackier mode for interactive fiction.

One puzzle involves removing the paint from a painting to reveal a more valuable one underneath. Another requires the player character to use two straight objects to make a vampire-resisting cross.

Numerous obscene inputs are recognized by *Haunt*. Marijuana is one of the treasures; smoking it makes the adventurer hungry. Stranger effects are brought on by eating the sugar cube. After winning the house, the player character is confronted with a final dilemma when James Watt arrives from the Department of the Interior and asks to buy the land. Written in CMU's OPS-4 (Official Production System 4), *Haunt* made its way to a few other universities but was not widely available. It was notable for being the first rule-based system to have more than 1,000 rules (Laird 1997). Laird (1998) wrote it without having played *Zork*; the creators of *Zork* played it at some point before *Zork* was finished (Nelson 2001, 353; Lebling 1997). Laird began a port of *Haunt* to OPS-5; this incomplete version has been used as an exercise by CMU students (Winalski 1997). CMU would later host the major academic effort in interactive fiction, Joseph Bates's Oz Project, discussed in chapter 7. Laird, now a professor of computer science at the University of Michigan, is currently developing a new domain for his artificial intelligence research, which he describes as "an adventure game where the player takes on the persona of a ghost-like energy creature trapped in a house" (Laird 2001). The graphical, 3-D system is being built using the Unreal Tournament engine and is known as *Haunt 2*.

The mainframe *Zork,* programmed at MIT beginning in May 1977, has a special place among the mainframe follow-ups to *Adventure. Zork* became the second widely known interactive fiction work. For less capacious home computers, it was split up and further developed into *Zork I, Zork II,* and *Zork III* —a trilogy of best-selling games that was the basis for Infocom's creative and financial success, which I discuss in chapter 5. Several specific improvements that had been made to the *Adventure* world model and parser were touted in an academic paper (Lebling, Blank, and Anderson 1979), and, later, in the manuals that accompanied Infocom's commercial products. Those familiar with the history of computer gaming recognize the significance of *Zork*. One contemporary IF author expresses a common view: "It's by far the most famous piece of IF and can be considered the father figure of the genre, much like *Super Mario Bros.* is with the side scroller or *King's Quest* for the graphic adventure" (Sherwin 1999). One rough measure of the overall popularity of *Zork* is that in mid-December 2001, the word "Zork" appeared in approximately 124,000 Web pages in the Google index; only about 22,000 such pages mentioned either "Space War" or "Spacewar," referring to the MIT program that is widely considered to be the first modern video game. Even taking into consideration that the word "zork" sometimes appears on the Web in its original sense—a nonsense word in MIT argot—the interactive fiction *Zork* is clearly well known; it is also important in the history of new media and of interactive fiction.

Zork in this chapter refers to the PDP-10 computer program, running on ITS and written in MDL, that was developed at MIT beginning in late May 1977 and augmented later that year and in the following years (Anderson 1985a, 7). For a few months *Zork* was called *Dungeon;* there is a version of a FORTRAN port of *Zork* that has been widely available since 1979 that uses this name. *Zork* also refers to ports from that FORTRAN port into Glk and from the original MDL into Inform. *Zork* is distinguished in this discussion from *Zork I–III*. I consider that trilogy and how it differed from the mainframe *Zork* in the next chapter. Where distinctions among different versions of *Zork* are important, the year of the version cited is given.

Despite the clear importance of *Zork,* with very few exceptions, the advances that this work brought about have been only superficially considered. This chapter describes three advances and their importance. First, *Zork* draws on a deep reservoir of technical humor, making its origins in the subculture of MIT evident and commenting on technology in interesting ways. It first realized the ability of interactive fiction to speak back to the culture in which it was produced. Second, while the technical advances made by the game's creators (known as Implementors) were in some ways incremental, they did lead to progress in interactive fiction. It is helpful to explain these advances and see how these proved important in the development of later works. Third, *Zork* was at least in some ways superior to *Adventure* as a system that generates satisfying narratives in response to user input. It produced narratives that were connected to adventure stories of the folktale sort in new ways—not just through offhand reference, but structurally. Neither programming improvements nor better writing, considered alone, made *Zork*'s thief the first memorable character in interactive fiction; rather, it was the way he functioned during an interaction and throughout a successful traversal of *Zork* that was fundamentally better than what had been achieved before.

SEEING *ZORK* AGAINST *ADVENTURE*

The potential narratives of a successful traversal of *Zork* involve the adventurer wandering through an outdoor area, a house, and then a vast complex called the Great Underground Empire. To succeed the interactor must direct the adventurer to collect treasures, almost all of which are located underground. A handful of living opponents thwart the adventurer: the troll, who stays put in a single room and serves as an obstacle; the vampire bat, who can carry off the adventurer; the cyclops, who can dine on the adventurer; and the thief, who wanders around the underground areas stealing items the adventurer either is holding or has already seen. To get through the mazes, detailed mapmaking (or else extraordinary luck, or cheating) is required. Riddle-like challenges require the interactor to understand the nature of a disguised object in order to use it properly; in some cases machinery must be manipulated in order to determine its purpose. Some puzzles, such as the Bank of Zork and the Royal Puzzle, are elaborate and extremely hard. A few require that the interactor "guess the verb" and perform an action that would not be obvious from the commands available in *Adventure.* If a magic word from *Adventure* is typed in *Zork,* a hollow voice says "Cretin."

It makes little sense to consider certain features in *Zork* as if they were original, because certain features are not. Attacking *Zork* with a detailed psychoanalytical reading that considers the subterranean world, beneath a forested area in which a lone building sits, is foolhardy—for several reasons, but most specifically because all of these features are lifted directly from *Adventure.* According to the small leaflet found in the mailbox in the 1978–1979 FORTRAN port of *Zork,* the program "was created . . . by Tim Anderson, Marc Blank, Bruce Daniels, and Dave Lebling. It was inspired by the Adventure game of Crowther and Woods, and the Dungeons and Dragons game of Gygax and Arneson." By 1981 the leaflet had been revised to replace mention of *Dungeons and Dragons* with "the long tradition of fantasy and science fiction adventure." This revision came after *Zork* was briefly renamed *Dungeon,* drawing the attention of certain lawyers to the Implementors and MIT (Anderson 1985b, 4). Both the original and revised statements have truth to them, of course.

Zork's Implementors had played *Adventure* earnestly, and they created *Zork* mainly in response to their enjoyment of that interactive fiction work and the opportunities they saw to improve upon it. The interests of the Implementors were not restricted to programming. As Anderson (2001) said, "One reason that some of the writing is good, if it is good, is that the people who wrote it were not nerds in the classic sense. Very few people are really nerds in the classic sense, I think. Marc, Dave, and I all exposed ourselves to a lot of really good writing." The *Zork* Implementors were also filmgoers, seeing *Star Wars* very soon after it came out, during *Zork's* early development; Marc Blank was on MIT's Lecture Series Committee, the student group that screens films on campus, and had an interest in classic films. The Implementors read books and viewed films eclectically, taking in much from outside the genres of science fiction and fantasy. This included history, as one might guess from the offhand reference in *Zork* to Octavian's general Marcus Vipsanius Agrippa.

Few people are struck by the powerful narratives that *Zork* produces when compared to those produced by *Adventure*. *Zork,* like *Adventure,* provided nothing special to set up the initial situation, in which the adventurer is standing near a building in the woods; certainly *Haunt* was much more innovative when this particular aspect of writing is considered. Although the humor of *Zork* is widely appreciated, in some ways *Zork's* writing may in fact be worse than the writing in *Adventure,* especially in the case of the accuracy and richness of geological description. Nelson (1995a) described *Zork's* underground setting as "based not on real caves but on Crowther's descriptions" and as "better laid out as a game but not as convincing." Lebling (1988) explains that those at MIT who weren't cavers still had their own underground empire to explore and to base interactive fiction upon:

> When I was a student at MIT, there was a pastime called "Institute Exploring" (also known as "Tunnel Tours"). A group of students would go over to the main part of the campus at around 3am and try to visit some of the more obscure and off-limits locations.

MIT is full of basements and subbasements, and these are often crammed with equipment left over from some cancelled research project.

However many levels of simulation are involved in the room descriptions, though, *Zork* did substantially improve upon the art of interactive fiction. Janet Murray (1997) describes one way in which *Zork* presents a compelling "moment of experimental drama," early on: when the adventurer first enters the dungeon, the trapdoor is closed and the way out is barred by an unseen opponent (81–82). This moment, which has no parallel at the beginning of *Adventure,* creates an ominous and interesting situation in the potential narratives of *Zork.* It also makes for a puzzle—the interactor must figure out how to escape, going deeper into the dungeon. This improvement, one of several that made interactive fiction and new media more compelling, came about by improving the design of the IF world, not by simply programming more cleverly or by writing better bits of texts.

SITUATED IN SUBCULTURE: TECHNICAL HUMOR AND CRITIQUE

Zork is a literary, gaming, and computing artifact, a part of the culture and subculture in which it was created. It has been noted that masculinist rationality underlies *Zork* and other interactive fiction (Sloane 2000, 100); other contexts of interest also exist. The Implementors were certainly influenced by, but not mere puppets of, male academic research and its perspectives and concerns. In *Zork* they sought to comment on academia and technology as technologists and as writers and designers of a new kind. They were marked in certain ways by their environment, and they marked back in *Zork,* the simulated environment they created.

To illustrate how an MIT-specific interpretation can help us understand *Zork,* consider that in the Entrance to Hades a large gateway bears this inscription: "Abandon every hope, all ye who enter here." Relating this inscription to literary tradition is, if not fruitless, misleading. *Zork*'s Hades has only superficial similarities to either Dante's Hell or the Hades of the ancient Greeks, with jeering "evil spirits" who prevent entry. Dante's Hell lies conspicuously open and unguarded—in contrast to the securely locked gate of

Purgatory, watched over by a sword-wielding angel (*Purgatorio* 9.76–138). Christian doctrine of Dante's time held that it was easy to enter hell; entering *Zork*'s equivalent realm is difficult, providing an intricate puzzle opportunity. A different approach to this Hades entryway is provided by Implementor Tim Anderson (2001): "You can think of it as a Dante quotation or you can think of it as something people say when they come to MIT, which is really more what we had in mind." MIT students come to learn that "Tech Is Hell," and admission to that Hell is indeed difficult. There was also a rather direct antecedent in computing, whether or not it was known to the *Zork* Implementors: The (rather arcane) source code for the Unisys A Series COBOL 68 compiler began with a comment containing the same quotation, in Italian (Stevens 1999).

The first glimpse of Hades reveals "a desolation, with a pile of mangled corpses in one corner." Hades is hardly a vast, mythical wasteland if it is small enough to have a pile of corpses in the corner, as in this tongue-in-cheek description. Actual lifeless corpses should also not have much of a place in either the Greek Hades (in which they would be wandering around listlessly) or Dante's Hell (where they might more appropriately writhe beneath their punishments). The rest of *The Inferno* is summarized in *Zork* at the entrance as "Thousands of voices, lamenting some hideous fate," and within as "the sounds of thousands of lost souls weeping and moaning." (The command *listen* is not implemented.) One reviewer's reaction to the corresponding region of *Zork I* is typical: "Here I am in Hades. *yawn* Wonder if there's a gift shop around" (Stevens 1997).

However, within the land of the dead is a room that didn't make it to the commercial *Zork I*. This area, except for the presence of severed heads and dead bodies, might fit in perfectly well at MIT:

Tomb of the Unknown Implementer
This is the Tomb of the Unknown Implementer. A hollow voice says: "That's not a bug, it's a feature!" In the north wall of the room is the Crypt of the Implementers. It is made of the finest marble, and apparently large enough for four headless corpses. The crypt is closed.
Above the entrance is the cryptic inscription:
"Feel Free."

There are four heads here, mounted securely on poles.

There is a large pile of empty Coke bottles here, evidently produced by the implementers during their long struggle to win totality.

There is a gigantic pile of line-printer output here. Although the paper once contained useful information, almost nothing can be distinguished now.

These signs of coding exertion (of no use to the adventurer) are situated in a place that is certainly not a direct reference to the Tomb of the Unknown Soldier, but rather to the Tomb of the Unknown Tool, a famously inaccessible area under MIT's Building 9. "Tomb" at MIT refers to, as one student publication explains, "an interesting, out-of-the way, unused spot" (Amonlirdviman 1996, 213). The heads are "securely mounted" because if they were removable the adventurer could carry them around and do things to them, thereby introducing unnecessary complexity to Zork's simulated world. The inscription punningly decorating the crypt was a common saying among the four creators (the spelling "Implementers" later being changed to "Implementors") in response to a suggestion that part of Zork be modified. It was a polite way of refusing, meaning "feel free to go ahead and make the change yourself if you like." For example, "How about you add an underwater area inside the reservoir that you can swim down into?" "Feel free."

This vein of technical humor continues into the south wall of Zork's temple. There is a prayer upon it, "inscribed in an ancient script which is hardly remembered these days, much less understood. What little of it can be made out seems to be a philippic against small insects, absent-mindedness, and the picking up and dropping of small objects." The prayer begins with an attempt to protect not against literal "small insects," of course, but against programming errors, or bugs. As for absentmindedness, it might be something the Implementors need to guard against in creating Zork, or it might be a professorial malady that students should watch out for. Clearly the last philippic is making fun of the adventurer, whose essential actions seem to be picking up and dropping things.

Zork has a purely numerical joke that may be the most elaborate in all interactive fiction—perhaps even in all computing. In the Clearing a command to *count leaves* brings the wry response "There are 69,105 leaves here."

This reply presupposes a superhuman (and in fact computer-like) adventurer, able to count a tremendous number of objects in the thin slice of time represented by a move. Perhaps this prodigious ability to count is in keeping with the adventurer's autistic nature, as manifested in the emotional understatement and the fixation on objects that Aarseth (1997, 115–117) has pointed out. Whatever the case, the absurd, impossibly accurate count is funny, as is the "364.4 Smoots and one ear" measurement first marked on the Harvard Bridge in October 1958 by MIT students who had just finished measuring the bridge with Oliver Reed Smoot's supine body. The same sexual innuendo is insisted upon twice in the digits "69,105"—the "69" to the left of the comma is repeated to the right of the comma, since decimal 69 is octal 105, and (as is not true in general) hexadecimal 69 is also decimal 105. This number appears again in Infocom works *The Witness* by Stu Galley (the gun receipt is number 69105) and in *Leather Goddesses of Phobos* by Steven Meretzky (which has another pile of leaves). In works from the late 1990s, Adam Cadre's *I-0* features 69,105 pieces of laundry in the trunk of car; Admiral Jota's in-joke *Pass the Banana* has a file size of 69,105 bytes. The number also is mentioned in Infocom's newsletter *The New Zork Times* and in the instructions to Douglas Adams's *Bureaucracy,* another Infocom work. But in case one's appetite for numeric allusion to mutual oral sex is not satisfied at the "Clearing," there is more in *Zork* along similar lines. The description of the "Studio" mentions that the "walls and floors are splattered with paints of 69 different colors."

Plenty of additional MIT-specific and computing references are to be found in *Zork.* Descending from the Dome Room to the Torch Room, the adventurer sees this: "Above you is a large dome painted with scenes depicting elvish hacking rites." "Hacking" at MIT refers to the exploration of restricted areas of campus and to the perpetration of extremely clever pranks, some of which are in fact ritualized. Although "dome" meant something else inside a cave, one of the most prominent sites for hacking has been MIT's Great Dome, which has had a phone booth and a model police car placed atop it (Haverson and Fulton-Pearson 1996; Leibowitz 1990). This makes it particularly appropriate for these frescos to appear in a "large dome."

There were also jabs at the large evil computer company of the day, IBM, found in the Machine Room and the Maintenance Room: "Along one wall of the room are three buttons which are, respectively, round, triangular, and square. Naturally, above the buttons are instructions written in EBCDIC." These indecipherable instructions are encoded in IBM's proprietary character code, a rival to ASCII. Other technically funny possible outputs of *Zork* include "Why, only last week I patched a running RSX system and it survived for over thirty seconds," and, on an unfortunate occasion, "According to Prof. TAA [Timothy A. Anderson] of MIT Tech, the rapidly changing magnetic fields in the room are so intense as to cause you to be electrocuted. I really don't know, but in any event, something has killed you." Engravings are seen to read "This space intentionally left blank," the same notice found on blank pages at the end of engineering and science textbooks, and possibly a reference to one of the Implementors as well.

Technology plays an important part in the world of *Zork,* which sports Flood Control Dam #3, a flashy public works project built for no discernible reason, as the Guide Book explains:

> Flood control dam #3 (FCD #3) was constructed in year 783 of the Great Underground Empire to harness the destructive power of the Frigid River. This work was supported by a grant of 37 million zorkmids from the central bureaucracy and your own omnipotent local tyrant Lord Dimwit Flathead the Excessive. This impressive structure is composed of 3.7 cubic feet of concrete, is 256 feet tall at the center, and 193 feet wide at the top. . . .
>
> The construction of FCD #3 took 112 days from ground breaking to the dedication. It required a work force of 384 slaves, 34 slave drivers, 12 engineers, 2 turtle doves, and a partridge in a pear tree. The work was managed by a command team composed of 234 bureaucrats, 2347 secretaries (at least two of whom could type), 12,256 paper shufflers, 52,469 rubber stampers, 245,193 red tape processors, and nearly one million dead trees.

FCD #3 is a concrete symbol of engineering as worshipped by the public, similar in this way to the impressive Hoover Dam. It is also amusingly useless, almost certainly incorrectly documented (it would take rather magical engineering practices to build a 256-foot-tall dam using nothing but 3.7 cubic feet of concrete), and apparently produced with an inefficiency more monumental than the dam itself. *Zork's* technical humor is an achievement not just because it is funny, but also because it delivers things like this effective parody of bumbling publicly funded technology projects. Although *Zork* was created more efficiently than was FCD #3, it did run on the spare time of computers purchased with, and was programmed by individuals who were supported by, Department of Defense money. It was in some ways an example of an amusingly useless public works project itself; the tongue-in-cheek tone of *Zork* seems to encode an awareness of this.

The structural innovations in *Zork's* world also reflect a technological subculture. To prevail the adventurer must use vehicles, riding in a balloon and a boat. This player character also must command a robot in order to get through one section of the work. Reading *Zork* against MIT makes it easier to see how the literary transformation of technology is accomplished in the work. The puzzles that offered riddle-like systems, called "problems" by the Implementors, often involve recognizing various technological artifacts, real and imagined, for what they are. In many cases, once the technology is recognized, the way in which objects are supposed to be used becomes obvious. A clear example is provided in the coal mine section of *Zork's* IF world.

Here, the player character finds a machine that might, in another place, be used for doing laundry; a tiny slot is noticable in the top of it. What this machine does, and how to turn it on, is unclear. The solution is to put some coal found nearby into the machine, and then turn the machine on using the screwdriver. This results in the coal being compressed with great force. (The switch is described as having the right dimensions to be turned with a screwdriver of the appropriate type—of course, a flathead screwdriver. One of these can be found near FCD #3.) To figure out how to turn on the machine, one need only recognize which ordinary tool is needed, based on a literal description. To figure out what the machine does, the interactor can act as scientist and put anything inside, then observe the results. Despite the absurdity of an underground flood control dam, many of the technologies found in the Great Underground Empire have purposes, and one could imagine why they might have been placed there by previous occupants of the realm. Understanding that useful machinery is found in this IF world, and using the process of experimentation and observation in order to learn what this machinery does, allows the player character to prevail in a way that is consistent with the overall scheme of Zork. The diamond-making machine is not a profound riddle, but it was a step toward systematic IF worlds of greater power.

Zork was not the last piece of interactive fiction to comment on MIT. Later, *Zork* Implementor Dave Lebling, working for Infocom, wrote an IF work that referred to MIT more directly. His 1987 *The Lurking Horror* was a Lovecraftian horror story set at the fictitious George Underwood Edwards Institute of Technology, or GUE Tech, which was laid out much like the MIT campus. MIT's Green Building was there with its meteorology dome on top, but it was called the Brown Building. (The actual Green Building is, in fact, brown.) Many other features were lifted from MIT, including an infinite corridor and an inaccessible "tomb." As independent IF authorship began to hit its stride, one of many IF works set on the authors' own campus was *GC: A Thrashing Parity Bit of the Mind,* written by Carl de Marcken, Dave Baggett, and Pearl Tsai for the MIT Artificial Intelligence Laboratory Olympics in January 1993. Excruciatingly difficult, it featured Marvin Minsky and other campus luminaries wandering about in the Acme Institute, an MIT-like place filled with computer science and AI references as well as inside jokes. *Zork* clearly influenced not only MIT-referential IF works like *The Lurking Horror* and *GC,* but all other interactive fiction that draws a connection between the simulated world, full of devious puzzles and fantastic elements, and our own contemporary and more mundane reality.

World Model and Parser: Software Advances

One might question whether *Zork*'s technical advances were actually so striking and of real importance to the interactor and to the development of interactive fiction. Certainly the Implementors did not think they were staggering; in reply to *help, Zork* stated, "You are dealing with a fairly stupid parser." Anderson (1985b) wrote that the early work was "in some ways . . . better than the classic Adventure at this time, but mostly it was the next game to come along, and it wasn't even the only contender" (4). But *Zork* did sport several advances that were used to good effect. These were in both essential components: the parser, which translates player-typed text into actions, and the world model, which simulates a narrative and puzzle-filled world to the degree required for an enjoyable interaction.

The parser, "fairly stupid" as it might be, was a substantial upgrade from that of *Adventure*, which only accepts commands of one or two words. When there was only one appropriate object for a requested action, the parser would assume the interactor wished to use that object; otherwise, it would ask a question to disambiguate the command (Lebling, Blank, and Anderson 1979). This worked particularly well in the case of actions like digging, which required tools. When a command was issued to dig with an inappropriate tool (e.g., *dig in the sand with the screwdriver*), the parser would generate a reply of the form "Digging with the screwdriver is slow and tedious." Since "the hands" were designated as tools, the parser, upon receiving the simple command *dig*, would assume—in the absence of any other tool—that "the hands" were to be used. It would then generate a response that—although unanticipated—was particularly apt and pleasing to the Implementors: "Digging with the hands is slow and tedious" (Anderson 2001). The parser folded prepositions into the different supported actions, so that "look at" and "look under" were considered as if they were separate verbs and were translated into different actions (Lebling, Blank, and Anderson 1979). Direct and indirect objects were recognized, and some verbs were allowed to take multiple direct objects.

The world model was enhanced to implement actors, who could perform actions in much the same way that the adventurer could, and could also be commanded by the interactor. The robot, who lacked many of the adventurer's abilities but who could be commanded to solve a puzzle, was the first actor implemented. Although not the most charming character in interactive fiction (in contrast to the robot Floyd from *Planetfall*, who is certainly ranked among the most engaging characters in the form), the robot is an interesting part of the world of *Zork*. The robot is a technological artifact, almost free of personality. The best pre-robotic entity to compare it to might be the golem of Jewish folklore. (There is no hint of the more sinister proto-robot, Frankenstein's monster.) When the robot is able to accomplish some task, it emits a "Whirr, buzz, click!," while all of its other utterances are what might be termed polite refusals. After the player character had asked the robot to read something, for instance, it would reply "My vision is not sufficiently acute to do that." If commanded to eat, it somehow speaks the reply "I am sorry but that is difficult for a being with no mouth." This robot, although an uninteresting conversational partner, did first allow the player character to direct another entity to accomplish tasks on his or her behalf. This opened up new possibilities for puzzles, and also brought on interesting narrative implications, to be explored later in works like *Planetfall*.

Vehicles were another new part of the world. They were implemented as if they were mobile rooms, contained in the top-level rooms of the dungeon (Lebling, Blank, and Anderson 1979). The boat and the balloon were the vehicles placed in *Zork*. By constraining them to linear paths, in order to avoid unusual situations that might rupture other parts of the world model or require inordinate amounts of new programming, the Implementors provided novel but carefully directed experiences of travel. Other aspects of the simulated world improved upon the *Adventure* universe:

> Containment: Objects may have contents. Bottles can contain water and be open or closed. Some objects are transparent. Some objects must be unlocked before they can be opened. The capacity of an object is limited. (For example, a paper bag won't hold as much as a bucket.)
>
> Weight: Objects have weight. A solid gold coffin weighs a lot more than a newspaper. The amount a player can carry depends on the total number of objects carried and on the total weight of the objects and their contents.
>
> Position: An object may be in, on, or under another object. (Lebling, Blank, and Anderson 1979)

Perhaps as important as these planned-out improvements were the ad hoc changes made by the implementors in response to email requests and based on their surveillance of other users' sessions. As Anderson (2001) said, "We spied on people playing *Zork*. This was ITS. You could see all the output from a terminal. We would 'watch' people this way." ITS was MIT's Incompatible Timesharing System, an intentionally insecure operating system made to facilitate group work. When the Implementors got a reasonable request or spied someone floundering due to what seemed like a parser failure, they would tweak *Zork*.

Had interactive fiction only accepted two-word inputs instead of being pushed by the *Zork* parser advances toward accepting text that is more like normal English, there is little chance that the appeal of interactive fiction would have lasted beyond the era of command-line home computing. Pointing and clicking would simply be good enough when compared to a verb-noun command. Instead, *Zork* took the first step toward a more symmetrical interaction between interactor and IF work, an exchange more like English conversation—one that cannot be easily replaced with mouse clicks (Montfort 2000). Improvements in the world model also paved the way for many interesting IF works. Michael Berlyn's 1983 *Suspended* (published by Infocom), for instance, used the "actor" enhancement to provide a fragmented sort of player character, whose senses were divided between different robots that could be commanded. Infocom also brought out, in 1985, Steven Meretzky's *A Mind Forever Voyaging,* which simulated an enormous city; some of the sense of scale was given by using vehicles of the sort developed in *Zork* and implementing a subway system. Hundreds of later works used containment and position to achieve a richer and more detailed world. While *Zork* made important progress as potential literature, its improvements to interactive fiction's technical infrastructure were definitely of value as well.

POTENTIAL NARRATIVE: IMPROVEMENTS IN VILLAINY

The thief, who appears randomly to steal treasures the adventurer is holding, is certainly the most memorable character in *Zork*. This is attributed variously to the better writing associated with the thief or to his nature as an IF daemon or bot (Leonard 1998, 84). In fact the thief is important to the development of interactive fiction because he functions as a true villain, not simply an obstacle or opponent. It is his role in the interaction and in the potential narratives that result that makes the thief so effective.

Phil Goetz (1994) writes that "*Zork* was . . . the first adventure whose non-player characters had personality. The thief was a gentleman gone wrong, with good manners, a cynical sense of humour and the willingness to slit your throat in a moment." That the thief has a true personality may be an overstatement. Comparing the descriptive text that constitutes *Adventure*'s pirate (a sort of proto-thief) with that of *Zork*'s thief can provide some insight into the difference in personality. From *Adventure:*

Out from the shadows behind you pounces a bearded pirate! "Har, har," he chortles, "I'll just take all this booty and hide it away with me chest deep in the maze!" He snatches your treasure and vanishes into the gloom.

There are faint rustling noises from the darkness behind you. As you turn toward them, the beam of your lamp falls across a bearded pirate. He is carrying a large chest. "Shiver me timbers!" he cries, "I've been spotted! I'd best hie meself off to the maze to hide me chest!"

Here is a selection of many brief descriptive outputs regarding the thief from *Zork:*

·   Someone carrying a large bag is casually leaning against one of the walls here. He does not speak, but it is clear from his aspect that the bag will be taken only over his dead body.

·   Your opponent, determining discretion to be the better part of valor, decides to terminate this little contretemps. With a rueful nod of his head, he steps backward into the gloom and disappears.

·   A 'lean and hungry' gentleman just wandered through. Finding nothing of value, he left disgruntled.

·   A seedy-looking individual with a large bag just wandered through the room. On the way, he quietly abstracted all valuables from the room and from your possession, mumbling something about, "Do unto others before . . ."

·   The other occupant just left carrying his large bag. You may not have noticed that he robbed you blind first.

·   The thief, a man of good breeding, refrains from attacking a helpless opponent.

·   The thief, forgetting his essentially genteel upbringing cuts your throat.

·   The thief, who is essentially a pragmatist, dispatches you as a threat to his livelihood.

Most of the thief's character is described apart from any encounter with him, in response to *info:*

Of special note is a thief (always carrying a large bag) who likes to wander around in the dungeon (he has never been seen by the light of day). He likes to take things. Since he steals for pleasure rather than profit and is somewhat sadistic, he only takes things which you have seen. Although he prefers valuables, sometimes in his haste he may take something which is worthless. From time to time, he examines his take and discards objects which he doesn't like. He may occasionally stop in a room you are visiting, but more often he just wanders through and rips you off (he is a skilled pickpocket).

Clearly, much more potential text is available to describe the thief than the pirate. The text by itself cannot tell the whole story of who the thief is and how he functions within *Zork*. Encounters with the thief will certainly tend to vary more than encounters with *Adventure*'s pirate. Still, this text demonstrates that Goetz's conclusion—that the thief is really endowed with personality the pirate lacks—is somewhat questionable. The thief is drawn from a stock *Dungeons and Dragons* player character class. The brief description of the startled pirate may be more original and humorous than any particular text associated with the thief. The pirate chortles and speaks with pithy but piratic diction that is a bit more pleasing than "Do unto others before . . ." However, the thief is a noticeable improvement over the pirate for one important narrative reason: the thief can be killed by the adventurer—indeed, must be killed in order for the interactor to successfully traverse *Zork*.

Writing about *Adventure,* Mary Ann Buckles (1985) noted that "[Vladimir] Propp believed villainy to be the most important function in the folktales he examined . . . In my view, the lack of true villainy constitutes one of the main structural and ideational differences between folktales and *Adventure*" (107). She described a villain as "the symbolic representation of forces working to seemingly hinder, but actually promoting, the hero's or heroine's development" (107), adding,

> In *Adventure* . . . I don't believe one can speak of villainy. The two types of figures who oppose the hero, dwarves and the pirate, are not capable of "evil." They do things that hinder and threaten the reader; they steal the reader's treasure and even "kill" the reader, although "death" is meaningless and not even always permanent in the game. But since *Adventure*'s "villains" are not representations of anything

else, neither parental figures nor psychological drives or impulses, their deeds are destructive without being "wicked."...They are stick figures which have nothing to do with ethics, "good" or "evil," or aspects of personal development. (107–108)

Buckles has one more complaint regarding the pirate: "when the pirate steals the reader's treasure in *Adventure,* the reader regains it by finding it. The triumph and revenge aspect [of the folktale] is missing entirely" (124).

Whatever the general applicability of Propp's theories to interactive narrative may be, these points about why *Adventure* is structurally unsatisfying are grounded in important concerns, and they help explain the effectiveness of the thief. He can be read as a manifestation of meaningless greed—perhaps even the same greed that is driving the adventurer to loot the dungeon. (One of the sections of the dungeon is a bank that the adventurer must rob, and in the Gallery, where a lone painting is found, the initial description notes that "there is still one chance for you to be a vandal.") Seen this way, *Zork*'s thief does begin to represent the villain Buckles finds lacking in *Adventure.* The most important feature of the thief is that he must be encountered and killed by the player character in a successful traversal of *Zork.* The adventurer can only prevail over the thief after significant experience has been acquired; a battle in which the adventurer is victorious ends with the demise of the thief and the recovery of the stolen treasures. The folktale revenge element lacking in *Adventure* is present in *Zork.*

Finally, the thief promotes the development of the adventurer in two ways: by serving as an incentive to explore more of the dungeon and improve in rank, and by unwittingly assisting the adventurer in gaining access to a treasure.

Specifically, the thief has to be "given" the jewel-encrusted egg that is found above ground, in a nest that is found up a tree outside the house. Since the egg can be taken directly to the trophy case with no chance of the thief stealing it, the interactor must choose to direct the adventurer below ground to either give the egg to the thief or have him steal it. After doing this, and then dispatching the thief in combat, the adventurer will find that the thief has carefully opened the egg, revealing another treasure.

These aspects of the thief make him a complex figure in comparison to *Adventure*'s simple and small menagerie; he is both a helper and a villain.

His role in the experience of *Zork* from start to successful finish, rather than his turn-to-turn behavior, is likely the reason that, in a letter to *XYZZY News* in which he reports a *Zork I* bug, one interactor wrote, "I always hated the stupid thief. Killing that lean-and-hungry not-so-gentleman with his own stolen stiletto is one of the more satisfying things I've ever done with my computer" (Gildemeister 1996).

Most of the opponents who deal with the adventurer violently and have the potential to kill the adventurer (i.e., the troll and the thief) must be killed to win *Zork*. An exception is the violent and potentially fatal cyclops, who is too mighty for the adventurer to dispatch but who can be dealt with conclusively in another way. (That the cyclops is dispatched non-fatally is consistent with the archetypical adventurer, Odysseus, escaping from Polyphemus without killing him.) The one opponent who never inflicts actual physical harm on the adventurer is the Wumpus-rejected vampire bat. To enter his lair without getting a one-way flight into the coal mine, the adventurer must use a nonviolent tactic, bringing an object that causes the bat to cower. The ways of dealing with opponents in *Zork* are therefore more consistent and systematic than they are in *Adventure*. In that IF work, a dragon who does not necessarily harm the adventurer must be killed—in a way that amuses but fails to even have literal meaning.

Other memorable characters in interactive fiction relied on the thief's success as a character who plays an essential role in the potential narrative. Not all of them were villains: Floyd in Steven Meretzky's 1983 *Planetfall* (from Infocom) had an important role as companion and helper.

Although successful, *Zork* was a very early and rough effort in the history of interactive fiction. The initial simple quest (accumulate all the treasures) saw an endgame added to it after 1977, incorporating an interesting twist that was absent from its contemporary IF works. As important as it was in the history of interactive fiction, *Zork* is not a masterwork by today's standards. MIT's answer to *Adventure* led interactive fiction onto a more satisfying course, however, making many advances by improving interactive fiction as an artifact that comments on technical culture, as world model and parser, and as a machine for interactively generating satisfying narratives.

Developments in the Other Cambridge

Many college campuses in the United States were one-hit wonders when it came to *Adventure* follow-ups. Students from MIT in Cambridge, Massachusetts, did go on to found Infocom. Another exception to the rule could be seen in Cambridge, England. Programmers there produced a massive work of interactive fiction that grew to dwarf *Adventure* and *Zork* and also devised a development system that helped others produce IF works throughout the 1980s. Shortly after *Adventure* and *Zork* made their way across the puddle, programmers at Essex University in England took off from interactive fiction in a different direction, creating the MUD, or Multiple User Dungeon, discussed in chapter 8. According to Nelson (1999b),

> The central computer of Cambridge University, England, an IBM mainframe usually called "Phoenix" after its operating system, was one of those to receive "Advent" (a.k.a. "Colossal Cave") and "Zork" (a.k.a. "Dungeon") in the late 1970s. Two graduate students, Jon Thackray and David Seal, began a game called "Acheton" in 1978–9: with the aid of Jonathan Partington it expanded for another two years. Possibly the first game written outside America, by 1981 it seems likely that it was also the largest in the world (it has 403 locations). "Acheton" was written with a game assembler contemporary with Infocom's proprietory "ZIL": unlike ZIL, Seal and Thackray's game assembler was available for public use, the public in question being all users of Phoenix c. 1980–95.

Acheton, like *Adventure* and *Zork,* features an outdoor area, underground area, and endgame part of the world—even a last lousy point is included—but it is, as one recent reviewer wrote, "quite a bit tougher and more cruel" than its American predecessors (Russotto 2000). The player character is frequently killed without warning, as when walking around, picking up a treasure, or closing an empty safe. There are numerous mazes. As Russotto recently put it, "When the player is tempted to write a Java program to discover a Hamiltonian path through a maze, the maze is perhaps a bit too difficult." While a non-programmer like Tracy Kidder could get the hang of *Adventure, Acheton* was clearly esoteric.

This extremely difficult challenge was appreciated, though, because *Acheton* effectively inspired programmers in Cambridge to create other works of interactive fiction using its development system. Fourteen such works were introduced (Meier and Persson 2001; Nelson 1999b), as shown in table 4.1.

Although, as already mentioned, another similar development system, F, was created at the University of Waterloo in Canada, that one did not see such wide use. By creating a free development system, even one for a small, local group of programmers, Seal and Thackray helped lay the groundwork for the broader authorship of interactive fiction by individuals. In the 1990s,

TABLE 4.1

Interactive fiction works developed at Cambridge in the Acheton system, with the authors' names and login names (frequently used in speech by Phoenix users) where these were available

---

Acheton, Jon Thackray, David Seal, and Jonathan R. Partington (JGT1, DJS6, JRP1)

Murdac, Jon Thackray and Jonathan R. Partington (JGT1 and JRP1)

Avon, Jon Thackray and Jonathan R. Partington (JGT1 and JRP1)

BrandX, Jonathan Mestel and Peter Killworth (AJM8 and PDK1), 1979

Hamil, Johnathan R. Partington (JRP1), 1980

Quondam, Rod Underwood (RU10), 1980

Hezarin, Steve Tinney, Alex Ship, and Jon Thackray, 1980

Xeno, Jonathan Mestel (AJM8)

Fyleet, Jonathan R. Partington (JRP1), 1985

Crobe, Jonathan R. Partington (JRP1), 1986

Sangraal, Jonathan Partington (JRP1), 1987

Nidus, Adam Atkinson (AJFA1), 1987

Parc, (JR26)

Xerb, Andrew Lipson

Spycatcher, Jonathan R. Partington (JRP1)

Note: The commercial release of *BrandX* was called *Philosopher's Quest.* Some dates are unknown, but the list is sorted into an approximately chronological order; *Spycatcher* was the last Phoenix game, around 1988-1989.

after commercial interactive fiction had foundered, the rise of this type of development would become central to continued progress in the form, as described in chapter 7. The most important contribution to independently authored interactive fiction in the 1990s was almost certainly Graham Nelson's development of Inform and his authorship of *Curses*. (Nelson (1999a) notes that Jonathan Partington, who was involved in authoring seven of the fifteen works listed here and was the most active Cambridge IF developer, was "by a curious coincidence" his topology tutor at Cambridge; Nelson was also a Phoenix user.) But before the era of individual authorship outside of academia, a commercial heyday would occur. Just as *Zork* saw commercial distribution to home computer users by Infocom, many of the previously mentioned works were ported to microcomputers and distributed by one of many companies in the United Kingdom involved with the development and publication of interactive fiction—a company that, in another interesting mathematical tie-in, was named Topologika. The next chapter chronicles the shift of interactive fiction development to places outside the university and the rise of commercial interactive fiction.

FIVE

INFOCOM AND COMMERCIAL BEGINNINGS

Adventure is considered the great original epic of interactive fiction. Infocom's works call for a grandiose comparison made on a slightly different metaphorical ground. Whoever the "Shakespeare" playwright actually was—common or noble, working largely alone or in close collaboration with a theater company—Shakespeare wrote, remarkably, not just the greatest English-language play, by critical consensus, but almost all of the greatest English-language plays. Similarly, the interactive fiction creators at Infocom devised practically all of the best-loved IF works in the history of the form. They certainly produced the favorites of the commercial era. Infocom's achievements were not surpassed, and the technical and thematic territory the company explored was not substantially extended, until independent interactive fiction authors started working in new ways in the 1990s. Infocom's development of interactive fiction as potential narrative and its refinement of the adventure-game puzzle far surpassed what was being done by any other company, including those that created graphical games. A critic writing in the commercial era said that for the text adventure category, "Infocom is considered by many clearly to be the industry leader" (McGath 1984, 27). Another author and critic of hypertext fiction has noted, more recently, that the company's more advanced text-based works "brought considerable sophistication and nuance to the form" (Moulthrop 1999).

The narrative aspects of the form were touted by Infocom. The term "interactive fiction" appeared on all its software packages and the company sometimes referred to its works as "stories." (Nevertheless, its works are usually called "Infocom games" by all who discuss them.) Infocom became the first company—in fact, the first entity of any sort—to openly declare that the text adventure had a literary aspect worth developing. At the same time, its works, with the exception of *A Mind Forever Voyaging,* were riddled with puzzles. In a 1984 issue of the company's newsletter, then called *The New Zork Times,* the company confirmed the central place of problem solving in its works, naming puzzles as the essential feature that distinguishes interactive fiction from a printed text:

> Although our games are interactive fiction, they are more than just stories: they are also a series of puzzles. It is these puzzles that transform our text from an hour's worth of reading to many, many hours' worth of thinking. . . . The value of our games is that they will provide many hours of stimulating mental exercise. (Infocom, Inc. 1984)

The company's stated belief in the centrality of problem solving should explain—if the nature of the market was not explanation enough—why Infocom did not focus on creating what might more easily be seen as artistic and literary works that favored exploration, communication with characters, or alternate plot progressions. Yet Infocom did make some progress along these lines, and advanced the state of the literary art by coupling the textually described worlds and situations with carefully crafted puzzles in ways that great riddlers might, in provocative and affecting ways.

Infocom helped establish many conventions of interactive fiction. As is often the case in art and literature, some of the most interesting work in recent years has sought to subvert these conventions and use the text adventure interface for novel purposes. As one technology writer explained in a subtly mangled metaphor that rings oddly true, technologically and artistically, "Infocom . . . broke important new ground that is still being explored today" (Garfinkel 1999, 83). Indeed, Infocom began work on the foundation of interactive fiction while the plot of ground that it was to be built upon had not yet been completely surveyed.

The thirty-five text-based Infocom games (see table 5.1) were all published during the 1980s. The early works, which contained no graphics at all, were available on a tremendous range of platforms. Infocom's publications spanned several popular literature genres, moving beyond the fantasy category into detective fiction, science fiction, modern-day treasure-plundering excursions, children's fiction, the spy thriller, and historical fiction/romance. A few of these IF works seemed to have more high-cultural aspirations (which were achieved in part) but almost all could be reasonably fitted into some popular genre, and Infocom did just that by conspicuously labeling them in the company's later years. Near the end of Infocom's independent existence, they created a few works based on classic stories, as many of their competitors had done.

Infocom's works, central as they were to the development of interactive fiction, were not known worldwide in the 1980s. For instance, Nelson reports that "Infocom's wares were rarely-seen exotica in England: a luxury brand for those in the know" (2002) and notes that while "Infocom was dominant for a period in the higher-end, chiefly American market . . . the company was not nearly so visible outside the USA, where disc drives were less affordable" (2001b, 350). Infocom's influence is indeed seen today in the worldwide IF community, but it did not extend across even the English-speaking world in the 1980s. Other important companies that were contemporaries of Infocom, inside and outside the United States, are discussed in the next chapter.

INTERACTIVE FICTION FOR SALE

Although Infocom was early to market and became the most important company of the commercial era, it was not the first to sell microcomputer text adventures. That honor goes to Scott Adams—no relation to the creator of the Dilbert comic—who released a tiny BASIC version of *Adventure* in 1978. He wrote the program, *Adventureland,* on his TRS-80 Model I. After selling a few copies of the cassette tape, he published it in a packaged format through the company he founded, Adventure International. His next work was *Pirate Adventure,* which was more original and cohesive. Its source code was published in the December 1980 issue of *Byte,* making Adams's work, and interactive fiction in general, more visible. His company would

TABLE 5.1

The thirty-five canonical interactive fiction works developed at and published by Infocom

---

Arthur: The Quest For Excalibur by Bob Bates (1989)

Young Arthur must find the pilfered sword-in-stone. Graphical; Infocom's last.

Ballyhoo by Jeff O'Neill (1986)

A circus visitor snoops to discover a kidnapping mystery. A darker, wry humor.

Beyond Zork: The Coconut of Quendor by Brian Moriarty (1987)

Had hit points (like *Dungeons and Dragons*), an on-screen map, and a rich world.

Border Zone by Marc Blank (1987)

A spy thriller in a made-up East European country. Events happen in real time.

Bureaucracy by Douglas Adams (1987)

Absurd red tape and procedural challenges are joined with Adams's wit.

Cutthroats by Michael Berlyn and Jerry Wolper (1984)

A diver recovers an undersea treasure with help from unreliable team members.

Deadline by Marc Blank (1982)

A detective interviews suspects at a family house to find the murderer.

Enchanter by Marc Blank and Dave Lebling (1983)

A novice spell-caster must defeat a warlock. A follow-up to the Zork Trilogy.

Hitchhiker's Guide To The Galaxy by Douglas Adams and Steve Meretzky (1984)

Arthur Dent explores space in his bathrobe. A clever reworking of Adams's book.

Hollywood Hijinx by Dave Anderson and Liz Cyr-Jones (1986)

The will calls for a treasure hunt at the dead Relative's California mansion.

Infidel by Michael Berlyn and Patricia Fogleman (1983)

Abandoned by the dig team in the desert, an archaeologist plunders a pyramid.

James Clavell's Shogun by Dave Lebling (1989)

In 1600, an Englishman enters a feudal Japan straight from the book. Graphical.

Journey: The Quest Begins by Marc Blank (1989)

A party of five go adventuring. Graphical and with role-playing game elements.

Leather Goddesses of Phobos by Steve Meretzky (1986)

A space opera with an impending alien attack and more bondage than most dungeons.

The Lurking Horror by Dave Lebling (1987)

During late-night studying, alchemical secrets are uncovered at an MIT-like campus.

TABLE 5.1 (CONTINUED)

A Mind Forever Voyaging by Steve Meretzky (1985)
Several dystopian trips to explore the possible futures of a city.

Moonmist by Stu Galley and Jim Lawrence (1986)
A night in a haunted castle gives a visitor the opportunity to uncover mysteries.

Nord and Bert Couldn't Make Head Or Tail Of It by Jeff O'Neill (1987)
Wordplay replaces the usual adventure actions in saving the town of Punster.

Planetfall by Steve Meretzky (1983)
The robot Floyd helps in a comic sci-fi quest for rescue from a strange planet.

Plundered Hearts by Amy Briggs (1987)
A romance-novel adventure with pirates, swords, and a female player character.

Seastalker by Stu Galley and Jim Lawrence (1984)
A monster threatens an undersea research lab. The first for younger interactors.

Sherlock: The Riddle Of The Crown Jewels by Bob Bates (1987)
Watson, accompanied by Holmes, takes the lead in recovering the crown jewels.

Sorcerer by Steve Meretzky (1984)
An evil demon menaces a land whose most powerful enchanter is missing.

Spellbreaker by Dave Lebling (1985)
The head enchanter faces the final crisis: the breakdown of magic itself.

Starcross by Dave Lebling (1982)
An alien craft holds logical challenges. Hard, and in the genre of hard sci-fi.

Stationfall by Steve Meretzky (1987)
A Planetfall sequel aboard a space station that's deserted—except for Floyd.

Suspect by Dave Lebling (1984)
The suspect must prove that someone else committed the murder at the masked ball.

Suspended by Michael Berlyn (1983)
A quiescently frozen controller directs robots to save a far-future complex.

Trinity by Brian Moriarty (1986)
A fantasy world offers passage back in time and a way to stop nuclear catastrophe.

Wishbringer by Brian Moriarty (1985)
A daydream turns real and a letter carrier quests through a magically changed town.

Witness by Stu Galley (1983)
Blackmail turns to murder in this hard-boiled detective game, set in the 1930s.

TABLE 5.1 (CONTINUED)

Zork I: The Great Underground Empire by Marc Blank and Dave Lebling (1980)
The generic adventurer visits a dazzling, below-ground kingdom—and loots it.

Zork II: The Wizard of Frobozz by Marc Blank and Dave Lebling (1981)
Another segment of the underground kingdom holds an annoying, spell-casting wizard.

Zork III: The Dungeon Master by Marc Blank and Dave Lebling (1982)
The final dungeon segment is intricate, with perhaps the hardest Infocom puzzle.

Zork Zero: The Revenge of Megaboz by Steve Meretzky (1988)
A silly object-collecting romp through a pre-Zork underground. Graphics.

publish thirteen other text adventures before going bankrupt in 1985
(Granade 1999a). Written for cartridge- and cassette-based computers with
very little memory, his works have been described as "strong on imagina-
tion and filled with clever puzzles. Their main weakness is rather poor
English usage and spelling" (McGath 1984, 45). These works are not known
for their literary qualities. As Nelson (2001b) reports, their descriptions had
"weirdly errant grammar" (348) and seemed to be written "in pidgin
English, like telegraphese" (200).

Language understanding was limited, too, but the terse descriptions and
two-word parser allowed this limited sort of interactive fiction to fit into 16k
of memory; frequently repeated phrases, which only had to be stored in
memory once, also helped to trim down the size of programs. The player
character was conceived of somewhat differently, as a reviewer noted: "the
Adams programs let you give commands to a more or less obedient 'puppet.'
Instead of saying 'you are at the top of a tree' . . . the program says 'I am at
the top of a tree'" (McGath 1984). Adams (2002) described his software
development process and how feedback from testers was important to it:

> I'd set my theme, I'd set my locations, and I'd start putting items in
> and putting in puzzles. I'd get the game about two thirds done and
> then I would stop. The next one third of the game literally came
> from the people I gave to play the game. I'd watch how they played
> the game, I'd watch what they tried to do with the items that I
> never thought they might try to do.

Although not very interesting to consider either as an interactive system or as potential literary art, Adams's works were widely available and influential. They remain good examples of how to cope with very limited computer resources. Many interactive fiction authors active today (e.g., Adam Cadre) first learned of the form through Scott Adams's works. The term interactive fiction itself was first popularized by Adventure International. It seems to have been coined by Robert Lafore, who started a company called Interactive Fiction and produced BASIC programs for the TRS-80, including *Six Micro Stories,* which were distributed by Adventure International (Lafore 2002). Although *Six Micro Stories* generated some critical enthusiasm for the possibilities of the form (Niesz and Holland 1984), it was exceedingly primitive, with long passages of text punctuated occasionally by a binary choice. The user could type in an English reply in order to indicate this choice, but formally, as potential literature, these programs had more affinity with Queneau's "Un Conte à votre façon" or with a Choose Your Own Adventure book than with *Adventure* and the interactive fiction works that followed it, those works that simulated complex worlds beneath the generated texts.

The type of entertainment software development that Adams and Adventure International exemplified—the single person serving as programmer and designer who worked with software testers—would change dramatically during the 1980s, as project budgets swelled and the development of games became a more complex affair. With some notable exceptions, commercial interactive fiction would, through the 1980s, follow the Scott Adams model, with a single person serving as programmer and writer. This was even the case at the flagship company of the form, founded by a group of programmers not long after Adventure International was started.

INFOCOM'S BEGINNINGS

Infocom was founded on 22 June 1979 by alumni and other affiliates of MIT's Project MAC (Multi Access Computing/Machine Aided Cognition), the group that later became the Laboratory for Computer Science. Three of the four *Zork* creators (Marc Blank, Tim Anderson, and Dave Lebling) were founding members of Infocom. There were seven other founders, including Joel Berez, Mike Broos, Scott Cutler, Stu Galley, and Chris Reeve. The other two were Al Vezza, head of the Dynamic Modeling group at MIT, and J. C. R. Licklider, Vezza's mentor and the founder of Project MAC. Infocom was not chartered as an interactive fiction company. The founders put the company together to sell some type of money-making software and planned to figure out exactly what that would be later. In August 1979, Blank became director; that November, Berez was elected Infocom's first president.

Berez and Blank became the first paid employees in June 1981; they were paid, at first, in IOUs. But as the early Infocom games began selling well and the company obliged customers with more, Infocom grew rapidly: by mid-1985 sales exceeded $10 million and the number of employees had topped one hundred. Before the close of the decade, however, fortunes had reversed and a tiny remnant of Infocom—five people—was all that was left. Those five moved to California to work at the headquarters of Infocom's new parent company. Despite the extremes that Infocom went thorough, when compared to the heady successes and abrupt downfalls of recent Internet start-ups or earlier video game makers such as Atari, this corporate rags-to-riches-to-rags story is not particularly dramatic. Considered in the context of interactive fiction, however—and as part of the overall intellectual history of computing—the rise and fall of Infocom is certainly of importance and interest.

The widespread availability of Infocom games was important to Infocom's commercial success during the era of the home computer, when a huge array of platforms were in use and no single one dominated the market. Cross-platform availability also broadened the audience for text adventures to include the users of business computers and other systems that were traditionally not seen as gaming platforms. Infocom didn't code up different versions of each work for Apple and Atari and Commodore, as many game makers of the 1980s did. Implementors were able to develop a single program to be used on any platform; they worked on terminals connected to the company's DEC System 20 using a special development system (Addams 1984). In order to deploy their games across different platforms, Berez and Blank specified and programmed a virtual machine called the Z-machine. This software computer could be implemented on many different platforms, including almost all of the popular microcomputers in the United States during the 1980s. (The only exceptions were very early or severely underpowered machines, such as the Commodore PET.) This approach was not only efficient with memory, it was also what allowed Infocom to develop for only one platform: the Z-machine. Since the Z-machine, actually software itself, was then widely implemented on many home computers (and could be implemented on new computers as the need arose), any new interactive fiction creation could instantly work on every major platform and many minor platforms. Developing twenty implementations of the Z-machine and twenty IF works would result in four hundred saleable products. Mike Dornbrook (2000), Infocom's director of marketing, said this cross-platform availability was important to the company's bottom line: no single computer platform ever accounted for more than 25 percent of Infocom's revenue in any quarter.

The Z-machine served as the interpreter for Infocom story files. To create the story files themselves—the code that the Z-machine ran—a compiler was programmed by Blank to convert high-level, more English-like instructions into executable form. The high-level language that was used was an Infocom original, based on the Lisp-like language MDL, which had been used to write the mainframe *Zork*. The new language was called ZIL, Zork Implementation Language. Here is the ZIL for the living room in *Zork I*:

```
<ROOM LIVING-ROOM
    (LOC ROOMS)
    (DESC "Living Room")
    (EAST TO KITCHEN)
    (WEST TO STRANGE-PASSAGE IF CYCLOPS-FLED ELSE
        "The wooden door is nailed shut.")
    (DOWN PER TRAP-DOOR-EXIT)
    (ACTION LIVING-ROOM-F)
    (FLAGS RLANDBIT ONBIT SACREDBIT)
    (GLOBAL STAIRS)
    (THINGS <> NAILS NAILS-PSEUDO)>  (Infocom, Inc. 1989, 6)
```

From the standpoint of IF developers, ZIL made several advances over MDL (Galley 1985). For one thing, it replaced what one developer called "more-or-less incomprehensible verb definitions" with more legible ones (Lebling 1996). The virtual machine concept was first implemented commercially in the Z-machine. (The earlier, noncommercial implementation was UCSD's P-Machine, which ran Pascal (Foust 2001).) This same concept is what enables Java programs to work across different platforms by running in Java virtual machines.

Infocom's successful product line was based on the mainframe *Zork,* a group project. Unsurprisingly, Infocom became a collaborative environment. Although one Infocom author said "We don't brainstorm as much as you might think" (Moriarty 1987), the author or authors listed on the packaging were seldom the only ones who helped to shape the games. One journalist who visited the company wrote that "a single writer originates each project, but the process soon becomes collaborative, with solutions and scenarios proffered, swapped, or stolen" (Suplee 1983). Also, a new IF work would be developed by starting with the code from an earlier project and modifying it; according to one Infocom IF creator, "5 to 10% of a game's total code comes from the 'generic' shell" (Moriarty 1987). This reuse, although a small part of the overall program, helps to explain a feature of IF works noted by Nelson (2001b)—namely, that "the strongest unity of style between the Infocom games is that they seem to be told by essentially the same narrator" (354). Usually either one individual or a team of two, working in slightly different roles, would head up the creation of a particular interactive fiction piece. One person would often serve in what would, in some other organizations, be several roles: as the main writer of the texts involved, the designer of interactivity and puzzles, and the ZIL programmer. "Too little credit has been given to department heads who were at least as responsible for Infocom's artistic texture" (350), Nelson noted. These included Jon Palace, a former book editor who managed the Implementors, and the heads of quality assurance: first Dave Anderson (who then became an Implementor), then Liz Cyr-Jones (Lebling 2002).

ZORK COMES TO THE MICROCOMPUTER

Infocom made its first sale in 1980: an 8-inch floppy disk containing the PDP-11 version of *Zork I.* To make the sprawling *Zork* fit on personal computers of the era, Blank and Lebling had implemented only one somewhat embellished segment of the game in their first commercial program. (At that time, home computers usually featured about 32 KB of RAM and one 100 KB floppy drive. The PDP-11 was a more powerful computer, but *Zork I* was developed on the Z-machine, which would work on less powerful platforms as well.) Blank and Lebling finished *Zork II* in 1981 and *Zork III* the following year, incorporating elements from the mainframe work but also adding more original text and code. The modifications make these three games new works, distinct from the mainframe *Zork* and different from one another. Infocom initially sought distribution for its first products through other companies—one implementor said that "by the time *Zork* fan Bill Gates heard of our offer, Infocom was deep in negotiations with Personal Software Inc." (Galley 1985)—but it chose to publish the works itself after a short period in which *Zork I* and *Zork II* were distributed through Personal Software.

The fame of *Zork I* eclipses its actual importance to interactive fiction. That game brought the more advanced elements in mainframe *Zork* to the home computer user, to be sure, and it became the basis of Infocom's commercial success. Yet Infocom's first release, when compared to its mainframe ancestor, features only slight improvements, whether considered in traditional terms of puzzlecraft and literary merit or seen in the context of world and riddle.

One important novelty was introduced in *Zork I,* however: The microcomputer work provides alternate ways to solve certain puzzles. The order in which puzzles were solved might have varied from session to session in the mainframe *Zork* and in *Adventure,* but this change provided a new way in which interactors could influence the generated narratives. Mike Dornbrook, who served as the game's main tester (he had never played the game on the mainframe and was appropriately naïve) said he suggested several alternate solutions to *Zork I* puzzles that he found obscure; Blank and Lebling took some of his advice (Dorbrook 2000).

In *Zork I,* the cyclops can be still be frightened away by shouting "Odysseus," but he can also be lulled to sleep with an offer of food.

Upon acquiring all of *Zork I*'s nineteen treasures and placing them in the white house's trophy case, a passage to the Stone Barrow becomes accessible. The interactor can direct the player character into this area, the threshold of *Zork II,* to win.

Zork II is an important early example of an interactive fiction sequel. This is seldom discussed, no doubt because of how the *Zork* trilogy originated from fragments of a single mainframe work. *Zork II* had several noticeable

elements not found in the mainframe *Zork,* though. There was a new antagonist, for instance: the Wizard of Frobozz. The description of the underground surroundings was also considerably enriched. The player character
enters this new part of the underground complex through a long and well-
described "corridor" of different areas, which serve only to introduce the
world of this work. *Zork II* demonstrated that an effective work of interactive fiction could be both extended and improved upon in a sequel.

The Wizard of Frobozz is, as described in *Zork II,* a "strange little
man in a long cloak ... wearing a high pointed hat embroidered with astro-
logical signs. He has a long, stringy, and unkempt beard." This Wizard is
Zork II's thief figure, coming and going before there is opportunity for
input, so that the interactor cannot command the player character to speak
with him or otherwise act on him. The Wizard simply appears, casts a spell
by waving his wand and uttering a word beginning with the letter "F,"
cackles, and vanishes. Certain spells immobilize the player character. Some
doom the player character (requiring the interactor to start over), while
others such as "Fireproof" do not even particularly annoy. Sometimes the
Wizard's spells fizzle and fail, frustrating him. Although the Wizard's reper-
toire of spells and amusing misfires were in some ways an improvement on
the one-trick thief in *Zork I,* there was little hint of what might motivate
the Wizard's actions. This antagonist of *Zork II*'s potential narratives did
incorporate some interesting new behaviors. The Wizard is hardly even a
very good caricature, though, much less a character; he is as flat and static
as a stock folkloric figure.

One of the puzzles in *Zork II* simply provides a riddle directly: "What
is tall as a house, / round as a cup, / and all the king's horses / can't draw it
up?" Not only is this a decent riddle, it is also tied in to another puzzle that
lies beyond the area where the riddle is inscribed. Other parts of *Zork II*
(taken from late additions to the mainframe *Zork*) allude to *Alice in
Wonderland:* In the Tea Room, where an evidently mad group has set the
table for tea, there are four cakes that seem to be labeled "eat me"; eating one
of these allows passage through a rabbit hole to another room, where there
is a pool of tears. Here, too, the player must be something of a scientist in
order to solve the puzzle posed, trying to eat various cakes and observing the
sometimes lethal effects so that the proper course of action can be figured
out. *Zork II* also features a dragon who must be defeated to rescue a princess.

The magic sword is not sufficient to dispatch the dragon, who must be defeated through cleverness.

Gathering treasure is an important part of *Zork II*, but assembling the booty in a trophy case is not the ultimate goal. In order to win, the interactor must have the player character supply these treasures to a powerful demon. This demon (like the robot) will do the adventurer a critical service—after he is propitiated. From the standpoint of the adventurer, *Zork II* adds a new and innovative motivation to the usual drive to plunder: Satanism. Such demonic elements were also found in *Zork: The Malifestro Quest*, a spin-off book for children that used a format similar to those of Choose Your Own Adventure books. A Cape Cod newspaper, *The Register*, reported a denunciation of this book in its 16 May 1995 issue. Jan Leary, the mother of one of this book's readers, called for the book to be removed from the school library and school book fairs. "Such reading promotes demonic worship," Leary said, "and glorifies violence for school children" (qtd. in Infocom, Inc. 1985). The more detailed and interactive Satanic experience of *Zork II*, in which the player character must summon a demon, enlist him to service, and (essentially) instruct him to murder someone, would no doubt have raised even more severe concerns—if it had even been noticed by parents. Text adventures were inaccessible, however, to those not adept at puzzle solving and not fluent in the dialect of English their parsers understood. This marginalized the form, but it also may have helped it elude strict parental control. By being esoteric, interactive fiction was less likely to be noticed by those who would suppress free expression. It was still noticed by some, though, who seized on any mention of magic (e.g., in the packaging or in advertisements) as proof that, as Steven Meretzky (2002) said, "Infocom was actually the Great Satan."

Zork II contains the Oddly-Angled Room, a particularly confounding pseudomaze. In order to get through it, the player character must move through the rooms in a diamond pattern, as if playing baseball. This puzzle has been rightly decried as involving a confusing intrusion of contemporary culture into a subterranean fantasy world. Similar complaints are not often made about the anachronistic placement of contemporary machinery, engineering, electrical devices (e.g., the brass lantern) and even a robot in different parts of *Zork I–III*. That sort of juxtaposition appealed to most of the interactors who played the games in the trilogy early on—anyone who used a computer in the early 1980s was necessarily fascinated with technology and was often amused to see it placed in a fantasy context. Since recent technologies are distributed throughout the IF world and cleverly incorporated into puzzles, they help to create a distinctive atmosphere. The baseball pseudomaze is different in that it relies on rules that are not a part of physics, engineering, or logic. The puzzle also points out how Infocom's works, although often set in other countries or in alternate or future worlds, were created in the context of the United States, with American assumptions. A puzzle about baseball is hardly the only case in which American cultural assumptions can be seen to underlie the IF world and its structures and potential narratives; it is only one of the more obvious and easily explained.

The shadowy, misty warrens of *Zork III* are something of a contrast to the worlds of the earlier *Zork* works, although a similar blend of technology, fantasy, and swordplay is seen in this final installment, and some of the same Great Underground Empire figures are mentioned. Part of the bleak landscape has hills, an ocean, a lake, and a massive cliff, all of which seem to have been casually transported underground. A "hello, sailor" puzzle refers to something amusing (a prostitutes' greeting and classic computer test message, first referred to in a holy book in *Zork I*), but most of the game lacks such humor. The player character in *Zork III* must overcome the puzzles presented and confront the Dungeon Master, an entity familiar from *Dungeons and Dragons,* as mentioned in chapter 3.

A few signs of life are present in the desolate dungeon. Beside a lush, sunlit cliff, the player character encounters a man who is somewhat reminiscent of the thief in *Zork I*. A frail old man is found sleeping in one room.

Extensive conversation is not possible with these figures—who turn out to be the same protean individual—but the interaction required to make progress does go beyond the troll slaughtering and thief slaughtering of *Zork I*.

Locations like the Crystal Grotto add color to the otherwise dim subterranean setting. More dominant in *Zork III* are the several areas that constitute the Land of Shadow, "a land of dark shadows and shallow hills, which stretch out in all directions." Puzzles in *Zork III* are few but intricate, as is suggested by the top score of 7 points.

One of *Zork III*'s challenges, the Royal Puzzle, is often singled out as Infocom's hardest. Typical room descriptions are not used, as seen when the player character first enters the puzzle:

> The architecture of this region is getting complex, so that further descriptions will be diagrams of the immediate vicinity in a 3 x 3 grid. The walls here are rock, but of two different types—sandstone and marble. The following notations will be used:

> .. = your position (middle of grid)
> MM = marble wall
> SS = sandstone wall
> ?? = unknown (blocked by walls)

> Room in a Puzzle
> ```
>          +MM      SS +
> West  +MM   ..    +   East
>          +??      SS    +
> ```

To solve the puzzle (without recourse to a walkthrough), the interactor has to map the area, discovering which portions of the puzzle will shift about and which are fixed in place. As soon as the player character drops into the maze, this adventurer is trapped, and pushing the wrong block the wrong way can make it impossible to get out. Beneath one of the puzzle's great blocks is the prize, a book. Two other blocks have ladders affixed to their sides. One of these can, after some shifting about of the blocks, be moved into place beneath the original entryway to allow the player character to escape the puzzle.

The elvish sword of the previous *Zork* works is found early on wedged into a stone in a throwaway reference to Arthurian legend. When the player character later encounters a hooded figure in *Zork III*'s Land of Shadow, the sword magically appears in hand. After typing "kill figure with sword" again and again, the interactor will (eventually) be able to have the player character defeat this figure. Then, on removing the hood, a moment reminiscent of the 1980 *The Empire Strikes Back* (when Luke encounters Darth Vader's figure on Dagobah) is played out: "You slowly remove the hood from your badly wounded opponent and recoil in horror at the sight of your own face, weary and wounded. A faint smile comes to the lips and then the face starts to change, very slowly, into that of an old, wizened person. The image fades and with it the body of your hooded opponent." The misty setting of this duel even recalls the thick atmosphere of the planet Dagobah, although the caverns of *Zork III* are mostly lifeless, in contrast to the teeming Dagobah jungle. (This correspondence was noted by a reviewer who wondered "whether George Lucas played this game before creating *Return of the Jedi*" (McGath 1984, 32).) In this part of the Great Underground Empire, no Yoda figure is on hand to explain the significance of the player character's vision.

In one somewhat dramatic moment in *Zork III,* Blank and Lebling poked fun at the strict input requirements placed on users by computers, and in particular the Infocom parser's inability to understand typed input that would be clear to a human but might differ by a single character from what the computer would accept. When the player character is near the end of his or her quest and has encountered the Dungeon Master at a door deep within the complex, the old figure says:

> "When you feel you are ready, go to the secret door and 'SAY "FROTZ OZMOO"'! Go, now!" He starts to leave but turns back briefly and wags his finger in warning. "Do not forget the double quotes!"

In winning *Zork III,* the adventurer fulfills this prophetic encounter by entering the Treasury of Zork, store of the greatest treasures of the land, and becoming the Great Underground Empire's Dungeon Master:

> "Long have I waited for one capable of releasing me from my burden!" He taps you lightly on the head with his staff, mumbling a few well-chosen spells, and you feel yourself changing, growing

older and more stooped. For a moment there are two identical mages standing among the treasure, then your counterpart dissolves into a mist and disappears, a sardonic grin on his face.

The final reply is a happy one for the player character, however, who begins "to feel the vast powers and lore . . . and thirst for an opportunity to use them."

A SET OF STANDARD INTERACTIVE FICTION INPUTS

A set of special inputs, beginning with *Zork I* and based on some special inputs that were useful in the mainframe *Zork,* were implemented in almost all of Infocom's works. Some are directives, some commands. Many of these special inputs (among them, *quit* and *inventory,* discussed in chapter 1) were found in similar form in *Adventure* and in other earlier interactive fiction, and many were adopted by other companies. Since Infocom's works were the best known of this era, it is worth listing (with some explanation, in brackets) the company's description of what some of special inputs do in their works. These appear in table 5.2.

In later Infocom works two additional special inputs were supported: *oops* (to allow a one-word typo to be corrected without the interactor having to type the whole line over again) and *undo* (to make it as if the previous command had not been issued).

DEADLINE, A DUNGEONLESS, DRAGONLESS GAME

Deadline, by Marc Blank, is a detective mystery, significant in that it broke from the *Dungeons and Dragons*–style worlds of *Adventure, Zork, Haunt,* and the early works from Scott Adams's Adventure International. By departing from fantasy and offering a set of characters with whom the player character could converse, *Deadline* attracted some new sorts of attention, such as a mention in *The New York Times Book Review* (Rothstein 1983). Much later it would be the main work discussed in the adventure-game chapter of *Cybertext* (Aarseth 1997).

TABLE 5.2

The special inputs supported by *Zork I,* most of which are extradiegetic, help to explain a good deal about the way an interactor actually experienced interactive fiction

---

AGAIN

ZORK will respond as if you had repeated your previous sentence. [Particularly useful in combat situations, which require the interactor to simply type *kill opponent with sword* over and over.] . . .

DIAGNOSE

ZORK gives you a medical report of your physical condition. . . . [Used to assess the damage from combat and, in *Planetfall,* from illness. *diagnose* did not play an important role in later Infocom works.]

LOOK

ZORK describes your surroundings in detail. . . . [Often used after the room description has scrolled off the top of the screen.]

RESTART

This . . . starts the game over from the beginning. [The interactor was expected to run into dead ends frequently, and need to restart.]

RESTORE

Restores a game position you saved . . .

SAVE

Saves a game position . . . [Saving and restoring are critical to most puzzle-solving. Trying a variety of actions, including some that are likely to kill the player character, is usually necessary.]

SCORE

ZORK shows your current score with the number of moves you have made, and your rank. . . . [Some sort of scoring is used in most interactive fiction, even when the game aspect of the work is not predominant. The score often the only indicator of how far the player character has progressed through to possible narratives or through the world.]

SCRIPT

. . . commands your printer to begin printing a transcript of your game session. [Useful for offline study of tricky problems, this directive also allows those who have won a game to print out the final reply as proof of their victory.] . . .

Table 5.2 (continued)

UNSCRIPT

This command stops your printer from printing. [To distinguish those inputs that influence the IF world from those that do not, this is considered a directive in this book, not a command.]

VERSION

ZORK responds by showing you the release number and serial number of your copy of the game.

WAIT

This command causes time in the game to pass. Normally, between moves, no time is passing as far as ZORK is concerned . . . For example, if you encounter an alien being, you could WAIT and see what it will do.

Source: Infocom 1981, 7.
Note: quit and *inventory*, already discussed, are omitted from this list.

Reviewer Edward Rothstein described some important ways in which *Deadline* differed from video games and offered the first bit of credibility to the emerging interactive fiction form:

> I am not some forensic Pac-Man, proceeding through a pre-existent maze. From my arrival at the Robner mansion, I am a character whose actions affect the world I enter. I arrest a suspect only to find that the grand jury isn't convinced by my evidence. I follow a suspect too obviously, and he just retires to his room. My questions can lead to a second murder—and my carelessness to my own. But there is a unique solution. And to find it, I must often start the case over, re-experience it from different perspectives. The average complete investigation lasts 20 hours; I have spent many more exploring the program's intricate universe. *Deadline,* in fact, is more like a genre of fiction than a game.

Rothstein pointed out that Infocom's works made use of the power found in mythology and folklore; he compared the resourceful adventurer in *Zork* and the clever detective in *Deadline* to Odysseus. He also mentioned that *Deadline's* limited vocabulary makes interaction less natural than one might hope for.

Cybertext provides a detailed discussion of the nature of adventure-game interaction. One of the many interesting points made with respect to *Deadline* is that the interactor, who is ignorant of the proper outcome and of what he or she is supposed to do, is not really a "wreader" with authorial power. Instead, the interactor is the target of authorial intrigue. This is a kinder interpretation than, but similar to, one made in the parodical Web periodical *Suck.com*. An article there suggested that the interactor is usually in the same situation as the protagonist of Christopher Durang's *The Actor's Nightmare*—thrust upon the stage without any warning, and without having had time to learn lines (Internick 1997).

Aarseth (1997) finds that some of the replies *Deadline* provides are "pure nonsense" and gives the example of the reply to the command "fingerprint me": "Upon looking over and dusting the me you notice there are no good fingerprints to be found" (116). Actually the response, although unhelpful in the context of trying to win, is sensible, amusing, and perfectly apropos. Aarseth no doubt wanted his detective player character to perform an odd behavior: to stop, ink his hands, and record his own fingerprints on paper in the middle of an investigation. For the work to parse his command differently and come up with an even more odd interpretation was not nonsense, but felicity. Interactors have been encouraged to have fun by prodding the parser in similarly unusual ways. One computer gaming magazine carried this suggestion: "After you've given up for the night trying to find out who the murderer is in *Deadline* or *The Witness*, have some fun with the computer. Tell it a joke. Insult it. Type in a sentence which makes no sense" (Gutman 1984). This sort of subversive interaction is not particularly uncommon in any sort of gaming or play situation, since children often use toys for purposes that are different from or even contrary to those intended by toy manufacturers. In interactive fiction, this subversive typing is an interesting way to interact. The interactor is engaged with the work and enjoys the text responses that are provided, but seems to be ignoring the overriding purposes for which the work was created.

Deadline included an interesting touch of metalepsis: A book within its world was supposedly a novelization of the interactive fiction work *Deadline*. One critic found the fatal effect of reading the ending of this book to be a sign that "the writers at Infocom seem afraid to be taken too seriously" (McGath 1984, 29); another identified it as "one of the more brutal types of metalepsis yet invented, or perhaps *dyslepsis* is a better word for it" (Aarseth 1997, 118). A sort of dyslepsis can also be seen in *Suspended* and can occur in non-interactive narrative also, as in Julio Cortázar's short story "Continuidad de los Parques" (Continuity of Parks). In the final reply of *Deadline,* after the interactor has figured out who committed the crime, another linear story is revealed, the "author's summary of the story." Interestingly, this text suggests that the interactor devise an independent summary first. This might be done so the interactor can see how close to the author's version he or she can get, but it might also suggest that the author's version of the story is not the only valid one. Solving the crime isn't the only possibility, of course: "The variety of possible outcomes is very impressive" (McGath 1984, 33).

Deadline has a different sort of appeal than *Zork* and *Adventure* do. The player character in those earlier two works quests through a fantasy landscape, and the important story (however dull it might be) transpires during the interactive exchange; it was told when the potential narrative was actualized. In *Deadline,* the interactor is not a party to any of the important events—those events that Blank calls the "story," of which the previous conclusion is a summary. This entire story takes place before the first opportunity for the player character to act within *Deadline's* world. The detective simply uncovers that earlier, hidden story through exploration, interrogation, and investigation. Treasures are to be found in *Zork,* while secret events are the treasures of *Deadline.* This is a better reward for some, but it means that the interactor has control over only how this earlier story is discovered. In contrast, although the particular story elements of *Zork* might be uninteresting, the interactor can exercise some influence over what important episodes might occur and in what order. A very different work that nevertheless has the uncovering of previous events as its goal would later be seen in the independent era. This was the 1997 *Babel* by Ian Finley, a detective-free science fiction work.

The Witness by Stu Galley was the next Infocom mystery, published in 1983. It was a more hard-boiled detective story, clearly influenced by pulp detective fiction and film noir. Lebling's *Suspect* followed, taking place at a costume ball. It began with the player character being framed for a murder. The interactor had to direct the player character to conduct an unofficial investigation in order to try to prove that someone else committed the crime. *Suspect's* debut was notable. It was unveiled at a party in a mansion during the 1984 Consumer Electronics Show, around the time of Infocom's greatest financial success. Despite the spectacular rollout, *Suspect* did little to revitalize the detective genre of interactive fiction.

The two other works Infocom published with a "Mystery" label were *Ballyhoo* and *Moonmist*. These two had some similarities to the three early mysteries and are more akin to them than to some treasure-collecting *Zork*-style work. They were fairly different from *Deadline, The Witness,* and *Suspect* in many respects, however.

ENCHANTER AND OTHER ZORK-WORLD STORIES

Infocom published three spell-casting adventures, set in the *Zork* world. The first of these was *Enchanter* by Blank and Lebling, in 1983. Meretzky's *Sorcerer* was released the following year; it incorporated the sort of humor for which that author became known. Lebling's *Spellbreaker* was published the year after that. These three added spells to the *Zork* world. The player character is a Wizard, who grows in ability throughout the series and can cast an increasingly powerful array of spells—after locating the scrolls upon which they are written. This power was hinted at in the end of *Zork II,* when the player character gained the Wizard of Frobozz's magic wand and could go about casting spells. In the *Enchanter* trilogy, spell-casting becomes the usual way of solving problems and making progress.

While the adventure-game puzzle in *Zork* and *Adventure* usually required the interactor to think about the way machines work, or to consider physics, or to imagine the interaction of different everyday objects, the spells of the new trilogy required a different kind of thinking. To solve an earlier puzzle, the interactor might think, "What object that I'm carrying or that I have found earlier will work to get me past this obstacle, given the usual way that objects work and the familiar laws of nature?" In *Enchanter,* this thinking had to be broadened to include very unusual, supernatural powers conferred on the player character by means of spells.

Spellbreaker dealt most directly with the waning of magic in the *Zork* world, a situation much like the one in Ursula K. Le Guin's *Earthsea Trilogy,* which Lebling has named as an inspiration for the *Enchanter* series (Masterson 1986). The work has several very difficult puzzles, deeply related to the themes of the works and its possible narratives. *Spellbreaker* is considered by aficionados to be one of Infocom's best.

Beyond Zork by Brian Moriarty, published in 1987, incorporated elements from role-playing games, but also (as might be anticipated from Moriarty, the author of *Trinity* and *Wishbringer*) had a well-described IF world that was rich with interesting situations. The *Dungeons and Dragons* influence is certainly noticeable when beginning *Beyond Zork,* since the interactor is required to assign ability points to the player character before the main textual exchange even begins. Combat plays a small but noticeable part in *Beyond Zork,* as does the use of magic items. One interesting feature is seen in how the world itself is subtly reconfigured each time a new traversal is begun, although the same areas are present in each. Despite this randomness, mapping is unnecessary, since an on-screen map is implemented (in this all-text work) by use of a special font. The current room description is always visible beside this map, at the top of the screen.

The overall goal of *Beyond Zork* is, rather farcically, to acquire the powerful Coconut of Quendor. Nelson (2001) described its prologue as "Self-indulgent, self-parodying, slack, told in the past tense, uninteractive and basically dumb" (371). While this work brings in references to Frank Baum's *The Wizard of Oz* alongside mention of earlier interactive fiction, such as *Wishbringer* and *The Hitchhiker's Guide to the Galaxy*, it was not among the finest of Infocom's works in terms of its writing. Its IF world—the land of Quendor—is above ground, very expansive, and populated, quite unlike the Great Underground Empire. The overall plot is no masterpiece; one reviewer noted that "one does not learn anything about the whereabouts of the coconut until well into the game, and finding it at the end amounts to stumbling over it. What plot *Beyond Zork* has is often entertaining, but it hardly makes a coherent whole" (Stevens 1988). But despite these mediocre aspects, as an interesting program and at the level of interface, *Beyond Zork* made some progress.

Steven Meretzky's *Zork Zero,* released in 1988, is far wackier than Blank and Lebling's *Zork I–III*. This work features graphics (some puzzles, such as a rebus puzzle, cannot be solved by looking only at the text) and a slick interface, but text remains central. Meretzky expands Blank and Lebling's sketchy historical notes regarding the origins of the Great Underground Empire to create a prequel that is consistent in many ways but different in tone. *Zork Zero* lacks grim elements such as earnest demonic summoning or mortal combat with underground denizens. The player character has inherited a valuable fragment of parchment from an ancestor. The original parchment owner (who is controlled by the interactor in an introductory segment) saw the wizard Megaboz slay Lord Dimwit Flathead and place a curse upon the land. In the main IF world, almost a century later, the curse's maturity date has arrived. The player character must race around, aided by the parchment, and gather a bunch of items (of course) in order to dispel the curse. Non-interactive texts like the parchment scrap are often important in interactive fiction—particularly if they hold needed instructions, since that gives them an affinity not only to magical spells but also to computer programs. The most interesting character that *Zork Zero* supplies is the jester, who is in some ways like the Wizard of Frobozz. The puzzles are many, but most are, as Duncan Stevens (1998) noted, "classic logic puzzles cribbed directly into the game." Infocom's last text-centered *Zork* work seemed, for the most part, to indicate the sterility of the treasure hunt format.

Three graphical games that were also set in the *Zork* world were pro-duced by Activision in the 1990s—extending the lifespan of the original *Zork* concept through twenty years of game development. These Activision games are *Return to Zork* (1993), *Zork Nemesis* (1996), and *Zork Grand Inquisitor* (1997). As a tie-in to the launch of the last of these, Activision com-missioned original *Zork* creator Blank and Implementor Mike Berlyn to design an all-text interactive fiction, *Zork: The Undiscovered Underground*. The player character in this instance was a feeble parody of an adventurer who had only a plastic sword. Grues at a grue convention wandered around like businesspeople. Perhaps this was appropriate for this rare piece of interactive fiction that was funded by a software company in the late 1990s: Two of the most prominent IF authors of the 1980s had been asked, after all, to put together a little promotional gimmick for a graphical game.

CONSCIOUSNESS SHATTERED IN *SUSPENDED*

Interactive fiction had, before 1983, generally presupposed a single heroic character whom the interactor would control. Hence the player character had been, up to this point, the protagonist of all possible narratives of the interactive fiction work. In Berlyn's *Suspended,* released that year, this assump-tion was shattered—as were the central consciousness and perceptions of player character. As mentioned in the discussion of hypodiegesis in chapter

1, there is, supposedly, a protagonist of *Suspended,* who rests in a cylindrical chamber in semiconsciousness, charged with responsibility for managing the infrastructure of a planet from within a far-future underground complex. The interactor does, as before, control this one main character. In *Suspended,* however, the usual commands to effect action and motion are futile. The interactor instead types instructions to and senses the world through six robots, each with a different set of sensors and effectors. The player character's perceptions and abilities are therefore fragmented into those of six hypodiegetic player characters: only one robot can see in color, only one robot can hear, only one robot is well-equipped for lifting heavy items. To solve *Suspended,* the interactor must direct these robots to act, deploying the right one to handle each problem that arises.

Berlyn was one of the few who came to Infocom early on from someplace other than MIT—it was Colorado, in his case. Berlyn describes his first encounter with interactive fiction as follows:

> I kind of tripped into it . . . In 1979, I was writing novels and decided to purchase a personal computer to use for word processing. After six months, I discovered the original adventure game, *Colossal Cave.* I just thought, "Wow, this is really interesting. I should learn how these are done, because it's writing and computers and a lot of fun . . ."
>
> I set about teaching myself how to program computers . . . In about six months, I'd written a game, and my wife and I started a software publishing company, called Sentient Software. (qtd. in Katz 1996, 153)

Through Sentient, Berlyn published the science fictional work *Oo-topos* (written with his wife, Muffy Berlyn) and then his *Cyborg,* both in 1981. The player character in this latter work was in need of repair. *scan* replaced the familiar *look* command. The text was in the first person, with the "I" of the generated text representing the cyborg's computer component. Other possible commands to this computer side included *opinion,* to ask for advice. When conversing with another character, the interactor would select responses from a menu rather than typing them in. Although *Cyborg's* parser was not as capable as Infocom's, it worked well. Three years after its release one reviewer called it, even in comparison to Infocom's works, "one of the best-written adventures available" (McGath 1984, 74).

In *Suspended* Berlyn broke that damaged cyborg even more severely—into six robots controlled by a motionless human. Even figuring out what exactly the objects were in different parts of the complex made for a riddle for the interactor. Here are two descriptions of the same area, by different robots:

> P O E T : Internal map reference—Gamma Repair
> Oh, to reach the end of one's previous existence, to travel the road-ways of life when they are most needed, only to end up here, reborn.
> The glider is not in motion.
> In the room with me is Waldo.
> A cage to hold our ancestry sits on the floor, meek and timid, yet unwilling to openly share.
> W A L D O : Internal map reference—Gamma Repair
> I have reached the south end of this area. The walkway ends here.
> The walkway is not in motion.
> In the room with me is Poet.
> A large object sits before me. Sonar indicates it is hollow, but not empty.

As intriguing as the different sensory perspectives and capabilities were, and as effective as the incorporation of board game and simulation elements was, *Suspended* suffered in terms of its possible narratives. It was essentially a sort of complex system toy, like *SimCity,* with a few interesting events that could transpire. McGath (1984) noted that certain final replies, "the messages you get for finishing . . . with a mediocre score [. . .] are unnecessarily insulting, considering that you have just saved the world" (36). The extreme difficulty of *Suspended* caused much of the interactor's focus to be on thinking about how to manipulate variables and about the layout of the world and the position of the robots. (A map and six robot tokens were included in the package to help the interactor deal with this aspect of the game.) Once every robot had visited every possible area and the world was fully explored, different sensory perspectives did little to enhance the original sense of strangeness and wonder. While the robots had different ways of describing the world (sometimes, as with Poet, fanciful ones) and could do different things to act within it, these essentially emotionless and correctly functioning beings only hinted at the possibility of a more interesting and multiple subjectivity in interactive fiction. Nevertheless, *Suspended* was a trailblazing work that too few have tried to follow.

A similarly hard science fiction work, Lebling's *Starcross* was released in 1982. *Starcross* was Infocom's first science fiction work. (*Zork I–III* had a few clearly science fiction elements, but these were installed in a fantasy framework.) *Starcross* brought the space-traveling player character onto a large and fairly desolate alien vessel. The work, which was most directly influenced by Arthur C. Clarke's *Rendezvous with Rama,* was full of puzzles requiring logical and mathematical reasoning.

The only Infocom work to follow the example of *Suspended* by providing multiple characters, all under the control of the interactor at once, was *Journey: The Quest Begins.* This very late work by Marc Blank, published in 1989, included graphics and a well-designed interface but did not accept natural language input and so was not, strictly speaking, interactive fiction as discussed in this book. It was touted as a role-playing game. The group under control—a party of adventurers à la *Dungeons and Dragons*—was less original in concept than was the group in *Suspended,* but the characters themselves were less robotic, as one might expect from their being human and from the later date of this title.

INFIDEL'S TREASURE-COLLECTING CRITIQUE

Infidel (1983) took on some interesting social and political issues, offering the first strong critique of traditional adventuring goals. It was at one point called "the most literary of Infocom's adventures to date" (McGath 1984, 41), but those interested in the literary qualities of early interactive fiction have preferred to look at *Deadline.* In form, *Infidel* is a typical, puzzle-filled adventure, set in a pyramid that the archaeologically inclined player character is supposed to loot. This nameless character awakens alone in the Egyptian desert, abandoned by the hired dig team. They have left in anger, a note explains, "after what you said of our rites." Most supplies are gone, although the note explains that the crew intended to leave enough for the player character to make it back to civilization alive. To successfully traverse the work, the inter-actor must figure out how to locate the pyramid, get inside it, and explore it. In the pyramid the interactor must have the player character avoid traps, must decipher "hieroglyphs" (which are analphabetic ASCII characters), and must have the player character manipulate parts of the structure to allow access to its deeper reaches. *Infidel* was created by *Suspended* author Mike Berlyn and Patricia Fogleman.

The highly successful film *Raiders of the Lost Ark* came out two years before *Infidel* did, and it was clearly a strong influence. One puzzle requires the player character to knock over a heavy statue, as Indiana Jones did in the film. Descending doors of stone and a weight-sensitive, treasure-bearing altar evoke the opening sequence of *Raiders*.

One room features walls that close in on the player character, who must brace them open with a beam. This puzzle comes from the garbage-disposal crisis in an earlier adventure film starring Harrison Ford, *Star Wars*.

The player character in *Infidel* is no charming, whip-wielding profes-sor, however. The materials packed with the game make that character's greed clear, indicating the character has abused the dig team. In the game's pro-logue, the player character recalls forcing them to work on a holy day. (The crew is never identified as Muslim, but everything suggests that they are.) The text generated deeper within the world indicates the greed of this character, too, as in this initial description of the royal barge's Fore Cabin area: "The cabin is bare with none of the luxuries you expected to see. You close your eyes for a moment, picturing the barge you'll someday own, the yacht fully rigged and crewed. You open your eyes and shake your head, anxious to make your dream reality." As McGath (1984) noted, "Even the messages you get in response to silly commands have a nastier edge than usual and rub in the character's worthlessness" (41). There is none of *Zork*'s treasure-collecting humor (such as the joke about the player character being a vandal) to make light of such unpleasant character traits.

The conclusion to *Infidel* comes after picking up numerous precious artifacts and using them to work further into the pyramid. In the final chamber, the player character unlocks and then opens a sarcophagus to reveal an enormous stash of treasure. The final reply is worth quoting in full:

> You lift the cover with great care, and in an instant you see all your dreams come true. The interior of the sarcophagus is lined with gold, inset with jewels, glistening in your torchlight. The riches and their dazzling beauty overwhelm you. You take a deep breath, amazed that all of this is yours. You tremble with excitement, then realize the ground beneath your feet is trembling, too.
>
> As a knife cuts through butter, this realization cuts through your mind, makes your hands shake and cold sweat appear on your forehead. The Burial Chamber is collapsing, the walls closing in. You will never get out of this pyramid alive. You earned this treasure. But it cost you your life. And as you sit there, gazing into the glistening wealth of the inner sarcophagus, you can't help but feel a little empty, a little foolish. If someone were on the other side of the quickly-collapsing wall, they could have dug you out. If only you'd treated the workers better. If only you'd cut Craige in on the find. If only you'd hired a reliable guide.
>
> Well, someday, someone will discover your bones here. And then you will get your fame.

Clearly this text is cliché-ridden and highly moralistic. Yet it is a powerful critique of the assumptions of adventure gamers.

Consider the effect of reading this unprecedented conclusion at the end of twenty or more hours of challenging interaction, when the expected outcome of your long toils is some form of outright triumph accompanied by a "You have won!" message. One reaction was denunciation:

> *Infidel*'s apparent goal of moving in a realistic and literary direction is a commendable one. But there is more to reality than self-destructiveness, and more to literature than anti-heroes. Of all Infocom's adventures, this has the least to recommend it. (McGath 1984, 42)

An extremely interesting response to this one possible "winning" final reply is given by the maintainer of the Infocom Bugs List:

> You receive the full 400 out of 400 points when you turn the final statue, not when you open the sarcophagus and trap yourself. Why not just turn that final statue, and then leave the pyramid, taking the five jewelled clusters [some of the artifacts found during exploration of the pyramid] . . . as your retirement fund? The farewell note at the beginning of the game establishes that your workers left you enough to get back to civilization safely. The game won't officially end of its own accord if you leave the pyramid, but so what? Leave the pyramid, QUIT with the full number of points, and if that isn't winning, I don't know what is. (Cree 2001)

The interactor who follows these steps is not rewarded by an alternative final reply; unlike the dig crew, Berlyn and Fogleman did not provide for the player character to return alive. Those who follow this path enable themselves to imagine their own ending, consistent with the framework of the text adventure. Even a third party examining a transcript of such a game could plausibly read it as having an outcome that Berlyn had not thought of and had not provided for in implementing *Infidel*. This demonstrates that reading against the grain (and writing against the grain, by interactors) is possible even in a work of interactive fiction, where the system of the world and the possible textual outcomes are programmatically fixed.

Interactors can choose their own adventures in other ways besides providing input to the program, and it is in this realm of interpretation—not in helping to understand how the actual operation of the text-machine occurs—that theories of reader response are likely to be of most help. In some cases, as in *Infidel,* interactors may even be able to operate the IF work in a way that is consistent with an unanticipated interpretation.

PLANETFALL'S FLOYD WANTS TO PLAY

Meretzky's first creation, the 1983 *Planetfall,* had the player character crash-land on a planet and try to survive to be rescued. The work included a few innovations that were wisely not emulated later: a requirement that the player

character eat and sleep, for instance, which seemed appropriate for the sur-
vival situation but did not make for particularly interesting challenges. A
litany of other failings is provided by one notable independent IF author and
critic, who called *Planetfall* "the worst Infocom game I've played yet" (Rees
1993). But Meretzky also added one element that made *Planetfall* a memorable hit and advanced the state of interactive fiction. He implemented one
of interactive fiction's best-loved characters: the robot buddy Floyd.

Meretzky started at Infocom as a game tester in November 1981 after
two years of working in the construction industry. While he went to MIT and
said that he had "some components of nerditute," Meretzky did not start off
as a programmer and was not initially as taken with computers as were most
of the other Implementors (Greenlee 1996). Yet he became one of the most
prolific Implementors and was credited as author of seven Infocom games. He
has continued to create games (such as the *Spellcasting 101* series, which anticipated Harry Potter in having a school for wizards) since leaving Infocom.

Floyd is the player character's sole bit of company in the deserted complex on the planet Resida. His antics and his enjoyment of games provide
amusement as the interactor contends with the puzzles at hand.

Yet solving one such puzzle requires that this childlike robot helper sacri-
fice himself:

"Looks dangerous in there," says Floyd. "I don't think you should go
inside." He peers in again. "We'll need card there to fix computer.
Hmmm... I know! Floyd will get card. Robots are tough. Nothing
can hurt robots. You open the door, then Floyd will rush in. Then
you close door. When Floyd knocks, open door again. Okay? Go!"
Floyd's voice trembles slightly as he waits for you to open the door.

>*open the door*

The door opens and Floyd, pausing only for the briefest moment,
plunges into the Bio Lab. Immediately, he is set upon by hideous,
mutated monsters! More are heading straight toward the open
door! Floyd shrieks and yells to you to close the door.

If the interactor has the player character close the door and wait, Floyd will knock; opening the door (and then immediately shutting it) allows Floyd to emerge from the room without the mutants escaping:

Floyd staggers to the ground, dropping the mini card. He is badly torn apart, with loose wires and broken circuits everywhere. Oil flows from his lubrication system. He obviously has only moments to live.

You drop to your knees and cradle Floyd's head in your lap. Floyd looks up at his friend with half-open eyes. "Floyd did it . . . got card. Floyd a good friend, huh?" Quietly, you sing Floyd's favorite song, the Ballad of the Starcrossed Miner . . .

Floyd smiles with contentment, and then his eyes close as his head rolls to one side. You sit in silence for a moment, in memory of a brave friend who gave his life so that you might live.

Although Floyd is well loved, as a part of the overall workings of *Planetfall* he is, as one reviewer wrote, "tragically underused. . . . He is only used to solve two or three puzzles, puzzles which could have been written with only minor changes to have them be solved by the player, and probably would have been stronger" (M. Murray 1997).

As a character who is also a technological artifact, Floyd is more important than his immediate function in the IF world suggests. He is a figure for the sometimes emotional relationships that people have with computers, or that are mediated through computers. Floyd represents the subtle emotional capacity of computers in how his antics provide amusement. Meretzky (2002) noted that Isaac Asimov also "found it easier to write silicon-based characters than carbon-based characters," adding that in the case of interactive fiction

I wouldn't be surprised if it's an issue of expectations; with a human character, people expect a full range of human emotions and reactions which games then (and still today) couldn't begin to come close to doing. But with something like a robot or an alien the reader/player doesn't have the same set of expectations and there-fore the character can come closer to matching them and seeming like a real, believable, fully-realized creation.

Despite the many limitations of Floyd, his role was both affecting and provocative, causing critics to think about what made for a good character in an interactive work. In having little knowledge of his own, yet communicat-ing effectively within a certain scenario, Floyd hearkened back to Weizenbaum's ELIZA/DOCTOR. Although he was not fully developed as a part of the IF world of *Planetfall,* his comic value and critical function in the potential narratives of that work made him a more interesting character, in many ways, than predecessors like the thief and robot of *Zork.* Meretzky would go on to create a very effective robot player character named PRISM (a.k.a. Perry Simm) in his 1985 *A Mind Forever Voyaging.*

A follow-up to *Planetfall,* also done by Meretzky, was the 1987 *Stationfall.* With a different setting (a desolate space station) and a resuscitated Floyd, Meretzky blended the old and new well. One reviewer wrote that *Stationfall* "provides a quintessential example of what a sequel ought to be" (Cree 1995).

TRANSFORMATION IN *WISHBRINGER*

It is almost essential to interactive fiction that some things in the world change during interaction: Doors must open so the player character can proceed to new areas, objects must be lifted from the ground, and bigger alterations (e.g., the draining of a reservoir, the moving around of segments of the Royal Puzzle) must be made by the player character now and then. It wasn't until the 1985 publication of Moriarty's *Wishbringer* that interac-tors found this malleability of the IF world taken to a new and powerful conclusion. Early in a traversal of that work (which is in the juvenile fiction genre), the entire world was magically transformed in medias res. After wan-dering through a village and making a delivery, the player character, a letter carrier, returns to find the familiar seaside town of Festeron altered in dis-turbing and fantastic ways. *Wishbringer* used this transformative technique to great effect; it would be employed even more strikingly in Meretzky's dystopian science fiction work *A Mind Forever Voyaging,* which was released later in the same year.

Moriarty had worked for the magazine *ANALOG* ("Atari Newsletter And a Lot Of Games") before coming to Infocom to develop Z-machine interpreters in 1984. He had written two works of interactive fiction that were published in *ANALOG*: *Adventure in the Fifth Dimension,* written in BASIC, and *Crash Dive!* in assembly. Moriarty also worked on Infocom's first juvenile fiction title, *Seastalker,* before starting on *Wishbringer.*

One important IF author and critic finds *Wishbringer* "solidly mediocre" (Nelson 2001b, 354). The concepts behind it certainly don't have an impressive heritage. *Wishbringer,* as Moriarty explained, "came from a plastic rock"—the idea for the packaging and included goodies first motivated the design of the work, with an original idea for including magic rings developing into an idea to include actual rocks, then glow-in-the-dark plastic lumps in the shape of rocks—while work on software development was continuing (Rigby 1991). But the work was Infocom's highest achievement for young interactors and is a good introductory interactive fiction work for those of any age. It provides alternate ways to solve most puzzles—one grounded in realism and typical adventure puzzle solving and one that uses the power of the eponymous magical stone—so two interactors might have almost entirely different experiences of solving it. The transformation of the town leaves it a frightening but amusingly skewed place: The police have been replaced by giant boots who stomp around menacingly, for instance. The particular blend of sinister bizarreness and more lighthearted fantasy is not frequently found in literature written for adults but is typical in children's literature, from *Alice in Wonderland* to Norton Juster's *The Phantom Tollbooth.* This sort of transformation has antecedents in mass media fiction. Specifically, *Wishbringer* has been related to "Mirror, Mirror," an episode of the original *Star Trek* that presented a strangely transformed "evil Enterprise" with a sinister, bearded Mister Spock (Cree 1995). The Enterprise set, of course, did not change as radically as Festeron does in *Wishbringer.*

THE CHANGING, NESTED WORLDS OF *A MIND FOREVER VOYAGING*

While *Wishbringer* used its transformative effect to good effect, the surprising appearance of a wholly changed setting made Meretzky's *A Mind Forever Voyaging,* in development at the same time, an interactive fiction work of unparalleled power. One educator who has taught using interactive fiction for more than a decade names *A Mind Forever Voyaging* "a work of serious science fiction that many readers regard as the finest piece of interactive fiction yet written" (Desilets 1999). This work takes its title from *The Prelude,* was unveiled in a press conference at the New York Public Library (Infocom, Inc. 1985), and treats political issues of obvious contemporary relevance. Meretzky (2002) explained that Infocom "chose the NYPL in order to emphasize the 'literary' nature of the game; the PR for the game was all geared toward spinning the game as the computer game equivalent of *Brave New World* and *1984.*" While Implementor and author Stu Galley read an introduction to *A Mind Forever Voyaging* that came from the manual, the event was otherwise similar to other Infocom press conferences (Meretzky 2002). The attempt to connect with literature can be seen within the work as well: It is arranged in three parts with epigraphs at the beginning of each. Meretzky's well-known humor isn't evident in the dystopian *A Mind Forever Voyaging.*

In the frame world, the player character exists as a sentient computer in the United States of North America of 2031. This computer player character, PRISM, is gendered male and comes complete with a human-like, synthesized past, described in the documentation. The interactor can switch this computer between modes (e.g., to read communications or to view a news feed) and can peer through cameras situated around the complex in which this artificial intelligence is housed. PRISM has a job to do, of course. He must enter into a special mode, simulation mode, and try to learn what the future effects of the proposed right-wing Plan for Renewed National Purpose. He does this not as a disembodied intelligence, as in the frame IF world, but through the eyes of his human persona, Perry Simm. The mission must be carried out in an IF world within the first simulated world: the computer-generated landscape of Rockvil, a middle American city, as it is supposed to exist ten years in the future of this fictional future.

The inventiveness of *A Mind Forever Voyaging* should be clear from a description of the outer and inner worlds that are represented within it. Text adventures began as programs in which a human adventurer, who was supposed to be "you," undertook a fantasy quest. The player character of *A Mind Forever Voyaging* is, for the first time, not human; he is a computer. He is therefore definitely not "you" in the usual sense. This computer has a richer and more detailed background (explained in the accompanying manual) than any human player character who had been originally developed for a text adventure in 1985, with the exception of those in works based on existing literature, such as *Lord*. Although in the work's "real world" the player character is a computer, he exists as a person in a simulated world within. Furthermore, this simulated world, although it incorporates science fiction elements, is no fantastic landscape. It is the character's home, an ordinary American city extended into the future. Finally, although there is an overarching riddle involving the highest-level IF world, there are no puzzles at all in the simulated city. There is simply a list of things to be observed, and a city in which to observe them. *A Mind Forever Voyaging* radically reversed many assumptions of the early text adventure.

An initial visit to Rockvil's future (during the year 2041) reveals that everything is rosy: it looks as if the somewhat draconian Plan for Renewed National Purpose has had a good effect. After returning and dutifully submitting video records of the simulated future, it seems there is little else for PRISM to do.

Then, PRISM's chief developer explains that thanks to these explorations, the simulator has been able to grind away and create an additional simulation set further in the future. Rockvil of 2051 is now available in simulation mode, and PRISM can voyage there as well. During the return visit, Perry Simm's family members have grown appropriately older and some parts of the city have changed. Most interestingly, some signs of trouble can be seen. In Perry Simm's apartment, for instance, this can happen:

> You hear a commotion in the hallway and then a half-dozen Border Security Force officers storm in, rifles ready. You freeze as they tramp about the apartment wielding Rad-Detectors. After a few nightmare minutes, they seem satisfied and begin to file out. The apparent leader turns to you. "Sorry for the inconvenience," he says apologetically. "You know how things are. We're only doing it for your own protection." He closes the door behind him. You hear sobbing and turn to see Jill crying in the corner of the living room.

After recording scenes like this one, PRISM can manage to make the sympathetic scientist in charge aware of potential problems with the Plan. But more research has to be done.

PRISM is eventually allowed access to the Rockvils of 2061, 2071, and then 2081. In these visions of the city, the deterioration of the infrastructure, the increasing misery of the population, and the breakdown of Perry Simm's family become evident as increasingly harsh events play themselves out in the crumbling world. All this is accomplished by means of sparse descriptions of city locations that change very slightly. As is often the case in interactive fiction, a transcript can do little to suggest the power of an interaction with *A Mind Forever Voyaging*. As PRISM records the events that happen, it soon becomes clear that even with evidence of the Plan's danger, his scientist creator will not be able to stop the Plan from passing. The senator who is sponsoring this oppressive legislation decides that PRISM must be shut down to avoid negative publicity, and a black bag team of saboteurs enters the research facility where PRISM is housed. (This moment is reminiscent not only of an obvious incident in American history, but also of a moment in *Suspended,* when people enter the underground complex to fatally "replace" the player character with a backup planetary controller.) To solve the problem posed in the frame world requires a lateral leap of thinking; it requires, in fact, that PRISM become a sort of hacker and pirate broadcaster, achieving a victory through subversion of the media.

A Mind Forever Voyaging, although innovative, was a science fiction work, placing it in an often deprecated genre. It was also the first Infocom work to be released with more demanding hardware requirements, making it available for a smaller number of computers and contributing to its poor commercial performance. It clearly is aligned with dystopian novels such as *Fahrenheit 451, Brave New World,* and *1984,* although of course the text that emerges from it does not, by itself, stack up against that found in any of these novels. Still, moments of true power occur in the experience of *A Mind Forever Voyaging:* when transformed places are first visited, for instance, and when increasingly shocking events occur unexpectedly. The way that events transpire in the generated narratives, in the context of an increasingly familiar but collapsing city, show that interactive fiction can be a serious form, delivering a compelling experience that turns on typed contributions from the interactor. Current IF author Adam Cadre (2001) identifies this work as "the one that got me hooked on IF." One reviewer (who has almost 200 computer game reviews posted on his Web page) calls *A Mind Forever Voyaging* "a landmark title" that "never ceases to . . . amaze and enthrall throughout, which makes the game's ending—possibly the best ever presented in a computer game—seem all the more magical and special." He concludes that *A Mind Forever Voyaging* is "the finest computer game ever written" (M. Murray 2001). It certainly ranks among the top computer games; in addition, it deserves to be called one of the preeminent works of computer literature.

In 1986 two Infocom games came out that allowed the interactor to select the player character's gender. One was *Leather Goddesses of Phobos,* by Meretzky, which was as close as Infocom came to erotica. The work is better characterized as a bawdy space opera. The whole project originated as a running joke: Meretzky kept putting the title on the project board as if it were in development. Then, he was asked to actually develop a work with that title (Greenlee 1996). The interactor can set the computer-produced text to be "tame," "suggestive," or "lewd" (an interesting new type of control similar in some ways to the one type of control the interactor had over descriptive text so far—whether room descriptions are "superbrief," "brief," or "verbose"). But even in the last of these modes the text is hardly torrid, usually featuring little more than juvenile innuendo. By directing the player character to enter either the men's or the women's restroom at the very beginning of the game, the interactor makes another important selection, determining the gender of the player character. (Presumably the gender, or social role of male and female, and the sex, or biological nature of the character, are both determined in this way.)

Leather Goddesses of Phobos* was a hit for Infocom, but it was not the first work of this sort. Chuck Benton's *Softporn Adventure,* for instance—the basis for Sierra's later *Leisure Suit Larry*—was released in 1984. Today there is a whole genre of adult interactive fiction (or AIF) created by individuals; gender and sex of all sorts play a prominent role in it. Some of this may be worth examining from a feminist or gender studies perspective—but, alas, vita brevis. Probably more interesting is the way gender (or rather, the ambiguity of gender) has been treated in an important work from the independent era,

Graham Nelson's 1995 *Jigsaw*. Nelson (2002) discusses the response to the "most notorious feature" of that work, which involves a romance:

> not imposing genders on either of the main characters. I got angry mail from a few homophobic players who believed I was coercing them into the Forbidden Love of Another Man; equally, some gay women wrote to me to say how much they appreciated it. Actually I'd had no particular thought of the gay angle at all, and had simply wanted to have a romance where you could project whatever you liked onto your inamorata. Or inamoratum, I suppose.

Moonmist is the other 1986 Infocom work that allows gender selection. It provides a detective-like setup but without the murders of *Deadline, The Witness,* and *Suspect.* In that work, the player character stays overnight in a supposedly haunted house, discovering what is going on there. When the player character announces himself or herself at the gate, the title used can indicate that the player character is male (e.g., "Mister" or "Sir") or female (e.g., "Lady," "Countess"). Other titles not recognized by the work or not gender-specific (e.g., "Sister," "Professor," "Midshipman") will lead to other possible narratives in which the gender of the player character is consistently ducked; generated texts never mention it.

In both Infocom works the overall experience is similar whether one chooses a male or female player character—it is not really that different even if the "neuter" option is chosen in *Moonmist.* The same commands work to unlock the plot-controlling puzzles in both cases. There are only subtle differences in the differently gendered interactive experiences. These different experiences of the game and the treatment of gender in these works certainly invite a more extensive critique. The works seem to assert that gender is actually superficial, since the same sorts of events occur whatever gender is selected. The IF worlds that are set up (perhaps in a somewhat utopian mode) provide for men and women to have essentially equal sorts of experiences. Other interactive fiction might be created that provides a variety of experiences and makes a different sort of point. Still other questions remain: Why does the interactor in *Leather Goddesses of Phobos* get to choose what gender the player character is but not (due to the limited availability of potential paramours) the sexuality of the player character? Why can't gender and sex be determined independently, so that the player character might be a biological woman who performs the male gender, or vice versa? (For a work called *Leather Goddesses of Phobos* that is a racy space opera, these questions should not seem too distant or academic.) The ability to select a gender is significant not only because of the way it relates to the issue of gender, but because for the first time an interactor could choose not just what the player character would do, but who the player character actually would be, in a way that did affect the experience of the IF world and the generated texts. While selecting a character is a usual feature of computer role-playing games, this selection is seldom meaningful except inasmuch as it influences combat.

Gender selection was possible in a few later Infocom works as well: *Ballyhoo, Bureaucracy,* and *Beyond Zork.* The two different interactive experiences varied even less in these works than in *Leather Goddesses of Phobos* and *Moonmist.* One Infocom work, the 1987 *Plundered Hearts* by Amy Briggs, has an explicitly female player character. This was Infocom's only interactive fiction in the historical fiction/romance category. Four Infocom works based on print literature had male player characters: *The Hitchhiker's Guide to the Galaxy, Sherlock: Riddle of the Crown Jewels, James Clavell's Shogun,* and *Arthur: The Quest for Excalibur.* In addition, all three of the different characters commanded by the interactor in *Border Zone* are male, and the artificial intelligence Perry Simm/PRISM, the player character of *A Mind Forever Voyaging,* is gendered male. While *Wishbringer's* player character is always referred to as a "letter carrier," never a "postman," this character initially daydreams about rescuing a princess and seems, like the player character in *Infidel,* to be stereotypically male.

Moonmist is distinguished in another way, besides being one of the earliest works of interactive fiction that allowed the interactor to select the player character's gender. Unfortunately for posterity, and for those who purchased and interacted with *Moonmist* when it was first released, Infocom chose not to include the descriptions of the world in the software at all. In order to figure out what the player character's surroundings are like, the interactor has to consult the manual, which has to be kept on hand during play and read alongside the computer text. This was done to make illegal copying of the game difficult—the nondigital manual would have to be copied, too, for the software to be of any use. This technique was one of many antipiracy "bundling" approaches used by Infocom, and certainly the most irksome one. In *A Mind Forever Voyaging*, a difficult-to-duplicate code wheel was included in the software package. The code determined on it is required to enter that work's simulation mode. *Infidel, Starcross, Leather Goddesses of Phobos,* and *Trinity* were three of the many Infocom works that came with partial maps that provided necessary information. Some of the items packaged in Infocom works were more of a carrot than a stick, included to entice buyers rather than to actually obstruct potential pirates. These "feelies" included a scratch-and-sniff card and 3-D comic in *Leather Goddesses of Phobos,* the aforementioned glow-in-the-dark stone of *Wishbringer,* and a Don't Panic button and "peril-sensitive" sunglasses included with *The Hitchhiker's Guide to the Galaxy.* The original packages for *Suspended* and *Starcross* were based around a large injection-molded face and flying saucer. The packaged items that are required within the game, to be used as a printed key, are a clear detriment to the experience of interactive fiction, whatever commercial sense they made or seemed to make. As a result of these measures, interaction (already a cumbersome affair by virtue of the note taking and mapping required) has been made even less accessible to those with casual interest.

The techniques employed by Infocom were far less intricate and oppressive than was standard in the computer gaming industry. On most platforms, Infocom's disks could be copied freely, whereas labyrinthine schemes to prevent disk duplication were routinely employed by other companies. These involved making alterations to the boot sector or employing special properties of home computer disk reading and writing to distinguish duplicated disks, even when the copying was done bit by bit. These schemes, euphemistically called copy protection, introduced additional incompatibilities to the software and made it difficult for legitimate users to back up their software. Because of the further problems this so-called "copy protection" introduced, when a legal, original disk with a home computer game can be found today it can be difficult to get it running on a modern platform or emulator. If any examples of heavily copy-protected computer games survive through another two decades for study and discussion, it will be thanks to the loose, widespread network of teenagers and college students who assiduously cracked these programs, allowing the crippled disks to run freely both on systems at the time and on compatible computers today.

TRINITY: A LITERARY, POLITICIZED FANTASY

An Infocom work that has been mentioned among the literati—more frequently than others have been, at least—is Brian Moriarty's *Trinity*, published in 1987. It was based on Moriarty's first concept upon becoming an Implementor, which had been set aside because of its ambition and because a work for children (*Wishbringer*) seemed more commercially desirable. *Trinity* gets a place in academic discussions in part because, as Nelson (2001b) explains, "The game is bookish and purposeful—a research bibliography is supplied—and is obtrusively trying to be what today's critics most wish to find: literature" (354). *Trinity* is weighty while it is also fantastic; trying to be literature does not make it any less enjoyable an experience. Part of its literary texture comes from an interface element. *Trinity* incorporates pop-up boxes with short quotations throughout, of the sort *A Mind Forever Voyaging* used at the beginning of each of its three parts. These work to good effect, drawing connections between *Trinity* and texts of other sorts without being pedantic.

Trinity is divided into segments; the introductory one is set in the Kensington Gardens at the end of the Cold War. A nuclear missile is on its way while the player character is there on vacation, taking a stroll. A series of sometimes fanciful and sometimes sensible actions—which work well to set up the logic of *Trinity*'s world—takes the player character to another, more fantastic landscape. From here there is access to the other segments of *Trinity*, in which the player character must cause various nuclear tests to fail in order to reverse the course of history. Part of this work's power comes from, as one critic has written, "its juxtaposition of bizarre fantasy and depressing history. In *Trinity*, *Alice in Wonderland* collocates with the nuclear holocaust" (Randall 1988, 188).

The more serious and immediate theme of *Trinity*, in contrast to those fantasy works that are not juxtaposed with history in this way, is an important aspect, as is the treatment of this theme in effective ways that employ literary techniques. It is meaningful here, however, to simply look at this work as an example of how far interactive fiction had come in terms of the texts that could result from very ordinary sorts of interaction. Figure 5.1 compares texts from *Zork I* and *Trinity*.

The two bits of landscape description and interaction shown there are telling. Rather grating adjectives like "marvelous" and an inability to refer to

ZORK I

>*Go east.*

Canyon View

You are at the top of the Great Canyon on its west wall. From here there is a marvelous view of the canyon and parts of the Frigid River upstream. Across the canyon, the walls of the White Cliffs join the mighty ramparts of the Flathead Mountains to the east. Following the Canyon upstream to the north, Aragain Falls may be seen, complete with rainbow. The mighty Frigid River flows out from a great dark cavern. To the west and south can be seen an immense forest, stretching for miles around. A path leads northwest. It is possible to climb down into the canyon from here.

>*Examine the canyon.*
I don't know the word "canyon".

>*Look at the river.*
There's nothing special about the river.

>*Look at the path.*
There's nothing special about the way.

TRINITY

>*Go north.*
You ascend the gentle hill.

Summit

The hill you've climbed lies at the southwest edge of a vast wilderness. Towering forests are broken by long tracts of wasteland, rugged plateaus and marshes shrouded in perpetual mist. A brooding sun fills the distant valleys with a sad, dusty light the color of antique brass.

A giant triangle, thousands of feet high, rises above the eastern treetops. Its vertex casts a long shadow across the wood.

As your eyes sweep the landscape, you notice more of the giant toadstools. There must be hundreds of them. Some sprout in clusters, others grow in solitude among the trees. Their numbers increase dramatically as your gaze moves westward, until the forest is choked with pale domes.

>*Examine the sun.*
The sun broods silently in the eastern sky.

>*Look at the triangle.*
Its dark edge divides the sky like a razor.

FIGURE 5.1
A short transcript from *Zork I* compared to one from *Trinity.*

basic elements of the surroundings are seen in Blank and Lebling's *Zork I*. (Their IF works had improved by this time as well, of course.) A decade later in *Trinity*, although the text is still slightly ponderous with adjectives, a more sophisticated use of personification and metaphor is visible, along with a detailed narration of how the landscape actually comes into view for the gazing player character. The language understanding capabilities of interactive fiction were more advanced by this time, this having been achieved mainly by simple expansion of the vocabulary rather than with parser improvements. Nelson (1995) gives one example: "there is a charming statue of a carefree little boy playing a set of pan pipes. This can be called the 'charming' or 'peter' 'statue' 'sculpture' 'pan' 'boy' 'pipe' or 'pipes'. Objects often have more than 10 nouns attached." The original *Zork I* had a 600-word vocabulary. *Trinity* could understand 2,120 different words. The clarity of *Trinity* was not the only possibility for advances in interactive fiction. Complicating communication could also be effective, as another Infocom work released in the same year revealed.

HOURS OF PUN IN *NORD AND BERT*

Jeff O'Neill's *Nord and Bert Couldn't Make Head or Tail of It,* published in 1987, introduced an unusual command format. Progressing through that work requires the interactor to offer punning clichés or other forms of wordplay, often in a way that is only very loosely related to any immediate goal. By solving verbal puzzles, the interactor can allow the player character to rescue the troubled town of Punster. In *Nord and Bert,* the usual adventuring actions are greatly diminished in importance. Puns dominate the puzzles, which occur in eight independent segments, each its own world. Compass directions are not required to move the player character about in *Nord and Bert.* Instead, the status line always indicates where the player character can go, just as the exits are shown on-screen in Scott Adams games. The interactor can type English input such as *go to the barn* rather than *e* or *east*. This more topological, landmark-based way of navigating was available in some respects in *Adventure,* in which the name of a visited location could be typed in order to move the player character to that location. This ability had not been provided in earlier Infocom games, however—except in *Suspended* with its multirobot complexities and board game–style map—and the early *Adventure* did not even recognize a simple, full English sentence such as *go to the barn.* Because of the improved movement scheme, mapmaking is not necessary, or at all useful, in *Nord and Bert.*

In one segment, Act the Part, the interactor must type replies to complete a comedy routine: "Bob says, 'Hey Sammy, what is this fly doing in my soup?' / >*Swimming.* / The crowd eats it up." The replies to commands in this segment are often consistent with the comedy framework, as when a woman described as "a lady" enters the room: ">*Examine the lady.* / That's no lady, that is your wife." Another segment, Play Jacks, has the player character manipulate a device, the "Jack of all Traits." This contraption takes on different properties as things are done to it. It becomes several different objects, all of which contain the name or sound "jack," and all of which must be used in some way during that segment of the work. Spoonerisms are required in the Shake a Tower segment.

In the segment Visit The Manor Of Speaking, the replies are sometimes in the first person, answering the command *take the bottle* with "You can go ahead and have that old thing anyway. It was here before I moved in." The interactor must intersperse adventure-game commands with more conversational exchanges in order to progress through this segment.

In solving puzzles, the interactor is limited to filling in fixed phrases almost exactly, and almost every phrase anticipated by the author must be supplied in order to win. The required actions are not always obvious and have little to do with the usual adventure-game reasoning. During the Eat Your Words segment, for instance, the player character encounters an inattentive waitress who must be dealt with harshly. Examining her reveals that she has a chip on her shoulder. The correct phrase to supply is *knock the chip off her shoulder,* which brings this text: "'Come on, knock it off!' the waitress says defiantly, and the chip goes flying off into the air. . . ." This earns the interactor a point. The similarly clever response *brush off the waitress* is not recognized, as the work's vocabulary does not include the word "brush." Fortunately, a hint system is included within the program itself for occasions when filling in the blank is more difficult than this, such as when a cliché completely unknown to the interactor is required.

As with other interactive fiction, when considered only as a narrative-generating program, without considering the activity of the interactor in generating those narratives, *Nord and Bert* is uninteresting. The interaction that can transpire is certainly intriguing, however, and not only because it brings the parser out of the realm of typical adventure-game actions. *Nord and Bert* also provides a much more symmetrical exchange between interactor and computer than is found in other Infocom works. For instance, in the Buy The Farm segment, when the player character finds a sow's ear, the interactor can solve a puzzle by typing *make a silk purse out of a sow's ear.* The computer's reply begins "After working your fingers to the bone . . ." The interactor and computer are trading cliché for cliché, just as in other situations the interactor participates in the formalized conversation of a knock-knock joke. This makes for a more equitable situation for the interactor than does the typical adventuring exchange, in which the interactor types things like *n. e. x window.* and the computer provides detailed descriptions in reply. The exchange is less like a command-prompt interaction—in which, for instance, a two-letter command might result in a lengthy directory listing, and somewhat more like a normal conversation between people. Of course, the interactor has almost no choice in what to say in the situations described earlier in *Nord and Bert.* There is essentially only one set of responses that allow the game to be solved. Still, the sort of symmetrical interaction provided in *Nord and Bert* could potentially be used as a model for a work in which the interactor had more genuine agency.

Another Infocom work in the humor category, also set in a quotidian world rather than a fantasy or science fiction one and also published in 1987, is *Bureaucracy. The Hitchhiker's Guide to the Galaxy* author Douglas Adams is credited as *Bureaucracy's* sole author, although one Implementor writes that it was completed "by a cast of thousands including Douglas Adams's friend Michael Bywater, Tim Anderson, and others" (Lebling 2002). This work, like *Nord and Bert,* features a waitress opponent. Its plot is advanced as the player character overcomes bureaucratic challenges, eventually discovering that a malicious hacker is the main obstructing force. The challenges are unlike the typical adventure-gaming puzzles in some ways, but not as much of a break from the usual format as was the nonrepresentational wordplay in *Nord and Bert.* It is not enough for the interactor to key in appropriate puns, the player character in *Bureaucracy* must actually be directed to act, although sometimes absurdly. One reviewer called *Bureaucracy* "the standard by which almost all tongue-in-cheek games about real life are measured" (Cree 1995).

Other Infocom Innovations

Infocom's only publication in the spy thriller genre was the 1987 *Border Zone,* by Blank. *Border Zone,* set in the fictitious Eastern European country of Frobnia, is divided into three chapters that can be accessed in any order. The interactor commands a different character in each. Another unusual feature of *Border Zone* is that time in the IF world continues to pass even if the interactor does not type a command. Time in the IF world is advanced in other Infocom works only by typing a command and pressing the return key; only such an input moves the simulated world's clock forward. In *Border Zone* time passes while the interactor is thinking about what to type. This had been done previously in four 1985 works by Synapse which are discussed in the next chapter; the technique added some special urgency to *Border Zone's* spy-thriller interaction. It also required the interactor to puzzle through situations many times, getting killed and restarting or restoring the game perhaps even more often than is usual.

The underwater adventure *Seastalker* by Stu Galley and Jim Lawrence, released in 1984, was a work in the juvenile fiction genre, Infocom's first "junior-level" game. The interactor could name the main character in *Seastalker,* providing his or her own name, for instance. *Seastalker* came with floor plans (as did *Deadline*) so that children interacting with it wouldn't have to map out the game on their own.

One of Infocom's most popular publications was *The Hitchhiker's Guide to the Galaxy.* This work, which Steven Meretzky and Douglas Adams created in collaboration, is discussed in the next chapter, in the context of other interactive fiction based on print books. *James Clavell's Shogun* by Dave Lebling, the only other Infocom work based directly on a book, is also discussed there. Although not a direct adaptation, Infocom's *Sherlock: The Riddle of the Crown Jewels* featured characters from Sir Arthur Conan Doyle's stories. It was written by Bob Bates in imitation of Doyle's prose style, and it stands as a well-crafted late Infocom work. (Bates had founded Challenge, Inc., to compete with Infocom, and began working for Infocom in 1986. He went on to found Legend Entertainment, discussed in the next chapter.) In *Sherlock,* the interactor directs Watson, who conducts the investigation while being trailed about by Holmes. The puzzles presented in *Sherlock* do require Watson to pilfer objects in a way more appropriate to the player character-plunderer of *Zork* than to Holmes's friend, though.

ARTHUR AND LE MORTE D'INFOCOM

The last canonical Infocom work was *Arthur: The Quest for Excalibur.* Although it included graphics, they were optional and the game could played from start to finish in text mode. *Arthur,* like *Sherlock,* centered on a famous character from British literature, and it was also written by Bob Bates. The sophisticated interface (used only in this Infocom work) allows the interactor to switch among a view of the current location, a textual description of that location, a map of the surroundings, a report on the state of the player character, and a listing of the player character's possessions. The player character, the young Arthur, gains the interesting ability to change into different animals. He needs this ability because the animal forms endow the main character with different capabilities, not because a new type of perspective can be gained by seeing through an animal's eyes.

Arthur's setting included an underground maze with a novel lateral-thinking challenge: The player character, transformed into a badger, is unable to carry objects about and use them as tokens. Instead, the badger-Arthur must scratch the walls to distinguish one room from another.

According to the manual, the young Arthur's goal is to "earn the wisdom, experience, and chivalry points" to prove to Merlin that he is ready to ascend the throne. Doing this involves the usual puzzle solving and object collection, however, only some of which is relevant to the particular virtues named. Even the subtitle of the work emphasizes that acquisition of a talisman is the main point, after all.

Infocom had foundered in 1985 after venturing into business software. Although it seemed reasonable to use the cross-platform Z-machine for business purposes, Infocom's relational database, Cornerstone, came to be called "tombstone" or "our worst game" (Masterson 1986) by the Implementors. Interactive fiction revenues essentially funded its development. The product shipped in January 1985, selling fairly well, but not well enough to make up for the very high cost of development. The layoffs started that September. By February 1986 Infocom was desperate to unload the blue "lunchbox" packages of Cornerstone, and dropped the price from $495 to

$99.95. Then Infocom itself went on sale. On June 13, 1986, the video game company Activision, then under CEO James Levy, bought Infocom for $7.5 million. An extensive report later chronicled Infocom's decline as a business (Briceño et al. 2000).

A series of late Infocom-branded publications, the Infocomics (which are not interactive fiction as discussed in this book), have features that suggest a different model for narrative interaction in text adventures. Infocomics were comic-like works with crude graphics, developed by Tom Snyder Productions. Some used settings and characters from Infocom's text adventures, while one, *Gamma Force in Pit of a Thousand Screams,* used an original story line. The Infocomics were available for computers—such as the Apple II, with its six colors—which had very limited graphics capabilities even by late-1980s standards. These works allowed the user to view different narrations of the same story. The user had to choose which character or group of characters the narration would follow at different points. Although the stories and graphics were of no interest, the interface concept, which did not involve any manipulation of the events in the narrated world, was somewhat novel. It may have been an influence on some later interactive fiction along the lines of *Exhibition.* By the time Infocomics appeared, Bruce Davis had succeeded Levy as Activision CEO and Infocom was in its twilight.

At the end of the 1980s, what was left of Infocom—now located at Activision's California headquarters—had stopped producing text adventures. Some software made by other companies was marketed using the Infocom brand, including the graphical game *Mines of Titan.* The brand was about all that was left of Infocom by 1990. The former corporate Shakespeare of interactive fiction had no existence separate from its parent video game maker. Some of Infocom's intellectual properties were used by Activision in graphical games during the 1990s. Three graphical *Zork* revivals were produced during that decade, as previously mentioned. *Leather Goddesses of Phobos 2: Gas Pump Girls Meet the Pulsating Inconvenience from Planet X* was another graphical Activision/Infocom release, designed by Meretzky, creator of the original *Leather Goddesses of Phobos.* A graphical *Planetfall* game was also begun and a demo video clip was released on the Web, but the project was never completed. On a happy note, by releasing collections of Infocom's interactive fiction—first in the two-volume *Lost Treasures of Infocom* (on floppy disk for PC and Macintosh) and later on the dual-format CD-ROM *Masterpieces of Infocom*—Activision has done a great deal to keep Infocom's works available to the public. The company has also been supportive of independent efforts to develop interactive fiction, a form that clearly no longer has the sort of commercial viability it did during its 1980s heyday.

D I F F E R E N T   V I S I O N S   W O R L D W I D E

Numerous companies sought a piece of the U.S. market that Infocom dominated, and companies in other countries sought to cash in on interactive fiction
abroad. The works that resulted during this commercial era varied tremendously
in terms of what they aspired to be and to what degree they attained those aspirations. Although it was possible to list the canonical publications from the most
important American company, Infocom, and to give a sense of the creative
breadth of all the work done there, this chapter focuses instead on the most
important remaining companies and on their specific creative efforts.

A Picture's Worth Along with Words

The most visible change in the commercial era of interactive fiction came
early on. In 1980 Ken and Roberta Williams founded On-line Systems (later
called Sierra) and released *Mystery House* for the Apple II. This piece of interactive fiction, originally called *Hi-Res Adventure,* was a minimal, bizarre treasure hunt with a two-word parser so primitive it made *Adventure* seem as
intelligent as HAL from *2001. Mystery House* was notable, however, because
it was apparently the first adventure game to show graphical representations
of different rooms and objects alongside (or, to be literal, up above) the usual
text. The pictures were spare green-on-black line drawings, placed on the
screen line by line as each room was entered. A special graphics mode on

the Apple II left room for four lines of text beneath such an image. In the first room of *Mystery House,* seven people are initially seen. The player character begins to find them dead one by one as the house is explored. They are shown as little more than stick figures, and the prose is just as sketchy: "YOU ARE IN A SMALL BEDROOM. THERE IS A DEAD BODY HERE."

Still, *Mystery House* sold 10,000 copies (Meier and Persson 2002), helping Sierra succeed and defining a noticeably different form of interactive fiction. Dozens of companies created adventure games that combined a few lines of text at the bottom with an image of the current location. Many of these were better to look at than to read, and many were not even particularly pleasant to look at. Interesting works did follow the example of *Mystery House,* though. One was a demonstration program for the IBM PC Jr. that Sierra developed, with an animated avatar situated in a similar sort of illustrated text adventure. The player character, visually represented in this way, could be directed to walk around using the keyboard or joystick. This was Roberta Williams's *King's Quest* (1984), which turned out to be much more successful than the IBM PC Jr. on which it first ran. It led to several series of similar graphical adventures for Sierra. Eventually the text was omitted entirely in these sorts of works, and the mouse alone was used to control the player character. This is the format of the later Sierra works and of the excellent, witty productions of LucasArts, but the purely graphical adventure is another story altogether. In 1990, celebrating ten years in business, Sierra officially released *Mystery House* for free distribution, setting a precedent that only a few other companies have followed.

While some U.S. companies published enjoyable text-and-graphics interactive fiction, the ones that could stand alongside Infocom's better works of this sort (*Zork Zero* and *Arthur*) were mostly developed abroad. Companies that became adept at working in this format included Level 9 and Magnetic Scrolls, both based in the United Kingdom and discussed later in this chapter. First, it's worthwhile to look at one notable text-and-graphics interactive fiction work from Australia, since it was also part of another trend, that of converting novels into IF works.

BOOKS INTO INTERACTIVE FICTION

In Australia, as in the United Kingdom, the typical 1980s home computer was the Sinclair Spectrum. This machine, released in 1982, had 48k of

RAM. That was an improvement over the first Sinclair, which offered only 16k, but it did not match the more capacious 64k of the Commodore 64 or of the Apple IIe that would be introduced the next year; these would quickly become typical computers in the United States. Moreover, the Spectrum ran programs from cassette tape rather than disk, which was the typical storage medium for a C64 or Apple IIe. Melbourne House, founded in 1977, catered to Spectrum users, first as a book publisher and then as a developer of software—and most notably, interactive fiction. In 1983 the company brought out Philip Mitchell's *The Hobbit,* which was a hit despite its many bugs. *The Hobbit* was one of the earliest commercial works of interactive fiction to be based on a book. It, like *Lord,* was inspired by a J. R. R. Tolkien book. The puzzles were at times obscure and would require knowledge of the book; the major incidents in Tolkien's novel were the direct basis for the situations of the IF work. (This would turn out to be the case often in interactive fiction that was "converted" from print fiction.) *The Hobbit* had graphics, drawn on the screen a line at a time, as in *Mystery House,* but they were in color, and noticeably less primitive. The non-player characters could be commanded to do things, and in fact such commands had to be issued to successfully traverse *The Hobbit.* The parser, a system called Inglish, was purportedly sophisticated in that, as one reviewer noted, "the analyzer . . . takes the input through several checks that ensure that the words are in the program's vocabulary, that the syntax makes sense in the game's context and that they make sense in the context of the game's development to that point" (Mangram 1984). If in fact the system added sensitivity to the progression of the generated narrative (not just to the state of the world and the immediate surroundings), it would be admirable, but much of this description applied to any contemporary interactive fiction parser. According to Mangram, "Mitchell has remarked on the fact that with the flexibility built into the *The Hobbit,* players still tend to under-use it, sticking to the verb–noun form." The parser's inability to understand simple commands like *look at the door* probably contributed to this underuse, although this work did, still, offer fewer frustrations than many competing titles. Despite being buggy and not nearly as capable of language understanding as a contemporary Infocom IF work (available only on more powerful computers), *The Hobbit* was a standout in the text-and-graphics category and became quite popular.

Other companies began creating interactive fiction based on the writings of well-known authors of different sorts, again, not involving those authors themselves. One creation of this sort that worked fairly well was the all-text *Robots of Dawn,* published in 1984 by Epyx. The setting and situation of the novel was easily transposed into an IF world and the initial situation of the work. The player character was to investigate a murder on a planet in where people found it distasteful to actually meet one another; furthermore, people lived very far apart and the player character was an agoraphobic. Hence it was natural that an isolated, depopulated area would make up the world of *Robots of Dawn.* The company Angelsoft adapted Stephen King's novella *The Mist* into an IF work with the same title, published in 1985—perhaps a surprise for those who thought that King's first electronic publishing venture was *The Plant.* It incorporated the text of King's story in a straightforward and, at times, even effective way. Angelsoft's parser did not advance the state of the art significantly, but it did manage to recognize some very unusual inputs simply by matching them against keywords. Some of the company's other titles—which all came out around 1985—featured James Bond and Rambo as player characters.

Perhaps the company most fervent about turning well-known books into interactive fiction works was Trillium, known as Tellarium after 1984. Their titles included *Fahrenheit 451* (1985, by Len Neufeld and Byron Preiss), *Rendezvous with Rama* (1984, by Ronald Martinez), and *Nine Princes in Amber* (1985, by multiple authors)—based on books by Ray Bradbury, Arthur C. Clarke, and Roger Zelazny. There is little evidence that any of these books' authors had much to do with the development of the Trillium/Tellarium titles, although Bradbury was quoted as saying he was "thrilled to be participating in the evolution of my *Fahrenheit 451* into a computer adventure" (Meier 2002). Some Trillium/Tellarium works integrated arcade-like games at different points—although the term "included" is probably more appropriate, as these did not fit into the overall work very well. They also incorporated graphics that, within a single work, would appear in different configurations by the text: sometimes with the two elements laid out side by side, sometimes with the text atop the graphics.

The greatest success in all based-on-a-book interactive fiction was the collaboration between Douglas Adams and Steven Meretzky that resulted in *The Hitchhiker's Guide to the Galaxy,* published by Infocom in 1984. This was clearly the best-selling work of this sort and probably the greatest creative achievement as well. While the novel *The Hitchhiker's Guide to the Galaxy* did precede the interactive fiction work of the same name and clearly has many affinities with it, this IF work differs in some important ways from the other efforts that have been discussed. First, *The Hitchhiker's Guide to the Galaxy* was originally a radio play, so in a sense the well-known novel is already a "conversion" from a different format. Second, and of most interest, is that Infocom involved Adams rather deeply in the process of designing the interactive fiction work itself. Other companies were pleased to license the rights to a novel and assign a programmer (who might have little interest in the original book, and might receive no royalties or credit for the new creative effort that was involved) to piece together a work of interactive fiction from pre-existing material. Infocom, on the other hand, sought to develop a new sort of collaboration between a well-known author and one of their Implementors—and succeeded.

Adams's "world-class procrastination abilities," as Meretzky called them, did cause some problems for the project, which began in February 1984 and was slated (ambitiously) to be completed by the following Christmas. Meretzky (2002) said of Adams that "being a successful person with tons of interesting acquaintances, he had an extremely distracting life. Plus, he wasn't fond of the actual task of writing. He loved coming up with ideas, but hated wrestling them into a properly-formed work." There was also the issue of developing an interactive fiction work based on an earlier creation—an issue that was new for Infocom. Another implementor, Michael Berlyn, said of IF works, "Nobody can sit down and write one of these as if they were writing a novel. They are too interactive and they are too complex. Take it from someone who's done both. It can't be done" (qtd. in Addams 1984). Meretzky described some of the general differences he discovered in writing a work of interactive fiction that is based on a previous work:

> It's easier because you have some constraints on the universe you're going to be designing, and on the characters you're going to be using . . . On the other hand, there's more of a challenge because you want to take advantage of the features of an interactive game, and you don't want it to be just a translation of the book, because the book is necessarily linear. If it was just a translation . . . there

wouldn't be any reason to do it at all. You have to avoid getting into the trap of "well, this is the way it was in the book, so this is the way it has to be in the game." (qtd. in Darling 1985)

The result, according to Adams, was a work "bearing as much relationship to the books as *Rosencrantz and Guildenstern are Dead* does to *Hamlet*" (qtd. in Gaiman 1993, 151). *Hitchhiker's* ended up being divided into a series of discrete segments, giving it more of a "rail game" sense than many other Infocom works had with their broad and interconnected worlds. The conclusion—devised by the two when Meretzky visited England for a week—was not as satisfying as the general texture of the work, in which Adams's humor worked very effectively in the context of interactivity. But the result was clearly a popular and critical success, earning praise from the *London Times* and becoming a best-seller in the United States (Gaiman 1993). It was also a new type of collaboration. At one point, Adams mentioned that he couldn't tell which parts of the work were written by him and which were written by Meretzky (Darling 1985; Meretzky 2002). While interactive fiction was a collaborative enterprise from the very beginning (as with *Adventure* and *Zork*), *Hitchhiker's* was the first case in which a veteran IF author and programmer worked closely with a famous author to produce something that was almost certainly greater than what either would have devised working alone.

DOCTOR VIRGIL'S TECHNOLOGY: *MINDWHEEL*

While the collaboration at Infocom between a veteran IF author and an established novelist was a first, a company called Synapse had earlier brought in several accomplished authors of printed literature to work intensively with programmers on interactive fiction. As the company sought out interested authors who didn't have preconceptions about the form, programmer William Mataga worked on an IF authoring language called BTZ (Better Than *Zork*), expressing the company's desire to produce works that, although quite different from *Zork,* could also be compared to it and seen as better. Founder Ihor Wolosenko, one Synapse author said, "was eager to avoid the concept or terminology of a 'game' and had quite ambitious notions about dialogue with characters" and about associating qualities with objects in the

IF world (Pinsky 2002). The results were published during 1984–1986, after the company was acquired by Brøderbund. They included the messianic science fiction *Breakers* by Rod Smith, a literary adventure dream called *Brimstone: The Dream of Gawain* by James Paul, and the spaceship-based *Essex* by Bill Darrah. It was a title by a poet that Synapse published in 1984— *Mindwheel*, a fantastic science fiction work with a bizarre premise—that turned out to be the most intriguing of these.

Synapse was founded by Wolosenko, who had studied drama and psychology in college, and Ken Grant, who had been in charge of data processing at San Francisco's Federal Reserve Bank. Both programmed on the Atari 800; the company was formed to work on a piece of business software for that computer, FileManager 800. In direct contrast to Infocom, Synapse moved from developing this type of software into the entertainment software market. Other programmers working for the company developed action-oriented games. One of these was Steve Hales, whose first work for Synapse was redoing a partially completed game called *Slime*. Mataga came to the company with a game similar to the arcade hit *Berzerk* (Wolosenko 1983). The writer Synapse had found to work on *Mindwheel*, Robert Pinsky, was teaching English at Berkeley at the time. He had studied at Rutgers with Frances Fergusson and then at Stanford with Yvor Winters; there, he did his Ph.D. dissertation on the poetry of Walter Savage Landor. When he started on the project he had published two books of poetry, *An Explanation of America* (1980) and *Sadness and Happiness* (1975). He was just finishing up another, *History of My Heart*. That book would be published the same year that *Mindwheel* was. Synapse had found a rising star to work on the project: By 2000 Pinsky's publications would include six books of poetry and an acclaimed translation of Dante's *Inferno* (1994). Pinsky later served as poet laureate of the United States from 1997 to 2000.

In retrospect, then, it is not surprising that in *Mindwheel,* as one reviewer noted, "The imagery is definitely something out of Dante's Inferno" (Friedland 1984), with an initial situation in which Doctor Virgil is ready to launch the player character on a fantastic journey. (Since Pinsky's work on *Mindwheel* preceded his translation of Dante, which is widely read today and is the way that many people know Dante's poem, *Mindwheel* can be considered the first work of interactive fiction to have influenced the *Inferno*.) Although *Mindwheel* is harder to come by and does not have the cult of Infocom's canon or of *The Knight Orc,* many interactors and reviewers loved *Mindwheel* when it came out. Its fantastic world represented the minds of four dead celebrities. The player character ventured into this array of puzzles and lively phrases in a quest to acquire the Wheel of Wisdom and save the planet.

Pinsky (2002) said he gave Wolosenko "four or five treatments, with *Mindwheel*—I think the title was there from the start—being the wildest. I probably wrote it as a semi-parody of Ihor's talk about discs and qualities ... He immediately said that was the one he'd like me to work on." As with all of Synapse's self-styled "electronic novels," a hardback book was included. This book was mostly written by Pinsky, although credited to another Synapse employee at Pinsky's request (Pinsky 2001). The book's "The Beginnings of Mindwheel" begins with an section told from the point of view of an "arch-senator" named Hay-Seuss Pederson. Randall (1988), who mistook this character for the player character (Pederson actually is not mentioned in the interactive fiction work *Mindwheel* at all, and section III of the book is devoted to "The Mind Adventurer," a different character who is never named and whose gender is never specified), noted that this name is "a rather clumsy and obvious rearrangement of 'Jesus' and 'Son of Peter'" (187). In his high-cultural enthusiasm, Randall seems to have overlooked the allusion, also rather obvious, to an American illustrator and author of children's books, not to mention the suggestion that this futuristic political leader is Hispanic. (It's also interesting to note that the president in this unusual future is named Helen Honda.) "The Beginnings of Mindwheel," with its bizarre and futuristic political situation, has some affinity with science fiction, but it seems equally connected to Mark Strand's "The President's Resignation," a famous bit of unusual prose by a poet (1985).

While *Mindwheel* was written up in one literary journal after its publication (Campbell 1987), the response of academics interested in computer literature was at best tepid. From the perspective of those working with hypertext literature, *Mindwheel* was described as having "not networks of possibilities to be explored but arrangements of traps and obstacles to be overcome in an insistent drive to a goal" (Moulthrop and Kaplan 1991). It is indeed possible to conceptualize the system of *Mindwheel*'s world this way, just as one can reduce a hypertext fiction to nothing but an arrangement of texts to be clicked upon and shuffled through. Both formulations miss the point, though, and overlook the possibilities these two types of potential literature offer. The obstacles and spaces in the IF world of *Mindwheel* make for a pleasing text-generating system, one arranged for explicit solution, just as literary riddles are. But the solution, as with a great riddle, results in more than the simple attainment of a goal. It leads to a new realization with its own new possibilities, both the possibilities of seeing things in a new way and the possibilities of operating the system differently to uncover new texts. As Pinsky (1997) put it:

> My experience of the computer is the experience of a puzzle that is an aperture. That is, each time I learn to do something new with the computer I try to find my way through a maze—the software or hardware manual, the protocol, the peculiarities of some new application. There is a blend of happiness and frustration, a forceful need to see one's way through the bottleneck. Through the narrow neck or aperture of this maze, I know, a vast world will open.

More than any previous work, *Mindwheel* (despite being called "an electronic novel") revealed the profound connection between interactive fiction and, not the novel, but poetry. Most obviously, there were poems on the surface of it. A central puzzle in the work involved filling in six words of a sonnet. This could possibly be accomplished by guesswork, but it was advisable instead to find the words in different texts that were scattered about, by exploring the IF world. Although filling in the blanks does not make for the most original and exciting activity, the puzzle is framed well. The sonnet is presented to the player character in *Mindwheel* by an amusing devil, Spaw, who stands amid references to lawyers and the IRS and checks over player character's works as if grading an assignment. The incomplete sonnet he offers is not an original either; it was one of many texts and incidents in *Mindwheel* drawn from earlier sources. In this case it was based on a sonnet by Fulke Greville (1554–1628): poem 100 from *Caelica,* a turning point in that work in which Greville dismissed devils as illusion. Pinsky had planned to use the poem, but he encountered a problem when it came to actually putting it into *Mindwheel:* Its lines were too long to fit on a forty-column screen of the sort many home computers of the era had, and it would not do to break them (Pinsky 2001). Rather than finding a poem with shorter lines, he became a clever Procrustes, converting the pentameter lines (except for line 11) to tetrameter. Here is the first quatrain of Greville's poem (as it was printed with modernized spelling in *Slate* in 2000), followed by the first quatrain of his tetrameter version from *Mindwheel* as it was printed in the documentation, with the words that were to be filled in indicated in italics.

> In night, when colors all to black are cast,
> Distinction lost, or gone down with the light,
> The eye, a watch to inward senses placed,
> Not seeing, yet still having power of sight,
>
> . . . . .

> In *night,* when color to black is *cast,*
> Distinction lost and gone with light,
> The eye, as inward watchman placed,
> Unseeing, but with power of sight,
>
> . . . . .

In creating *Mindwheel,* Pinsky (1996) also employed an early riddle and situations and imagery from earlier literature; he has mentioned a situation in which the player character is immobilized from the waist down as being "raided out of the *Thousand and One Nights*" (41–42). There were more contemporary references, too. In a crowd scene, some of the people brandished books from the Ecco Press, publisher of Pinsky's *History of My Heart.* (Another fill-in-the-blank poem that appeared in *Mindwheel* was Pinsky's "Sonnet," which also appeared in that book.) In a twist on the baseball puzzle in *Zork II,* the bums who huddled around a fire in one location could be seen, upon closer inspection and with the appropriate cultural background, to be "bums" of a different sort: the Brooklyn Dodgers.

The manifestation of poems was only the most obvious way in which *Mindwheel* brought the perspectives of a poet to bear on interactive fiction. When the interactor did nothing, different sorts of lines would appear from time to time, either "weather" (which had some emotional effect) or "drivel" (which did not) (Pinsky 1996, 41). This would allow *Mindwheel* to generate an atmospheric poem if left to its own devices, or to sprinkle whimsy throughout the interaction otherwise. Some examples from the initial crowd scene: "Held high in one pair of limbs you see a Twinkie and a silver revolver." "Gibbering reptiles dressed in antique finery whirl past and away from you." Some of the development work required Pinsky to enumerate all possible names of different sorts—for instance, all the possible taunts the interactor might type (Pinsky 1996, 42). Pinsky's love of naming things can be seen in later poems such as "Creation According to Ovid" and "Shirt."

Some of the best replies that *Mindwheel* produced in interaction were unanticipated, as with "Digging with the hands is slow and tedious" in *Zork* and "Upon looking over and dusting the me you notice that there are no good fingerprints to be found" in *Deadline*. Pinsky (1997) recounts one such reply from an encounter with his work:

> Demonstrating the game for a friend, I guided him to a room where he confronted a female character. She addressed him in some faintly provocative manner, and having typed in the "look-at" command he found that she was, say—I forget the details—attractive, dark-haired, wearing surgical scrubs. My friend addressed her:
>
> "You look like my mother," he typed. The machine, an antediluvian Kaypro as I recall, clucked over its hard drive, and the character responded:
>
> "I will look," she said to him, "any way you want me to look."
>
> To my pleasure, he looked startled, claimed he got goosebumps, and I got a little thrill myself—the pleasure of feeling that the clunky little game, on that yellow-and-black monochrome monitor, had made a plot that imitated reality: he saw her, he made a remark half-mocking and half-flirtatious, and she had responded in a way germane and unexpected.

While this experience is a pleasing one, the implications of such an interaction for the poetics of interactive fiction seem troubling, at least at first. If the most powerful moments of an interaction occur because of configurations of text that were not in any way anticipated by the author, how can authors hope to intentionally create better works? Improvement certainly will not come by piecing together appropriate replies for every input text in every context. Relying on chance combinations will not do, either, since by chance it is easier to arrive at a frustrating or otherwise unpleasant reply than a surprising and appropriate one. If moments like this one—in which Pinsky's female character outdoes ELIZA/DOCTOR with her noncommittal and dazzling response—are to occur more often, authors will have to recognize what *classes* of combinations of text have resonance. Not just the quality of an individual reply, but rather the ways of replying will have to be evaluated in the context of the immediate generated text, the interaction, and the overall traversal of the work—and also in the context of the culture or cultures in which the work and the interactor exist. Only then can beautiful accidents like this one be consciously worked into the texture of interactive fiction.

By investing four different parts of *Mindwheel*'s IF world with features representing four markedly different personae, Pinsky accomplished an interesting new communication between what, in a novel, would be the sharply divided elements of setting and character. (This innovation may have been prompted by Wolosenko's ideas about associating qualities with objects and the IF world.) It was impossible to have a literal conversation with those four who were, if not characters in a narratological sense, certainly the principal personalities of *Mindwheel*. Instead, the player character walked through connected rooms that presented the minds of these other characters in images and in the structures of simulated space. The inability of the computer to converse naturally was no longer a problem, since the personae of these dead celebrities were represented not through interactive conversation but in space; the compelling simulation of spaces had been, of course, the strong point of interactive fiction from the beginning.

The eschatological *Mindwheel* calls for comparison to two of its contemporary works. One is Brian Moriarty's *Trinity*, which also sends a hero on a quest to stave off global crisis. The other work is a poem, one that was included in Pinsky's 1984 *History of My Heart:* "The Figured Wheel." It shares a title word, of course, and Pinsky has said it was an inspiration for *Mindwheel* (Pinsky 2002), but an additional connection is that the final word that must be supplied to fill in the final blank in *Mindwheel* is supplied in the last line of "The Figured Wheel." The poem—which is printed, in part, in the documentation to *Mindwheel*—literally provides the answer to the final question posed in *Mindwheel*. The poem sweeps from "the Antarctic station of American sailors and technicians" to "the mineral-rich tundra of the Soviet northernmost settlements," and the wheel of the title moves through these places as well, "and through the dead-world of bomb, fireblast, and fallout."

The science fiction apocalypse of *Mindwheel* is a more distant, less threatening figure for the more immediate Cold War doom depicted in "The Figured Wheel," the same doom that is very explicitly present in *Trinity*. In *Mindwheel*—as in *Trinity*—the player character enters a fantastic world, leaving behind a familiar society on the brink of collapse in an attempt to rescue that society. In the poem the wheel of art is seen turning "even in the scorched and frozen world of the dead after the holocaust." Pinsky declares in "The Figured Wheel" that he too is completely subject to the destructive course of this wheel.

"The Figured Wheel" certainly is about the composition of poetry and the creation of art in general, but it applies particularly well to the process Pinsky went through in ornamenting *Mindwheel* with different types of language, "toys and messages, jokes and zodiacs." The process of creating *Mindwheel* involved not only festooning the figurative wheel represented by the work's title but also literally placing messages and jokes on a wheel, a slim magnetic one known as a floppy disk. A simple reading of the poem alongside the IF work might reveal the poem to be a sophisticated statement about the futility of art and the essential human drive to create art despite that futility, while *Mindwheel* might be seen as simply an example of such lighthearted (and futile) literary creation in the harsh shadow of the Cold War. A more interesting reading would not only see *Mindwheel* as a riddle that has "The Figured Wheel" as its solution, but also recognize that the poem's puzzle is in certain ways solved by the work of interactive fiction. The player character of *Mindwheel* is supposed to pursue a relentless quest but cannot help assembling art during the process: filling in the blanks of poems as well as performing actions that uncover new phrases and poems, spaces and conversations. Is *Mindwheel* a trivial game of no consequence next to "The Figured Wheel"? Consider a few of the assumptions that *Mindwheel* is founded upon: that the consciousness of individuals with unique minds persists after death as spaces of words that one can visit; that the solution to crisis comes in deep understanding of our past and our early origins; that fathoming a system of words can unlock new worlds. It may be easy to be distracted by the gibbering reptiles flying past, and by the way the program was sold on the shelf alongside entertainment software, but the structures and language of this work have much to offer besides whimsical amusement, and there has only been enough space here to begin a discussion of *Mindwheel*.

AMNESIA DRAWS A BLANK

It was in 1986, only two years after *Mindwheel* made its fairly successful debut and a year after *Hitchhiker's* was launched to record sales, that another interactive fiction work with similar origins—one created by a successful print writer, working with programmers—hit the shelves. This one, *Amnesia,* was by Thomas Disch, the author of the novels *334, Camp Concentration,* and *The Genocides;* he worked on it with programmer Kevin Bentley of the Cognetics Corporation. Disch was known mainly for his science fiction, although by that point he had gained a reputation as a book critic and had published four books of poetry as well as novels of other sorts. (His 1984 novel published just before *Amnesia* was *The Businessman: A Tale of Terror.*) While Pinsky chose a science fiction IF world, Disch gave his work the IF world of present-day New York City. Pinsky remained enthusiastic about the computer as a medium for literature; while he authored no other interactive fiction in the next decade and a half, he did become poetry editor of the online magazine *Slate* and he wrote about the possibilities of interactive fiction in *The New York Times Book Review.* In contrast, Disch (1990), who was initially quite excited about the new form and wrote a much earlier piece for *The New York Times Book Review* extolling the virtues of these "Youdunits," had quite different feelings about interactive fiction in later years, as he explained: "When I was working on *Amnesia,* I realized it was an art form unto itself; I saw visions of sugarplums dancing in my head. Now, all that is but a handful of ashes . . . *Amnesia* has been one of the quickest disillusionments of my life" (118).

Amnesia was not successful after it went on sale, and although some reviewers have found things to like about it, general opinion has not been favorable. Still, Disch's abilities as a writer and his enthusiasm about interactive fiction led to some notable accomplishments. The initial situation finds the player character waking up in a hotel room, with no idea of who or where he is. The conceit of having the player character wake up without any memory whatsoever positions the interactor and player character on the same level of awareness. Although this is a hackneyed premise in interactive fiction today—a similar idea had already been floated at Infocom, and in fact a graphical adventure with the same premise, *Déjà Vu: The Nightmare Comes True,* had been released in 1985 (Adler 1996)—Disch played the premise to the hilt, probably better than had been done before or has been done since.

An interesting play with the interactor's input can be seen when the player character first stands up from bed:

> The mirror over the dresser is angled so you can't see yourself from where you stand. So you decide to take a simple test, closing your eyes and taking an inventory of how you think you OUGHT to look.
> Your hair—is it light or dark?
> *light*
> Is it long or short?
> *short*
> Do you have a beard? Or a mustache? Or neither? Or both?
> *beard*
> What is the color of your eyes?
> *green*
> You could hardly be more completely mistaken! For when you look into the mirror, the stranger you see there has long black hair. He has a mustache but no beard. And his eyes are emphatically blue.

Starting over a few times and trying different inputs quickly reveals that however the interactor replies, the player character is always almost "completely mistaken." This is a compelling and literary use of the concept of computerized customization that has long been employed in different types of computer gaming to allow the player character to be specified.

This ability was particularly evident in role-playing games and appeared to some extent in interactive fiction, where the name or gender might be chosen. Instead of providing the interactor with control over what the player character looks like, however, any attempt to specify this in *Amnesia* is disrupted; a similar level of dissonance rather than customization is always provided. Yet *Amnesia* also offered a clever type of customization in another way: The player character would find a computer in the hotel room with him, which would always be the same type of computer that the interactor was using to run *Amnesia*. This IF work was also not lacking in terms of how it was implemented technically. It boasted a capable parser and a vocabulary of around 1,700 words, as well as an IF world that had a location for almost every Manhattan intersection. Of the approximately 4,000 different locations, few were described except for a bare reference to the street names.

As an interactive experience, *Amnesia* quickly runs into difficulties. The single path out of the hotel is laid on rails, with no alternative to the series of incidents Disch plotted out. Rather than allowing numerous different sorts of experiences and possible manipulations of the environment interspersed throughout the world of *Amnesia,* the work offers several major events, organized like cut-scenes with few options for variation, in a work that is otherwise open to many unimportant possibilities. One of these segments, in the hotel, consists of a dream in which the player character finds himself in a Texas jail, forced to beg for a meal by finding the correct two words to say. Later, appropriately, the player character is the groom in what is essentially a shotgun wedding. (The gun involved is actually a pistol.) Once out of the hotel and set free in New York City while wearing his white tuxedo but having discovered he is a wanted man, the player character can barely walk the distance of a few subway stops before keeling over dead from hunger, a difficulty that requires the interactor to constantly restore an earlier saved position in order to puzzle this out and get anywhere. As if these constraints on the interaction weren't annoying enough, the copy-protection scheme of *Amnesia* also constantly intrudes, requiring the interactor to locate cross-streets based on addresses. Perhaps such a design makes a point about the illusion of freedom in early interactive fiction.

Certainly, a tuxedo-clad player character in danger of starvation (and eventually reduced to squeegeeing windows and sleeping in a tenement, if the narrative is to progress at all) does provide an interesting social commentary, as other events in a traversal of *Amnesia* do.

But the gears of *Amnesia*'s text-machine are simply too sticky to make the overall experience of solving this Youdunit at all enjoyable, however transforming certain moments might be.

Disch (1990) dismissed those who were disappointed with *Amnesia* as wanting "trivial pursuits" and being uninterested in "reading and imaginative skills," and he decided that "trying to superimpose over this structure a *dramatic conception* other than a puzzle was apparently too much for the audience" (118). Whether he was right or not, *Amnesia* principally offered the interactors of the mid-1980s not a new type of interactive literary joy but a sort of textual torture device. It did include a collection of powerful cut-scenes and an overall framework that would have been much more compelling, if the experience of it were less of a struggle.

More Rooms on Level 9

Stephen Granade (1999b) writes that "Level 9 was one of the foremost British adventure game companies. . . . It was a family company which was started by Pete Austin and eventually employed Pete's two brothers, his sister, and his father." The company's first products were utilities and video games. The brothers—Pete, Nick, and Mike—started off in interactive fiction by publishing a knock-off of *Adventure* for the BBC Micro Model B and the Sinclair Spectrum in 1983. This was a feat, since the BBC Micro Model B had only 32k of memory, but Level 9's *Colossal Cave,* using text compression and a highly efficient programming language Mike Austin developed, a-code, actually managed to provide more rooms than the original had. The Austin brothers followed that success with two other works that year: the puzzle mélange *Adventure Quest* and the science fiction *Snowball.* The latter work is famous for having more than 7,000 rooms—6,800 of them part of a simple, color-coded maze. (The company boasted how many rooms their other works had, too; one writer noted that "'over 200 locations' would become a familiar quote on the Level 9 packaging" (Hewison 1992).) It also had a player character named Kim Kimberly, who might be imagined as either male or female. The company later brought in other authors and began adding graphics to every room in its works.

Level 9 ended up issuing twenty interactive fiction titles, more than any other company save Infocom (Schmidt and Schulz 1999). The company became, as Hewison (1992) put it, "the undisputed kings of adventure games in the U.K." The works it published were recently called "the most advanced adventure games ever available on tape" (Schmidt and Schulz 1999). The appeal of more rooms and the push for a larger vocabulary relates to concerns of the software market of the time. While other computer games in the 1980s could suggest what gameplay was like visually, with screenshots depicting the game in action, interactive fiction works could at best show an illustrated text. Moreover, interactive fiction was considered to be worthwhile only until the interactor won; it was not genuinely thought (regardless of Marc Blank's comments on the matter) that it would be replayed as other computer games might be. Thus the appeal to objective criteria was one way to advertise that a work of interactive fiction was both pleasing to experience and sizeable enough to provide many hours of interaction along the way to victory. There are connections to hacker and troubadour traditions, too; being able to simulate an IF world with thousands of rooms in a tiny program was an impressive feat.

As the business of interactive fiction in general went bust in the late 1980s, Level 9 managed to hang on for a while, finally succumbing in 1991. By then the company had made its mark on the form. Pete Austin's *The Knight Orc* is one well-loved work brought out by Sinclair, a cleverly twisted text-and-graphics piece that serves as an example of some of Level 9's innovations. The player character in the 1987 *The Knight Orc* is the orc Grindleguts, who, while drunk, was selected by his ill-intentioned companions to represent his vile race at a tournament. The initial situation finds him waking up while tied to a horse as a knight is about to charge him. After enduring defeat, Grindleguts must seek a long enough rope to escape from the clean, well-lighted realm in which he's trapped, completing a comic treasure hunt to finish the first of the work's three parts. Many non-player characters wander about aimlessly, without any essential function in the generated narratives, but they are described in such a bilious way, and wander with enough personality, as to provide amusement. The evil player character made *The Knight Orc,* as one IF author wrote, "one of the first games to give voice to a villain" (Sherwin 1999), although this player character was certainly not as nuanced and did not unfold in as interesting a way as in *Amnesia*. But that was not the point; Grindleguts and his quest worked instead to turn the conventions of sword-and-sorcery fantasy on their heads. One character, the Prophet, departed from the usual image of the fantasy cleric by being "a sweaty paedophile, quite happy to swarm on about the meek inheriting the Earth, turning the other cheek and the love of you know who . . . Until you mention liberation theology, disarmament, or anyone other than male humans becoming ministers."

At the end of the first part, the character sees that this fantasy world is an illusion. In the second and third parts of *The Knight Orc,* raising and lowering a visor would move the player character between two different worlds—a similar situation as with Level 9's sequels to *Snowball: Return to Eden* and *The Worm in Paradise.*

Just as Infocom games came packaged with "feelies" and *Mindwheel* shipped with a hardcover book, *The Knight Orc* included a novella by Peter McBride: *The Sign of the Orc.* While *The Knight Orc* was a hit, not all fans of Level 9 enjoyed it; one reviewer found it the first of Level 9's more formulaic efforts, "lacking the atmosphere and puzzles of [its] earlier games" (Hewison 1992). Other works written in the same development system, which was dubbed KAOS, followed. These included the "Ingrid Trilogy" that began with *Gnome Ranger,* the Time and Magik trilogy, *Lancelot,* and Level 9's final KAOS title, the afterlife detective story *Scapeghost,* published in 1989.

MAGNETIC SCROLLS PUSHES THE ENVELOPE

In 1985 an intriguing new work of interactive fiction was published in England, one of the first to run on the new 16-bit Spectrum Sinclair QL. It was *The Pawn,* written by Rob Steggles and based on ideas from several people at a new company, Magnetic Scrolls, a company chartered to create interactive fiction and aiming to be England's answer to Infocom. *The Pawn* featured a player character who had to seek freedom in a fantasy world while fettered by a silver bracelet and subject to events that were ordained from above. Although at times cruel to the interactor with its intricate requirements for puzzle solving, the parser was quite advanced and the work was both enjoyable and impressive. The company followed the original release with a version for the Atari ST; this and subsequent ports of *The Pawn* were published and distributed by another U.K. company, Rainbird. It was this company that convinced the Magnetic Scrolls founders, Anita Sinclair and Ken Gordon, to add graphics, using the art of Geoff Quilley. The text-and-graphics format became standard for the relatively few but memorable offerings this company brought out in the coming years, with the visual art functioning "more like illustrations than exact pictures of a room or scene" (Granade 2001b). This was a convenient approach since it meant that changes in the implementation of the IF world during the development process were less likely to require revisions in the associated graphics; the graphics were also not required for interaction. As with the Synapse and Level 9 publications, a novella (used in the copy protection scheme) was included with *The Pawn.* Programming of this first work was done by Hugh Steers and cofounder Gordon.

Before the company closed down in 1992—suffering from the decline of interactive fiction's popularity on software shelves—it published several renowned works and made several technological improvements. Interactors could use "go to" to specify a location and the player character would go there by following the shortest path. This was an interesting attempt (although not an entirely original one, since *Suspended* among other IF works had done something similar) to make mapping unnecessary. The company boasted that its parser could correctly handle the (syntactically uninteresting) input *plant the plant in the plant pot,* making sense of the same word being used as verb, adjective, and noun. But if the system was more advanced than Infocom's, this still did not allow a great deal more subtlety to be brought to the textual interaction. The capable parser did allow Magnetic Scrolls to surpass some of its competitors who had started out producing works for 8-bit computers, such as Level 9.

One well-received Magnetic Scrolls production was the 1987 fantasy *The Guild of Thieves,* also written by Steggles and with illustrations by Quilley. It featured a treasure hunt on an island, in which the player character was trying to acquire the loot necessary to join the eponymous guild. The following year saw the release of a work with a contemporary London IF world, *Corruption,* by Steggles and Steers and with illustrations by Alan Hunnisett and Richard Selby. The cover art of the U.S. package featured a stylized gunman clutching a briefcase; the player character was a BMW-driving suit. Like many Magnetic Scrolls works, this one is exacting. To traverse the work successfully requires that the player character be in several particular places at precisely the right time. Although those at Magnetic Scrolls were familiar with early U.S. interactive fiction works such as *Adventure* and *Zork* (Granade 2001b), the tendency toward such demanding and sometimes even cruel requirements can likely be attributed to earlier interactive fiction published in the United Kingdom, such as the Phoenix games that were made available commercially by Topologika. A different conflation of influences could be seen in *Fish!,* a work by multiple authors that has been called "something like bits of *Leather Goddesses, Stationfall, Lurking Horror, Border Zone,* and *The Pawn,* all rolled into one, with a bit of Monty Python thrown in for good measure" (Campbell 1988). The player character is a multidimensional agent incarnated, initially, in the form of a fish—and enjoying a relaxing vacation. The vacation does not last long; the player character must enter several different IF worlds in a pun-laden sort of wild fish chase.

In 1990 the new and very slick Magnetic Windows interpreter was released along with the company's *Wonderland,* which was based on Lewis Carroll's Alice books. The interpreter was essentially a cross-platform windowing system crafted particularly for text-and-graphics interactive fiction. Three works (*Guild of Thieves, Corruption,* and *Fish!*) were then ported to run in the new interpreter and released in 1991 as *The Magnetic Scrolls Collection Volume 1.* But the costly development of the new interpreter did not pay off in the waning market for interactive fiction of the early 1990s, and the company had scrolled to the bottom by 1992 without publishing another volume of this collection, or any other work.

IF IN OTHER LANGUAGES

Although this book has only sought to cover English-language IF works, interactive fiction is a phenomenon that has reached most all computer-using countries. Many works were created during the commercial era in languages other than English. A handful of English-language works were translated by the companies that made them—Infocom even had Jeff O'Neill begin a German translation of *Zork I,* which was never completed—but the nature of world software markets made such translations unappealing from a business standpoint. Brian Howarth's *Gremlins,* written in Scott Adams's system and published in 1984 by Adventure Soft UK, was translated to Spanish and sold in Spain. Few there had access to Infocom's works (as was the case in the United Kingdom), but English-language interactive fiction for the Sinclair Spectrum and Amstrad, such as that by Level 9, was fairly popular in Spain (Jan 1996a).

Interactive fiction companies in non-English-speaking countries were also founded; Aventuras AD in Spain, founded by Juan J. Muñoz, is one example. Today, numerous Spanish interactive fiction clubs exist. The Club de Aventuras AD (CAAD), which grew from Aventuras AD, is one of the most prominent (Jan 1996b), along with the Sociedad para la Preservación de las Aventuras Conversacionales (SPAC), which has a purpose similar to the English-language Society for the Preservation of Adventure Games (SPAG) founded earlier by G. Kevin Wilson. Although the Interactive Fiction

Archive was founded as an English-language resource (originally hosted in Germany), today it hosts works in Dutch, Esperanto, Italian, German, Spanish, and Swedish—and these include only those works that are available for free—either works authored by individuals or allowed by companies to circulate for free. English-language articles on the history of Italian, German, and Spanish interactive fiction will appear in an upcoming anthology (Short 2004).

LATE INTERACTIVE FICTION CAPITALISM

Legend Entertainment was perhaps the last 1980s-style commercial interactive fiction company, selling boxed software on store shelves alongside other computer entertainment offerings. It was founded by Bob Bates (the last person to become an Infocom Implementor) and Mike Verdu in 1989. All of Legend's interactive fiction featured graphics, although some works— namely, the *Spellcasting* trilogy—could be traversed with the graphics turned off. *Spellcasting 101: Sorcerers Get All the Girls* (1990), *Spellcasting 201: The Sorcerer's Appliance* (1991), and *Spellcasting 301: Spring Break* (1992) feature a college for wizards complete with curvaceous coeds (lovingly depicted on the package) and fraternity hazing. Infocom Implementor Steven Meretzky, whose IF experience included spellcasting (*Sorcerer*) and lowbrow sexual corniness (*Leather Goddesses of Phobos*), designed these works. One aficionado of Legend's interactive fiction described the first of this series as "not quite as mature as *Porky's Revenge*" and "not *Gravity's Rainbow*, but it's fun" (Marsh 1999). At least there were some interesting puzzles provided by these and the other Legend titles, such as Bates's more serious *Timequest* (1991) and the even less serious IF parody *Eric the Unready* (1993). At any rate, the shelves of Babbage's, Egghead Software, and Electronics Boutique had no other new interactive fiction to offer in the early 1990s, so there would have been little point in complaining. As of 2003, Legend is still in business, but its last piece of interactive fiction was published in 1993. This was *Gateway II: Homeworld*, a follow-up to the 1992 *Frederik Pohl's Gateway* and the last piece of interactive fiction to be commercially published for the usual game market (Granade 2002).

While that was the end of one sort of interactive fiction company, others have attempted to sell interactive fiction in different ways. David Baggett and David Leary started a company called Adventions in 1991 to offer "commercial quality text adventures"; they called their Unnkulian Unventure Series "Interactive Fiction for the 90's" (Baggett 1993). Their first two works were distributed as shareware; for a registration fee of $10 each, the customer would also get a map and hints. Former Infocom Implementor Michael Berlyn and his wife Muffy Berlyn founded a company in 1998 to sell boxed interactive fiction in the style of the 1980s. The venture, Cascade Mountain Publishing, published G. Kevin Wilson's *Once and Future* (which had long been in progress under the name *Avalon*) that year and then brought out an updated version of Michael Berlyn's *Dr. Dumont's Wild P.A.R.T.I.* After a few years in which no new works were brought out, and in which a promised book edition of the *Inform Designer's Manual* failed to arrive—years that left some people in the IF community even more wary of commercial ventures (Cadre 2000)—Cascade Mountain Publishing closed its Web site early in 2000. Reportedly, 300 copies of *Once and Future* were sold (leaving 1,500 in the warehouse) and only 60 copies of the later release *Dr. Dumont's Wild P.A.R.T.I.* were sold (Granade 2001a). A few individuals have since sought to sell their IF works, and the occasional company like Activision has rereleased older works. The main market for interactive fiction today, however, is on eBay and other auction sites, where packaged disks from the 1980s are bought and sold by collectors and IF enthusiasts. Fortunately, the end of the interactive fiction market is not the end of the story for the form.

SEVEN

THE INDEPENDENTS

The adventure game has been called a "remarkable, short-lived genre" (Aarseth 1997, 101). If commercial success were all that determined the life of a genre, it would be correct to declare that interactive fiction's brief life is over. But if one were to accept that way of defining an art form's lifespan, poetry, hypertext fiction, and short film would never have existed at all, since none of these achieved real commercial viability at any point. In the specific case of all-text adventure games and other sorts of interactive fiction, it is the mass popularity brought on by profitability and the presence of interactive fiction on software store shelves that has been exhausted. Interactive fiction itself certainly lives on. After the companies that produced IF works shut down or shifted their focus, as Edward Rothstein (1998) noted, "in a world beneath the thriving universe of video-game commerce, these text adventures thrived. In fact, they are still being written and are far different from the more precious experiments in participatory fiction that ask the reader to use hyperlinks." Interactive fiction has been passionately authored over the past two decades, with a surge of new works being released in recent years.

The still-growing community of interactive fiction authors first really began to demonstrate the vitality of the form in the 1990s, innovating in ways that early hackers and later game companies did not. Their IF works are usually even more widely available today than were the most successful commercial software of the 1980s, since they are typically free for download and, thanks to the Internet, available worldwide. These new pieces of interactive fiction have been created in an array of genres, with different amounts of time required for the typical traversal, and starting from widely varying conceptual and thematic points. A relevant FAQ notes that "interactive fiction [from the independent era] quite regularly achieves respectable rankings on the 'Internet PC Games Charts' . . . there were five interactive fiction games in the 1996 Year-end Download Top 40, the highest romping in at #12 (beating *Doom*), making these games some of the most popular non-commercial computer games in the world" (Glasser 2000). In fact the perspective of today's active community of IF authors and interactors is that interactive fiction didn't really get going until after the commercial era. Stephen Granade's timeline of inter- active fiction's history (2002), for instance, in an odd reversal of Aarseth's idea of interactive fiction, places about two-thirds of its events *after* 1991.

This era of independently created interactive fiction is the current one, so the innovative works of interactive fiction that are to come, at least in the immediate future, are likely to be from the authors discussed here or from other members of the community who are most familiar with these works. These independent IF works themselves and online reviews of many such works are freely available. The works can be found at the Interactive Fiction Archive, <http://www.ifarchive.org>, currently maintained by David Kinder and Stephen Granade. Capsule reviews can be found at Baf's Guide, <http://www.wurb.com/baf/>, while longer reviews are hosted on many sites and easily located with a Web search. This makes independent interactive fiction the easiest for today's interactors to approach. This author and others are already undertaking detailed discussions of a few of the works mentioned here (e.g., Montfort and Moulthrop 2003); several pieces deserve such treat- ment but have not even been mentioned in this chapter. Instead, the empha- sis here is on giving a sense of the shape of the current IF community or movement, while pointing out some important aspects of select works.

TOOL YOUR OWN ADVENTURE

While the current community of IF authors dates from around 1993, indi- viduals and hobbyists began programming interactive fiction much earlier. From the very beginning, *Adventure* and its imitators were programmed by hobbyists, not for commercial gain. *Adventure* has been described as folk art

(Buckles 1985), although the esoteric skills and expensive computing hardware required for early interactive fiction authorship prevented sophisticated authorship from becoming popular in a broader context.

The source code to this early interactive fiction was often closely guarded, not because authors were fervent about protecting their intellectual property but simply as a practical matter, to make cheating more difficult. This changed in the home computer era, during the 1980s, when magazines offered listings of interactive fiction written in BASIC. The listing of Lance Micklus's *Dog Star Adventure,* possibly the first of these, was published in May 1979 (Nelson 2001b, 46). Commercial programs were sometimes published in this way, as happened in December 1980 with Scott Adams's *Pirate Adventure.* It was also not unheard of for the authors of BASIC games, originally published in magazines, to go on to create more complex commercial interactive fiction; this was the case with Brian Moriarty, who became an Infocom Implementor.

Computer program listings of this sort served two main purposes. First, they helped educate the owners of home computers about programming. Programs provided an education in debugging, if nothing else, since the typist would inevitably introduce errors and need to correct them and since the program listings very often had errors in them to begin with. But beyond that, there was some idea that the workings of a program would be easier to understand after one typed it in, line by line. Second, the program so entered was supposed to be either useful or fun. Interestingly, in the case of a work of interactive fiction, these two goals were in fairly direct conflict. Either the program was obscured and incomprehensible—and thus of no educational value, not to mention practically impossible to debug—or else one would learn all about the IF world and its workings as one typed the program in, leaving nothing to be discovered as one interacted. Nevertheless, many BASIC adventure games found their way into print, and numerous books were published on IF programming (DaCosta 1982; Tyler and Howarth 1983; Vile 1984; Menick 1984; Horn 1984). Different editions were sometimes printed of the same book for the different BASIC dialects of 1980s home computers. As this author knows, it is not the most pleasant programming experience to implement interactive fiction in BASIC, but programmers have created text adventures under far less hospitable programming conditions—in, for instance, WordPerfect macros (McComb 1990, chap. 17) and obfuscated C (Noll et al. 2002).

Some special-purpose interactive fiction development systems were used by the ordinary home computer owner of the 1980s. An important early one was Donald Brown's 1980 freeware system Eamon, a system for creating text-based role-playing games; these are primitive interactive fictions that only accept one- or two-word input from a limited set of commands, all of which could be listed. Eamon was used to create more than 240 games; these ranged from works based (without authorization) on *The Empire Strikes Back* to educational games to a satirical samurai adventure rife with Eamon in-jokes. Several IF development systems were sold alongside games on store shelves, in keeping with the do-it-yourself spirit of the times that led many to learn how to program in BASIC and to purchase creative software like Electronic Arts' Music Construction Kit or Brøderbund's Dazzle Draw. Foremost among the IF systems was The Quill by Graeme Yeandle (1983), which ran on the Sinclair Spectrum, BBC Micro, and Commodore 64. Not only was this system popular with hobbyists, but more than sixty commercial works of interactive fiction developed with The Quill were released during the mid-1980s (Nelson 2001, 46). The Quill, as with many IF works developed in the United Kingdom, was hardly known at all in the United States. Another system released in the British market, the 1986 Graphic Adventure Creator by Sean Ellis, proved to be a capable system for creating text-and-graphics interactive fiction. (The Quill could also be used to create works with graphics; add-ons were available to expand its capabilities.) The numerous other systems, with varying capabilities and targeted toward different sorts of users of varying ages and ability levels, included the 1984 Adventure Master by Christopher Chance (Persson 1994). Computer game construction kits of many other sorts existed, too, including the Bard's Tale Construction Kit, HURD (developed by Level 9, which was also a prolific publisher of interactive fiction), Adventure Construction Set (actually for creating maze games), and various arcade-style games that came with "level editors," such as *Floppy* and *Mr. Robot and His Robot Factory.*

An important early shareware system for PCs was the Generic Adventure Game System (GAGS) by Mark J. Welch, first released in 1985. An enhanced version, with improvements made by David Malmberg, was released in 1987; it was called the Adventure Game Toolkit (AGT) (Welch 1997). This system was later ported to the Atari ST and the Amiga; a version for early Macintoshes was also available. From 1987 to 1992 Softworks sponsored the Annual AGT Adventure Game Writing Contest, held on the Gamer's Forum in CompuServe (Malmberg 1994). As one writer noted, "AGT did very well in the thriving BBS community of the day, particularly [on] the early online services like CompuServe, GEnie and Delphi" (Guy 2001). One AGT work was Judith Pintar's *CosmoServe: An Adventure Game for the BBS-Enslaved,* which pokes fun at CompuServe's online culture and at some points mimics a DOS command-line interface. Using the interface, the interactor has to sift through the contents of a simulated hard disk. *CosmoServe* won the 1992 AGT contest. Some AGT works were available on late-1980s bulletin board systems for online play, making them accessible even to those who didn't download and install them or who used computers that didn't run AGT works. As of this writing, more than eighty AGT works are available on the Interactive Fiction Archive. While this system provided only a two-word parser and had other limitations that were seen as irksome in the 1990s, it was written for a platform that survived through that decade, which wasn't the case with many early systems for home computers. Because of this and because it was effective enough for the purposes of many authors, it remained somewhat popular into the 1990s. Printed AGT manuals were advertised for sale on the Web after 2000, and one AGT entry even appeared in the 2001 Interactive Fiction Competition.

Of the interactive fiction development systems in wide use today, the one with the longest lineage is The Text Adventure Development System (TADS); the first version was offered by its creator, Michael Roberts, as shareware in 1987 and was, like AGT (which was released that same year), frequently distributed through bulletin board systems. One TADS aficionado writes that "Mike Roberts and his business partner Steve McAdam eventually set up a small dialup BBS in Palo Alto, California, where High Energy, the company they formed to sell TADS as shareware, was based" (Guy 2001). TADS was upgraded to version 2 in November 1992. The new version used virtual memory to allow much larger works to be created, exceeding Infocom's in terms of their file size and the complexity of their IF worlds. But even with the first version, according to Neil Guy (2001),

it was possible for even a hobbyist to sit down and write a near Infocom-quality game—you didn't need a minicomputer and vast budget to do it. You just needed a copy of TADS, with its excellent

parser, totally object-oriented internal structure and extensive documentation. And just as Infocom's games had been distributed on a
wide variety of OS architectures, TADS was ported to the most
common OSs of the day—MS-DOS, Macintosh, Atari, UNIX.

From the beginning TADS featured a C-like syntax; it was an object-
oriented language with classes and inheritance. The objects that encapsulate
data and methods correspond to things in the IF world—their states and the
ways one might interact with them.

At the beginning of the 1990s the important forum for IF discussion
was neither on the proprietary CompuServe nor on some email list or Web
bulletin board. Rather, it was on Usenet, where two newsgroups had been
formed for discussing the playing of interactive fiction (rec.games.int-fiction,
or rgif) and the creation of it (rec.arts.int-fiction, or raif). Postings to rgif were
made as early as 1991, and raif was founded in 1987, although when Adam
Engst created raif in 1987 he did so for the discussion of hypertext fiction
(Cole 1998). By 1993 both groups were hosting a great deal of discussion,
which included programming tips, requests for hints, and commentary on
things like Graham Nelson's (1993) proposed "Bill of Player's Rights." These
newsgroups (together known as r*if) have continued to be centers for the
discussion of interactive fiction. An important complement to the newsgroups in these early days of the Web was the resource mentioned at the
beginning of this chapter, the Interactive Fiction Archive. It was originally
hosted at the German National Research Center for Information
Technology and maintained by Volker Blasius, beginning in 1992. Those who
posted to and read the newsgroups, enjoying the interactive fiction that the
regulars made available on the Interactive Fiction Archive, came to refer to
themselves as the "IF community," a term that seems to have been used first
in the newsgroups in 1994 (Hale-Evans 1994).

THE OZ PROJECT AT CMU

Near the end of the 1980s, the first and as yet only major academic project
dealing with interactive fiction began to come together at Carnegie Mellon
University. This was Joe Bates's Oz Project, inspired in part by the work of
Brenda Laurel on interactive drama. During the 1990s the project pursued

the ideal of "highly interactive" experiences in which the interactor could influence what was happening at any point in time and in many ways, a different experience, one Oz researcher explained, from that of "other interactive media such as hypertext, where the interactor is given only a small number of fixed choices" (Kelso, Wayhrauch, and Bates 1992, 1). The Oz Project devised an architecture for such interactive drama systems, using a drama manager to coordinate different events. This was tested and refined in a live interactive theater experiment and in two different types of projects. One thread used real-time animation to present a graphical world that held inarticulate but amusing characters with underlying models of their emotional state: These creatures were the Woggles. It was this thread of research that has continued in the work of Bates's company Zoesis. The other series of projects was built in LISP and constituted interactive fiction in the sense used in this book. These included *Lyotard,* a simulated cat portrayed in text in a simulated world, and three text worlds built by Scott Neal Reilly: *Robbery World, Office Politics,* and *The Playground.* There was also impressive work done on a system called GLINDA for generation of surface text in interactive fiction from underlying knowledge representations. Using this system would enable an IF author to create a simulated world and control what types of descriptions were generated based on "knobs" that could alter grammatical or other features of the language (Kantrowitz 1990). While the results of the project's research are well documented in academic publications and reports, the systems and works themselves unfortunately have not been made publicly available.

In *The Playground* the player character can trade baseball cards with Melvin and Sluggo using rather fluent English. The descriptions of what was happening and of the appearance of characters in the world may seem primitive, but each was the result of an underlying event in the world—there was essentially nothing "pre-written" in the text that appeared:

PLAYER> Sluggo: How about Ted Williams and Hank Aaron for
Willie Mays?
You are speaking to Sluggo.
Player's voice says "How about Ted Williams and Hank Aaron for
Willie Mays?".
Melvin whistles.

Sluggo is now red.

Sluggo is now scowling.

Sluggo is now tense.

Sluggo is speaking to you.

Sluggo's voice says "You think you're cool with your fancy trades? No deal, dweeb!".

PLAYER> Sluggo: Well, how about just Williams for Mays then?

You are speaking to Sluggo.

Player's voice says "Well, how about just Williams for Mays then?".

Melvin whistles.

Sluggo is now frowning.

Sluggo is speaking angrily to you.

Sluggo's voice says "Get out of here before I pound you, twerp!".

The Oz Project had tapered to a close near the end of the 1990s, but it continued into 2002 in the work of CMU graduate student Michael Mateas and Andrew Stern. In 2003, they were completing a graphical interactive drama system called *Façade*. Using an interface that looks like that of a first-person shooter but that replaces the gun with a cocktail glass, *Façade* simulates an uncomfortable dinner visit, during which the couple that has invited the player character over stages a breakup (Mateas and Stern 2001). When finished, *Façade* will realize several of the Oz Project's goals, demonstrate how well an Aristotelian concept of drama can be adapted to an interactive experience, and offer lessons for interactive fiction and other forms of new media; it promises to be a rare academic project that is also interesting as art and fun to interact with.

NELSON'S INFORM AND *CURSES*

"Since its invention in 1993, Inform has been used to design some hundreds of works of interactive fiction, in eight languages, reviewed in periodicals ranging in specialisation from *XYZZYnews* . . . to *The New York Times*. It accounts for around ten thousand postings per year to Internet newsgroups," according to the creator of Inform, Graham Nelson (2001b, 1). With its object-oriented, procedural language that compiles to the cross-platform Z-machine format, Inform is responsible for much of interactive fiction's current popularity. In late April 1993 Nelson completed the first version of this system. Whatever its technical merits, Inform offered a winning combination by creating "story files" in a venerated format—the same one used by the highly regarded Implementors of Infocom—and by being available for free, at a time when the premier development system, TADS, was offered as shareware. Released almost concurrently, and contributing greatly to Inform's success, was the text adventure that would become the most popular IF work of the early independent era: Nelson's sprawling *Curses*.

To return to hyperbolic literary comparisons for a moment, by developing both the most important tool for the creation of interactive fiction in the 1990s, Inform, and the most important and popular work of that decade, *Curses*, Nelson served as both Gutenberg and Cervantes for the new movement of IF authors and interactors. Of course, Inform largely reproduced what Infocom had developed, and *Curses* did not challenge the assumptions that Infocom's works had made in the way that some later independent pieces would. But Nelson (2002) is right to say that while "Inform may be . . . a dog's breakfast in terms of its computer-science elements . . . it contains genuine thought about how the model world and the parser ought to work." Inform's parser and libraries, which process language and contain much of the "default" behavior and many of the standard replies, make good attempts at tackling tricky problems like pronoun resolution and the disambiguation of commands. While Inform is not cutting-edge in terms of language understanding when compared to systems devised by academic researchers (Inform fails to work as well as the 1972 SHRDLU in some cases), this freely available system exceeds the in-house development systems of 1980s commercial companies in many ways.

The New York Times named Nelson "one of the more ornately literate creators of interactive fiction. . . . The epigram from *Jigsaw* is from T. S. Eliot. And any player who manages to solve its problems will find untranslated Latin mottos and puzzles involving Proust and Lenin" (Rothstein 1998). Nelson, who lectures in pure mathematics in his official role at St Anne's College, Oxford, is also a poet and an editor of *Oxford Poetry*. Nelson (2001a) lists some of his recent publications: "'The Homology of Moduli Spaces over a Compact Riemann Surface as a Representation of the Mapping Class Group' . . . the editing of Louis MacNeice's previously unpublished play 'Blacklegs' (1939) and an introduction to his translation of

Euripides' 'Hippolytus.'" Nelson's literary tastes and his unusual perspective on language are both illuminated by his reply to an interview question about his favorite authors: "I greatly admire the poetry of Philip Larkin and Primo Levi, writers who have absolutely nothing in common except their initials" (1995b).

Before Nelson began work on Inform, a group of programmers called the InfoTaskForce had already reverse-engineered the Z-machine format, and the ZIP interpreter, a free program that ran Infocom IF works, had also been developed by Mark Howell. Nelson—who said he had never intended to write a complete Z-machine compiler—began by trying to get a program to simply print "Hello World" (not the more appropriate West Coast test message, "Hello Sailor"). After succeeding, he went on to develop the compiler. At first Nelson called it zass, since it assembled Z-machine files, and he used what he called a small "silly test game" as he developed it (1995b). Using an Acorn Archimedes and programming in ANSI C, he quickly abandoned his small game to begin developing *Curses*, using that to put the in-progress compiler through its paces (Nelson 2002).

Although never employed full-time as a game developer, by the time he started working on Inform and *Curses* Nelson had an extensive background as an interactor and as an IF author. A neighbor took Nelson to visit the Digital offices in Reading when he was about ten. There, he played *Adventure*. Nelson (2002) recalls, "I was entirely seduced by it and in some sense it entered my imaginary world." When his father assembled the Acorn Atom computer from a kit a few years later, Nelson began to devise ways to program adventure games on it—no easy task, since it came with 2k of RAM, only expandable to 12k. He continues:

> My only really viable game for the Atom had no name, but my family members referred to it as "the Adventure of Igneous the Dwarf," after a mercurial character appearing therein. I can only remember elements of the design: there was a volcanic crater; there was an underground stream, which flowed over a key. (Nelson 2002)

Prior to college, Nelson interacted with a handful of Infocom games (a rare experience in England) and wrote two BBC Micro text adventures, which a local company advertised in magazines and sold. He explained, "These were science fiction in style, and the treasures were hyper-high-tech alien gadgets. The more noteworthy was the second game, which ran on a pair of BBC Micros connected together by RS-232 cable, and in which the players alternated turns" (Nelson 2002). When studying mathematics at Cambridge, Nelson became acquainted with the Phoenix games (his login was GAN10) and even did some programming, attempting to get *Tera*, a multiplayer game, working.

Nelson's most famous piece of interactive fiction— and likely the most well known IF work since the demise of Infocom—is the first fruit of Inform, the 1993 *Curses*. This large, complex, and difficult adventure is set in an English country home and in certain other spaces that are linked in fantastic ways to it. Nelson (2002) said he "consciously wrote it in an Infocomesque spirit, aiming at the same epigrammatic style of wit." Richard Tucker and Gareth Rees were the principal early testers of *Curses,* which was made public beginning with release 7. This first version was about half the size of the final 1995 release, number 16 (Nelson 1995b), because *Curses* became, as Nelson (2002) put it, "an interactive sort of event, in that many players in the early months became dedicated play-testers, and the game slightly expanded with each release, often incorporating their suggestions." The magically numbered release 7 of *Curses* did a great deal to build momentum for Inform. Potential authors could clearly see what wonders could be accomplished in the language. Nelson (2002) calls it "the ultimate proof of concept: an indisputably Infocom-sized and -style work, composed using Inform."

"A hinged trapdoor in the floor stands open, and light streams in from below." This is the last bit of prologue in *Curses,* the part of the initial room description that comes just before the prompt for input. This text recalls the most famous visual art from Infocom, the *Zork* trilogy logo with its open trapdoor, light streaming from it. But here the player character starts off on the darker side of the trapdoor, and in the attic rather than in *Zork I*'s cellar. Nelson is right to note that *Curses* "is unusual among games of its period in having a main character with . . . a family, an imminent holiday, etc. . . . and in being in some sense rooted in real-world concerns rather than simply collecting gold from dungeons" (2002); it is also unusual to present the player character going on a real adventure in that character's own house—not an anonymous house in the woods of *Zork,* not a *Mystery House,* and not a relative's bizarre mansion. It was not just the inclusion of numerous witty epigraphs (in the style of *Trinity*) and the overt references to T. S. Eliot that gave *Curses* its literary texture. This different type of IF world also allowed new resonances to arise from brief phrases. Gaston Bachelard (1994) noted, with reference to poetry, that the "virtues of shelter are so simple, so deeply rooted in our unconscious, that they may be recaptured through mere mention, rather than through minute description" (12). Such mention works to similar effect in *Curses,* and here, as Bachelard writes of the image of the house in poetry, "the house image would appear to have become the topography of our intimate being" (xxxvi), with the IF world encoding the family history of the player character and giving clues not just to the solution of puzzles but also to this character's tendencies and personality.

Nelson has continued to improve Inform over the years and has also offered other IF works, the most significant of which is his intricate 1995 *Jigsaw,* a millennial fantasy that recalls *Trinity* in its opening sequence and in its structure. That was also the first work in the Z-machine version 8 format he developed; this expanded the file size for an all-text work to 512k, allowing later sizable projects to take shape. Nelson entered a *Zork*-like romp in the 1996 Interactive Fiction Competition, using the pseudonym "Angela M. Horns," an anagram of his name. That piece—which won first place—originated when Activision contacted Nelson about using Inform to write what would eventually become *Zork: The Undiscovered Underground.* Nelson (2002) said he wrote the first version of his *The Meteor, the Stone, and the Long Glass of Sherbert* "as a lure for them." He also created the impressive *Tempest,* an adaptation of the play, presented in verse and using the original text, along with replies that Nelson wrote. This was entered in the 1997 Interactive Fiction Competition under the name "William Shakespeare" and did not fare well, ending up in twenty-fifth place. (Many intriguing but unusual competition entries have suffered similar fates.) Aside from his work as developer of Inform and author of interactive fiction, Nelson has also made a great contribution with his *Inform Designer's Manual,* known in its current edition as the *DM4* (Nelson 2001b). Disguised as a manual for the Inform language— and fulfilling that overt role very well—this book, originally published online in September 1994, also contains an excellent summary history of the form, advice on the design (not just the programming) of interactive fiction, and commentary on many specific works. It has been widely read, even by those who do not program in Inform.

COLLEGES AND *CHRISTMINSTER*

Many IF authors felt the impulse to model an unusual space (the cave of *Adventure* or a fantasy landscape), but there seemed to be an almost equally strong impulse to simulate the familiar in an IF world. (Sometimes, of course, both could be accomplished in an interesting and literary transformation of the everyday.) IF creators have sought the inspiration for their worlds in their own apartment or house, and several have looked to their own college campus. As described in the discussion of the influence of MIT on *Zork* in chapter 4, this impulse led to two MIT-influenced works, *The Lurking Horror* and *GC: A Thrashing Parity Bit of the Mind*. These two examples show how broad the spectrum of college interactive fiction was: The former was sold as entertainment software and created for those who had no knowledge of MIT at all, while the latter was so laden with in-jokes as to prove completely inscrutable to those who hadn't attended MIT, and perhaps even difficult to understand for those at MIT who were not affiliated with the AI Lab. In between these two extremes was the TADS work *Save Princeton* by Jacob Weinstein and Karine Schaefer, released in 1991. Full of in-jokes and self-reference, its humor was also enjoyed by some outside Princeton. Later, in 1995, James T. Reese's *Veritas,* a scavenger hunt set at Harvard, was released, as was Neil deMause's *MacWesleyan*. There had also been some earlier interactive fiction (from the 1980s) with IF worlds that were generic colleges or universities.

The highest achievement in this college genre of interactive fiction is Gareth Rees's *Christminster,* an early Inform work that was released in 1995. It is set at the fictional Biblioll College. Christ's College, Cambridge, is the model for how this IF world is laid out (Rees 2002), and images of the Christ's College great gate and clock tower decorate Rees's *Christminster* Web pages (Rees 2001). The background of *Christminster's* college is drawn from the history of Balliol College, Oxford. Rees (2002) explained that "other Oxford and Cambridge colleges contributed miscellaneous features." The player character, Christabel, is visiting her brother Malcolm on campus.

The initial situation finds her at the gate, which on this Sunday is shut, presenting the first challenge.

After solving a series of puzzles that involve getting one non-player character to distract another non-player character, and that then get more convoluted, Christabel gains entrance to the college. There, she discovers that Malcolm is missing and that an alchemical intrigue is afoot. Sinister dons seeking the elixir of life have abducted Malcolm; Christabel must seek him as she solves puzzles that involve gaining access to the library, rewiring telephones, solving ciphers, and, near the final stages, acting properly at a particularly difficult dinner.

The conflation of the detective-style intrigue found in *Deadline* and *The Witness* with the college setting was one special feature of *Christminster*. Another could be seen in the numerous non-player characters who are essential to progress through the work. Epigraphs of the sort seen in *Trinity, A Mind Forever Voyaging,* and *Curses* introduce the different stages of *Christminster;* in this work they are taken from alchemical lore.

In newsgroup discussion in the years following *Christminster's* release, much was made of the fact that the player character in this work is female. What is more interesting is that she is an outsider; being female (when venturing into an all-male college) is only one way in which she doesn't fit in. Christabel has a map of the college—rendered on screen with ASCII characters, thus making *Christminster* easier to handle without pencil-and-paper mapping—as is appropriate for a visitor; her lack of knowledge about the layout, history, and workings of the college aligns with the interactor's initial ignorance of these things. While the interactor may not inherently share Christabel's wish to find Malcolm, who cannot be encountered for quite a while, the general curiosity about the IF world, and the secrets hidden therein, which is evoked as obstacles are overcome and new non-player characters are encountered, is enough to compel interaction. The non-player characters—ranging from a busker and policeman in the initial sequence to several dons, some rather bumbling and others more malicious, work remarkably well. Here again, neither reading a transcript in which these characters appear nor looking at the appropriate parts of the source code (which is publicly available) is extremely impressive, although the non-player characters are programmed very capably and the writing works well. The real achievement is in how the non-player characters are integrated into the workings of the puzzles and how they work to convey necessary information while managing to unobtrusively give a sense of their personality and their existence as people in this particular IF world.

Rees (1995) wrote, "One idea I used, following Legend's 'Gateway' and some Infocom games, was to split up long interactions over a number of turns, with some mechanism to keep the player sitting still while the interaction was going on." This kept the computer-generated replies shorter, and made them closer in size to the commands that the interactor could input, creating a more dialogic interaction than would have occurred had long "cut scenes" been used. In one case, the player character is physically trapped in a secret chamber with one of the dons, Wilderspin. As the interactor figures out how to escape, Christabel is a captive audience for what Wilderspin has to say. Escape also requires cooperation between the two, so the non-player character is important not only for the information he provides and as a character in a generated story, but also as part of the solution to a puzzle. While the puzzles are not always meaningful in the sense that a great riddle can be, they do constrain the interaction so that the potential narrative of *Christminster* is realized in pleasing ways, not only requiring that Christabel spend time near some of the non-player characters but also acting to withhold and divulge secrets in a way that keeps the interactor interested.

THE INTERACTIVE FICTION COMPETITION

An important tradition in independent interactive fiction began when the first Interactive Fiction Competition was announced on rec.★.int-fiction and took place in 1995. This competition took place in the summer of 1995 and was run by G. Kevin Wilson, a.k.a. Whizzard, who is also author of *Once and Future* and founder of the *SPAG Newsletter*. Initially conceived of as a contest for Inform works, a TADS division was added for the first year. (The IF Competition, also called simply the Comp, became an annual affair and later allowed entries developed in any system, even entries written in general-purpose programing languages.) Although the restrictions on development systems were part of the structure of the Comp, the famous "one rule" simply specified that "games must be finishable . . . in two hours or less" (Wilson

1995). Works of this sort had been imagined and executed prior to the competition. These included examples for development systems and John Baker's *John's Fire Witch,* completed the previous January, which its author called "a snack-sized text adventure" (1995). But the Comp not only encouraged more people to get involved in authoring interactive fiction, it also encouraged them to experiment with smaller IF worlds (with fewer locations and objects) and sometimes with concepts that would have been too complex or too tedious to implement in more traditional interactive fiction, where the time required for a successful traversal might range from ten to forty hours. The first Comp had six Inform and six TADS entries.

The Inform winner was *A Change in the Weather* by Andrew Plotkin, which begins with a four-line poem in bold. The description of scenery at different times of day and from different perspectives gave this work a different texture than most previous interactive fiction. Interactors also appreciated and commented on the fox, a character who served as helper. The player character had to devise a way to return after a foray away from picnicking friends and into the wilderness. Many interactors noticed that the reply to *score* is not a report of the score but the phrase "That's not how life works." For some reason, not keeping score has been noted by literary critics as a literary feature of interactive fiction (Randall 1988, 187), although whether or not a work keeps score has nothing to do with whether or not it has puzzles or how literary it is. A work can have no puzzles and still keep score (e.g., based on how much of the world has been visited), or, as with *A Change in the Weather,* it can have puzzles but not report the score. The lack of a score in such a case simply obscures from the interactor how much progress has been made—an effect that may be desirable but is not, in and of itself, literary. *A Change in the Weather* is remarkable, rather, for its attempts to integrate the typical sorts of adventure-game puzzles with the description of landscape, the simulation of an animal character, and the emotional situation of the "adventurer" player character who has wandered away to spend the night in the woods.

Uncle Zebulon's Will by Magnus Olsson took top honors in the TADS category. The initial situation is very much like that of the 1986 *Hollywood Hijinks* by Dave Anderson and Liz Cyr-Jones. The player character, favorite nephew of a recently departed eccentric, arrives at the mansion of his relative to explore it. (In *Hollywood Hijinks,* it is Aunt Hildegarde's, not Uncle

Zebulon's, mansion.) The work didn't forge into new territory as *A Change in the Weather* did, but it was a well-implemented puzzle game with a fantasy IF world that conflated the everyday with the magical. Even an interactive fiction book, à la *Deadline,* was included. Although the work didn't take nearly as long to traverse as the average piece of interactive fiction from Infocom, it was implemented about as well as Infocom's works were, and its smaller number of challenges fit together to provide a satisfying experience. Olsson made the well-commented source code of *Uncle Zebulon's Will* available, helping numerous TADS programmers to understand the workings of that development system.

The Interactive Fiction Competition entered its eighth year in 2002. There were more than fifty entries in 2000 and again in 2001; in both years more than two hundred people judged the contest by interacting with the works for up to two hours each. Several judges played all of the works, and several even wrote reviews of all of them—a tradition that began with the first Comp. The Comp has become a major motivation for people to complete works in progress, and it is almost certainly the most important means of publicizing work, although longer works released at other times do garner some attention on the newsgroups. One sign of the importance of the competition metaphor over that of publication is that numerous themed "mini-comps" have taken place—often without voting, ranking, or prizes. The first of these to bear such a name was Lucain Paul Smith's The First Ever (and Maybe the Only) IF Mini-Competition, announced in May 1998. Marnie Parker's IF Art Show (originally called "The First Annual Text Art Show"), announced in March 1999, was another notable contest of this sort, although it was one where entries were ranked by a panel of judges.

In general, mini-comps have functioned more like theme issues of a journal than like contests. Another sort of contest was inaugurated in October 1998 by David Cornelson, who had authors on ifMUD (a virtual environment for socializing among those in the IF community) engage in "SpeedIF." Participants created very small IF works within a time limit of one hour (the time limit later became two hours) based on a selection of unusual topics, characters, and items that were volunteered online. The results were uploaded for the "competitors," and anyone else, to enjoy. SpeedIF, occurring irregularly and often decided upon spontaneously, has also become a tradition. Although the focus on competition as a metaphor—even in noncompetitive events—may seem unusual, the many sorts of competitions that have transpired in recent years (including some for interactive fiction in other languages) have had clear benefits for the community. The Comp itself has functioned as a means of publicity for the IF community and an excuse not only for authors to experiment with works that have smaller IF worlds, but also for interactors to review a slew of different entries and evaluate which approaches and techniques are most effective.

PLOTKIN'S WORK FROM *A CHANGE IN THE WEATHER* TO *SHADE*

Andrew Plotkin, usually referred to on rec.*.int-fiction by his login name, zarf, is legendary in the IF community not only for creating some of the most enjoyable recent interactive fiction works but also for devising IF interpreters, the Glk interface standard, and the multimedia-capable IF virtual machine Glulx—among other innovations. Plotkin, a graduate of Carnegie Mellon University who works for Red Hat in Pittsburgh, has kept up his pace of innovation since winning the Inform division of the first Interactive Fiction Competition. One measure of his fame is that the winner of the 2000 Best Game XYZZY Award (given, based on a popular vote, by Eileen Mullin's IF newsletter *XYZZYnews*) was a tribute to him based on the movie *Being John Malkovich;* written by J. Robinson Wheeler, this IF work was titled *Being Andrew Plotkin.* In the 2000 Interactive Fiction Competition, voters even ranked that amusing send-up significantly higher than *Shade,* a pseudonymous entry by Plotkin himself.

This section focuses on Plotkin's 1998 *Spider and Web* and his 2000 *Shade,* but first provides a short description of his other IF works to give some idea of his eclectic range. In 1996, the year after *A Change in the Weather,* Plotkin released two quite different works. One was *So Far,* which won the Best Game XYZZY Award and three other XYZZYs. After a tedious start at the theater, the elaborate *So Far* shifts through bizarre landscapes; these IF worlds work in unusual ways. Reviewers in the IF community have called them surreal or referred to the style as magical realism, but the more ancient precedent here, and the more appropriate figure, is the literary riddle. The workings of the IF world and the themes of *So Far* must be enacted, as in solving such riddles, for the interactor to make progress.

Plotkin's other IF work released that year was *Lists and Lists,* an interpreter and tutorial for Scheme, a LISP-like programming language. This was created in Inform and did simulate a world, although vestigially; thus it was, formally, interactive fiction, although perhaps closer to SHRDLU than *Adventure* in terms of how thrilling it seemed to the average interactor. His 1999 *Hunter, in Darkness* garnered two XYZZYs; it offers a tensely narrated experience based on Gregory Yob's *Hunt the Wumpus,* an ancestor of interactive fiction. Among Plotkin's prodigious non-IF programming output, two works are worth mentioning. One, written in Inform, often is lumped in with interactive fiction but is actually a hypertext work, in that lexias appear in response to a word from the current lexia being typed; a world is not simulated and represented in text as with IF works. This is the short *The Space Under the Window* (1997), written as part of Kristin Looney's conceptual art piece. In March 1997, Looney called for people to create works of art with the title *The Space Under the Window.* As of 1999, Plotkin's was one of twenty-seven works that were created and submitted (Looney 1999). In a different region of new media space is Plotkin's 1993 *System's Twilight,* a graphical Macintosh game, originally released as shareware and now available for free. This is a difficult puzzle game, but set in a curious world and incorporating some text in the form of dialogue. A small iconic character encounters other icon-like creatures in this game and has conversations with them that frame the puzzle-solving activities.

Critics complained during the commercial era that "most interactive fiction today does not adopt the metafictional form of the infinite, hall-of-mirrors story but rather the tactics of the detective, spy, or adventure novel—an extremely complex puzzle whose specific key the reader may have great difficulty finding but which is, in principle, solvable" (Niesz and Holland 1984, 121). *Spider and Web* is metafiction *and* a spy thriller. It begins in an alley: A tourist to this country (the player character) is standing by a featureless door. It quickly becomes clear that this IF world is a memory, or more precisely, is being presented mentally as a sort of reconstructed memory. The player character is actually a spy who has apparently slipped inside a secret enemy intelligence complex, for this character comes out of this first, hypodiegetic world very quickly, fettered and faced by an interrogator who has been forcing the player character to interactively revisit the break-in. Only *yes* and *no* can be said (usefully) in this IF world in which the interrogation takes place—at least until the moment when the interactor solves the work's most exquisite puzzle, using knowledge gained from the other IF worlds.

Progressing through the interrogation, without any of the player character's knowledge, does have certain pleasures, but the bizarre situation of the interactor being given hints by the player character's interrogator usually runs aground before the interrogation ends. The interrogation does help in some ways to enrich the IF world and provides insight into the character of the interrogator, but it is sometimes too evident that it mainly exists to set up the work's major puzzle, which leaves the player character free (or at least more free than before) to explore the frame IF world and to seek escape from the complex. The hypodiegetic worlds that the interrogation device forces the player to enter, it becomes apparent, may not reflect the past accurately—in fact, cannot all reflect the past accurately—yet they do provide needed information and experience to allow the interactor to puzzle through to a successful traversal of the work.

The way that texts are presented, with some unusual exhortations in italics, suggests an interesting new voice that is speaking in order to control the hyponarrative being generated by the player character's simulated, and supposedly remembered, actions. As a genre piece, *Spider and Web* also works well, even if too much is left generic at times in the attempt to create a sense of enigma. It presents a sort of Cold War in a deep freeze, with the only battles being fought by people like the player character, equipped with nonmetal high-tech gadgets and perhaps uncertain (as the interrogator seems to be) about why they are continuing to wage this conflict. The "best" final replies that are possible are satisfying, in terms of completing the game, but they are also intriguing and provoke further thought about what exactly may have happened in the end and about what the implications of the player character's actions have been for this IF world.

Although Plotkin is master of the devious puzzle, his finest work may be the short piece *Shade,* which essentially is puzzleless. Certain tasks must be done to traverse the work, and it's possible to have trouble figuring out what those are, but there may not be anything to do that is non-obvious in the sense of a literary riddle, and so the work could be considered as puzzleless (Montfort 2002b). But *Shade* is a riddle of highest order, with one IF world leaking into another in a terrifying way.

The player character begins on a futon, in this character's own apartment: a single room, with a closet and with nooks that house a bathroom and kitchen. The shade is down, and it is not yet dawn. Here again is the sort of intimate space that Nelson presented so well in *Curses,* but at the opposite extreme in terms of its size and in terms of how much family history it encodes. The player character is about to leave for a sort of vacation, as in *Curses,* but, as having the player character putter around the apartment reveals, the destination this time is the Death Valley Om, a Burning-Man-like festival that features constant chanting. While waiting for a taxi, first thirst, and then not knowing where the plane tickets are, compels some quotidian actions. The apartment contains a primitive computer, on whose screen the player character can see the "you-have-died message" from an interactive fiction version of Adam Cadre's novel *Ready, Okay!*

But as the interactor undertakes ordinary tasks, sand begins cropping up in unusual places. First there's a bit on the floor; finding the vacuum cleaner doesn't help, however, because it seems broken and full of sand. Eventually, as the sun rises, the player character, simply by undertaking similar, ordinary actions, turns maniacal and frees sand from every unlikely location, transforming the apartment into part of the desert. The prologue began with the player character groggy in predawn; by now it seems evident that the apartment was experienced only in a delirium and was as false as the memories "recalled" under interrogation in *Spider and Web.* The friendly space of the apartment has, in the course of ordinary actions, been transformed into a lethal waste. Plotkin has made the one-room game in the apartment, often an occasion for wacky puzzles involving household objects, into an instrument of existential terror.

CADRE'S WORK FROM *I-0* TO *VARICELLA*

Writer and teacher Adam Cadre had played some interactive fiction when he was young, but what made him interested in actually writing and programming interactive fiction himself in the late 1990s was Plotkin's *A Change in the Weather.* This short and introspective work seemed to indicate that interactive fiction could take a different path. Still, Cadre said of *A Change in the Weather* that he "didn't actually like it much," finding something lacking in Plotkin's "left-brained lyricism" as it was expressed in that work, where the interactor had to figure out how to assemble a bridge. He went on to traverse Nelson's *Curses* and *Jigsaw* and Gareth Rees's *Christminster* in quick succession. "I concluded that all IF was written by British mathematics professors," said Cadre (2001), a native of California who graduated from Berkeley, "so I wanted to do something trashy and quintessentially American."

That's what he did in his first IF work, *I-0 (Interstate Zero),* which won the Best Game XYZZY Award in 1997. It was set in the desert, on the quintessentially American open road, in the fictitious Western state of Dorado. The player character is the succulently named college student Tracy Valencia; the initial situation finds her stuck in the desert heat, her car having broken down on her way home near the end of her first semester. (This places Tracy directly between two stereotypical IF environments: the college campus and one's own house.) Volker Blasius added an illustrative (and unofficial) subtitle when the work was added to the Interactive Fiction Archive; it is listed there as *I-0: Jailbait on the Interstate.* Cadre (2001) believes that most of what is compelling about *I-0* is its nature as a sort of text-based "virtual reality," an interesting simulation that has little to do with solving puzzles or discovering alternate plot progressions and more to do with simply offering the situation "you're a cute chick. What do you want to do?" Indeed, numerous possibilities for action, some of which would normally be met with a computer-generated polite refusal, are available. One can choose to have Tracy hitchhike or walk in search of help, for instance, but the interactor can also have her remove her clothes. While Cadre was working on a larger, darkly comedic work after *I-0* came out, his next release would be not be remembered for its humor or for this sort of "anything goes" capability.

As Cadre (2001) put it, "Whatever people think about *Photopia,* it isn't about hacking apart trolls." People in the IF community have thought a great deal about Cadre's pseudonymous 1998 entry in the IF Competition, which won first place. Its short, differently colored segments can only be experienced in one order, and it's not clear at first why they're being experienced. First the player character is a drunken fraternity boy in the passenger seat, beside a similar character. In the next segment, the player character is a female astronaut exploring a red planet; the world is presented with a sort of warm, pedantic narration in which difficult terms are explained in parentheses. Cadre (2001) cites Christopher Priest (who writes for comics) and the influence of

> the "Priest plot": a type of storytelling in which not only is chronology mixed up, but at the beginning, you don't even really know what you're looking at as you read ... but gradually you piece together who the characters are, what the events you've just witnessed mean, and by the end of the story, you can't imagine it any other way—the details have been related in exactly the right order for maximum effect.

What is unusual about *Photopia* is not that it has many IF worlds—although this is more noticeable here than in most previous works—but that it has no "frame" world. Instead, *Photopia* begins with the text "'Will you read me a story?' 'Read you a story? What fun would that be? I've got a better idea: Let's tell a story together.'" Arrows and shifts of color (in interpreters that support color) signal the transition to a new IF world. In terms of its subject matter, Cadre has named Atom Egoyan's movie *The Sweet Hereafter*, with its babysitter protagonist, as the main influence on *Photopia*. (Alison, the girl who is the main character in *Photopia*, is always seen as a non-player character; she is never controlled by the interactor.) He noted that Robert C. O'Brien's *A Report from Group 17* inspired his technique of presenting this main character from the perspective of those who adore her, making the reader more likely to care about her even when few events are related and when little descriptive text is provided. Specific characters and puzzles have their background in books, also; Ron Hansen's *Mariette in Ecstasy* is the basis for the puzzle in the sky blue segment, for example (Cadre 2001). *Photopia* has been translated to Spanish by an IF author who goes by the name Zak.

Cadre, whose first novel *Ready, Okay!* was published in 2000, has some background in programming as well as writing, and a strong interest in comics and gaming. He attended a high school magnet program in computer science, coding some computer games (none of which were interactive fiction) early on. Adventure games are not even Cadre's favorites on the computer; he has confessed that his favorite computer game is the space exploration game *Star Control II:* "The sense of discovery and solitude in that experience was the closest I've ever come to being there," Cadre said of the predecessor, *Starflight* (2001). He said that in high school he spent almost every weekend playing non-computer strategy games—"Axis and Allies, Diplomacy, Fortress America, Supremacy, and infinite home-grown variants of Risk, with 'Colony Risk' being most popular" (2001). Cadre named the graphic novel *Watchmen* by Alan Moore and Dave Gibbons as his favorite book.

In yet another very different Cadre work, *Varicella* (winner of the Best Game XYZZY Award in 1999) the single IF world is a palace that seems, at first, to be from the Renaissance. Slowly the interactor notices anachronistic elements here and there, and the nature of this IF world becomes increasingly clear. Primo Varicella, the player character, is a palace minister, scheming to gain the regency after the king's very recent demise. *Varicella* introduced a great improvement over the (unfortunately influential) menu-based system of conversation in *Photopia*. *Varicella* allowed the interactors not only to *ask* and *tell* characters about topics of their choice (as in the more conversationally capable *Deadline* and other Infocom detective stories) but also to specify a *servile, cordial,* or *hostile* tone.

There are wonderful non-player characters to converse with, too, who invite conversation by their appearance and presentation, and there is also a need to converse with them in order to figure out the intricate challenges posed by Varicella's rivals. A companion, helper, and trickster figure who is first encountered in the palace asylum is a standout (Montfort and Moulthrop 2003), but even the minor non-player characters have much to offer.

One difficulty in the conception of *Varicella* is that the player character's level of knowledge is so much greater than that of the controlling interactor: This character is supposed to know everything about his rivals and about the palace itself, while the interactor knows nothing at first. Cadre handles this challenging gap in knowledge quite deftly, turning it to some advantage by loading each text that is generated with something that hints at the nature of the IF world or of the player character, who is greatly concerned with outward appearances. In *Varicella,* even trying to go in a direction where there is no exit is amusing: "You walk into a solid wall. How unseemly!" While *Varicella* proves quite difficult to traverse successfully, even finding new ways to wander around and get killed can be a joy—not just because it amuses, as the player character's death frequently did in certain graphical adventure games, but because it adds to the interactor's understanding of the world. Primo Varicella can be commanded to kill, or try to kill, anyone—he is that sort of guy—just as Tracy Valencia can be made to remove her clothes on the side of the road, if that's what the interactor types.

Cadre has also released numerous smaller IF works, including *Shrapnel* (set in a house that seems, at first, to be the one from *Zork*), *9:05* (set in another house), and *TextFire Golf* (referring to the TextFire hoax) as well as more recent multimedia pieces.

NEW DIRECTIONS

Besides exploring smaller worlds and works that have shorter successful traversal times than were seen in commercial and early academic works, authors have also taken on a broader range of themes and subjects, worked in new genres, developed certain aspects (like non-player characters) much more thoroughly, and attempted new sorts of formal innovation. This last look at some of the most recent efforts of independent IF creators includes work that—while it is too early to see its influence on the development of the form over the long term—demonstrates the vitality of interactive fiction today.

By taking interactive fiction to one extreme, it is possible to create a work that allows for *at most* one command from the interactor during any traversal; in such a work, the first reply is also the final reply. This seems to have been done first by Sam Barlow, whose *Aisle* (released in 1999) places the player character in a supermarket. Almost any command is properly handled, but after the reply to that command is generated nothing further can be narrated; the world reverts to the initial situation. There is nothing to solve, but many interesting texts wait to be revealed. Not only can different replies result in radically different courses for the brief generated narrative, they can also reveal that the initial situation is actually different depending upon the command provided. The loop cannot be interrupted, as a similar loop is in the movie *Groundhog Day;* in that movie, the main character eventually escapes from the longer repeating circumstance, which always begins with the same suppositions. While interactors found Barlow's approach fascinating (and certainly worth the slight effort and commitment of time that was involved in interacting with *Aisle* a few times), it seemed that *Aisle* had exhausted this "one command only" format of interactive fiction. Then, in 2000, Andrew Pontius released *Rematch,* a puzzle-based one-move work of interactive fiction. It required the interactor to figure out, over several one-move traversals that ended with the player character's (or his friends') death, what one complex action would work to save the group from its seemingly unlikely but imminent fate.

Another recent direction for interactive fiction has involved new sorts of parody. Today's IF community considers the canonical IF parody to be by C. E. Forman. He entered *Mystery Science Theater 3000 Presents "Detective"* in the first IF Competition in 1995. This lampooned Matt Barringer's buggy and bizarre 1993 *Detective,* à la *Mystery Science Theater.* There had been earlier parodies, such as David Malmberg's 1988 *Pork 1: The Great Underground Sewer System* (a *Zork I* parody done in AGT) and the 1986 work *The Boggit* by Fergus McNeill and Judith Child, a commercial piece of software developed in The Quill that specifically parodied the interactive fiction *The Hobbit* from Melbourne House. More complex parodical projects took shape in the late 1990s, when a whole fake interactive fiction company was formed. On 1 April 1998, the "TextFire 12-Pack" appeared in the /games/demos directory of the Interactive Fiction Archive. In the twelve short IF works (developed in Inform, TADS, and Hugo), which purported to offer previews of upcoming commercial interactive fiction, typing *about* would elicit short and funny bios of the purported authors. The readme file that came in the pack promised that TextFire would have a booth at the upcoming First Annual Festival of Interactive Fiction. After great discussion and speculation on the newsgroups, the parties responsible for the hoax were finally revealed (Britton 1998). Although the works themselves— which include *Revenge of the Killer Surf Nazi Robot Babes from Hell, Zugzwang: The Interactive Life of a Chess Piece,* and *Verb!*—are tiny and offer only brief amusement, the project, however loose a collaboration it was, was still the first large-scale collaboration of authors from the independent era. A similar large-scale parody was released on 1 January 2001: the Interactive Fiction Arcade, with sixteen works that provided textual versions of arcade favorites. But the April Fools Day offering found in the 1999 archive was a *Coke Is It!,* a conflation of segments from many other interactive fiction works by independents, augmented so as to amusingly incorporate product placement.

The most significant work in creating non–player characters that function in new and effective ways has been done by a classics Ph.D. candidate who uses the pseudonym Emily Short in the IF community. Short, who is editing a forthcoming book of essays from the IF community on craft, history, and theory, has released works with intriguing and puzzling IF worlds, including her 2000 *Metamorphoses* and her 2002 *Savoir Faire*. Authors and players have shown the most interest, however, in her implementation of interactive conversations. Her *Galatea,* which won Best of Show in the 2000 Interactive Fiction Art Show, featured a living statue. The player character, who approaches this eponymous statue in a museum, can take a few of the typical adventure-game actions and can also converse with Galatea by asking or telling her about certain topic words. While the language that can be understood by the work is very limited, *Galatea* implemented a complex discourse model and an emotional model, with variables for Galatea's mood, her sympathy with the player character, and the amount of tension. Depending upon what topics had already been discussed and what the current topic and emotional levels were, a wide range of different conversations, leading to very different conclusions, could ensue.

If taken to their conclusions they can in these different cases reveal different, even contradictory assumptions that the IF world was founded upon. In one final reply, Galatea would be seen to be a fake, in others, a magical or mythological being, and in yet others she would seem to be an artificial intelligence on display in a technology (not an art) exhibit.

Galatea essentially provides a chatterbot with a more sophisticated architecture for behavior than had been seen in IF before; the statue's presence in an IF world is not very important to the work and the interaction. But *Galatea* does begin to unite new sorts of discourse and emotional modeling with the usual sorts of world modeling; that such an impressive chatterbot was implemented as a non-player character in interactive fiction, rather than as a stand-alone system, is a good sign for the form.

Short introduced a new conversation system in her 2001 *Best of Three.* In that work, the potential conversation was also well implemented, but the situation of the player character was less than compelling and provided the interactor with too little motivation—a difficulty in the puzzleless *Galatea* as well, although one that some interactors worked around by devising a challenge for themselves and attempting to find every possible final reply.

Another IF author who has released impressive works recently is Jon Ingold, a recent graduate of Cambridge University. His 1999 *My Angel* used a "NOVEL mode" in which new text produced by the computer would appear as normal prose sentences would, sometimes being added to the end of the current paragraph and sometimes to the beginning of a new paragraph. The interactor's input is not incorporated into this text. The result is a generated text that looks much like a passage from literary fiction. The player character communicates with a strange presence in this generated story; flashbacks are employed at times.

In Ingold's 2001 *All Roads*, winner of that year's Interactive Fiction Competition, the player character seems to be some sort of entity who shifts between the minds of different people in Renaissance Italy, controlling them; from the beginning, though, as this character's "host" waits on the gallows, about to be hanged, it is not clear to either the interactor or the player character exactly what is going on.

While Ingold (1999) has said he seeks "puzzles that . . . integrate well into the story" and while he does manage to devise such puzzles, his works, for all their innovation in structure and interface, do not yet bring puzzles together with the process of generating narratives as powerfully as in the riddle-like works of Plotkin. Nor are the generated prose and the possible narratives exceptional when considered as a whole, although some of the descriptive text in *All Roads* creates compelling images of light and shadow. Ingold's main contribution so far has been in his greater sensitivity to the levels of the interactor's and player character's awareness, as seen in the way he provides for a confused player character whose thoughts clarify as the interactor traverses *My Angel,* and in the way he provides for the interactor's level of awareness, at crucial times, to exceed that of one of the player characters in *All Roads,* as this understanding gradually rises to the level of the work's mastermind. Fortunately, in neither case do these structural clarifications, satisfying as they may be on certain levels, completely answer the deeper, complex questions raised by these two IF worlds.

Other recent developments have included development systems themselves. Andrew Plotkin's Glulx offers a way around the harsh memory limits of the Z-machine. Instead of compiling Inform programs to Z-machine targets, programmers can compile Inform to Plotkin's cross-platform Glulx virtual machine, which allows files to be up to 4 gigabytes and provides—using Plotkin's Glk interface standard and his Blorb standard for packaging multimedia resources—the ability for programmers to integrate nontextual media elements. Meanwhile, a similarly expanded version 3 of TADS (called T3) neared completion in 2002. The virtual machine for that system was completed in 2001, with ports to several platforms being made early the next year. There is also further development of systems that have smaller followings than TADS or Inform but have seen recent use: the shareware system ADRIFT by Campbell Wild, which runs on Windows and is popular with non-programmers, and the more capable cross-platform multimedia system Hugo by Kent Tessman. New interpreters for many of the existing formats are also being developed and released: 2002 saw the release of new Z-machine interpreters Zoom (for several platforms) and Windows Frotz, for instance.

Efforts have also been made to offer IF works to interactors outside the IF community. They include hosting IF readings and in other ways bringing interactive fiction to the attention of the computer literature community, activities in which this author has often been involved. (The readings involving interactive fiction have included the Boston T1 Party, the readings in New York City sponsored by Wiresight, and a reading at UCLA sponsored by the Electronic Literature Organization.) David Cornelson has started the IF Library, a Web site and small press offering manuals to aid IF authors. While About.com shut down its IF site, which had been run by Stephen Granade, that author continues to offer Web resources to the community at his new site, Brass Lantern.

Rumors of the death of interactive fiction have been greatly exaggerated. Although it is easy to find unimaginative recent works of interactive fiction, it is hard not to notice the formal, thematic, computational, and literary innovation that is happening today and that promises to continue.

EIGHT

INTERACTIVE FICTION IN OUR CULTURE

Throughout this book several connections between interactive fiction and its cultural context have been discussed. This final chapter seeks to explain in a bit more depth how interactive fiction has influenced other aspects of computing and other sorts of cultural production. The chapter closes with some predictions regarding the future of interactive fiction—not in terms of what the shape of individual works will be like or even what sorts of creative trends will predominate, but concerning, rather, the place the form might occupy within computing and literature.

In Computing and Beyond

MUDs and MOOs, online social spaces that simulate worlds just as interactive fiction does but that involve multiple characters controlled by different people, have recently received some attention from scholars. These systems are direct descendants of interactive fiction. Specifically, the "D" in "MUD" stands for *Zork*. MUDs are sometimes euphemistically called "Multiple User Dimensions" or "Multiple User Domains," but as everyone who has been involved with these environments for a while knows, the acronym actually stands for "Multiple User Dungeons," as it did when the first MUD was developed by Roy Trubshaw and Richard Bartle at England's Essex University in 1979. As Bartle explains, "The 'D' does stand for 'Dungeon', but not because the original MUD (which I co-wrote) had a dungeon in it; rather it was because there was a hacked-up version of Zork doing the rounds at the time, which bore the name 'Dungeon'" (qtd. in Smith and Cowan 1999). These environments were similar to works of interactive fiction, but multiple interactors could log on at the same time and interact with one another. The nature of the experience changed dramatically as a result, and interacting with others, rather than interacting directly with the simulated world, became the really important aspect of most MUDs. The advent of MOOs (with MOO standing for "MUD Object Oriented") brought a powerful new paradigm to this virtual space, making it easier for many MUD users to create new objects on MUDs and to carve out their own virtual spaces. Although the presence of multiple interactors makes many things about the MUD or MOO experience different from the experience of an IF work, those systems have many affinities with IF works. Studies of one of these types of systems will surely yield results about textual and interactive properties that will apply to the other.

The influence of interactive fiction on different sorts of computer games has already been discussed with reference to the graphical adventure game, of the sort that Sierra and LucasArts pioneered and that, in one fairly simple formulation, Robin and Rand Miller's *Myst* (1994), attained widespread popularity. But another type of computer game, the RPG or role-playing game, also drew its inspiration from the first work of interactive fiction, *Adventure*. One very influential early RPG, *Rogue*, used letters and other characters to visually depict the map of a dungeon, through which the intrepid adventurer (represented by '@') quests. To move, the player presses individual keys. Michael Toy and Glenn Wichman developed the game in 1980. In the 1980s it was ported to many different computers.

> Most of the existing adventure-type games had "canned" adventures—they were exactly the same every time you played, and of course the programmers had to invent all of the puzzles, and therefore would always know how to beat the game. We decided that with Rogue, the program itself should "build the dungeon", giving you a new adventure every time you played, and making it possible for even the creators to be surprised by the game. (Wichman 1997)

This *Adventure*-inspired game in turn was an inspiration for computer role-playing games, although not the only one. Richard Garriott, who created the popular *Ultima* series of computer RPGs at his company Origin (using the pseudonym Lord British) had programmed a similar sort of game using graphics on his Apple II in 1979, when he was in high school. For that game, called *Akalabeth,* Garriott drew inspiration from *Dungeons and Dragons*. *Adventure* was one of several predecessors to computer RPGs, however, which have (along with the ideas of the MUD and MOO) led to a successful new format, the MMORPG or Massively Multiplayer Online Roleplaying Game, of which *EverQuest* and *Ultima Online* are examples.

One sign of the pervasive influence of *Adventure* and interactive fiction is seen in the way it influenced the most talked-about information system of the 1990s. Tim Berners-Lee, who conceived of and originally implemented the World Wide Web, was inspired by interactive fiction in his work, as seen when he tested his earlier system, Enquire. Two of the original developers of the World Wide Web wrote that "Tim made bits of labyrinthine hyper-routes in Enquire that served no better purpose than to exploit the program's capacity for making them. 'I made mazes of twisty little passages all alike,' he explains, 'in honour of Adventure'" (Gillies and Cailliau 2000, 170). In his original proposal for the Web, Berners-Lee (1989) described the way Enquire worked in terms of *Adventure:* "In 1980, I wrote a program . . . Enquire . . . it allowed one to store snippets of information, and to link related pieces together in any way. To find information, one progressed via the links from one sheet to another, rather like in the old computer game 'adventure.'"

Interactive fiction has been used extensively in education to teach students about computers and about language; interactors have encountered it in the middle-school classroom (e.g., Desilets 1999) and, as was already mentioned in chapter 4, it has been used for programming exercises at the university level. Interactive fiction has also served in less formal educational roles as an introduction to the computer. As a curator once commented in conversation, *Adventure* teaches two essential principles of computing: Try absolutely everything you can think of and save all the time. It has been the inspiration for some people to learn to program and to discover more about the workings of computers. Interactive fiction has also been used to aid in language learning, both in classroom contexts and independently by individuals. Graphical adventure games that do not accept natural language input have been developed especially for language learning; *No Recuerdo* by Douglas Morgenstern and Janet Murray is an early example. Begun in 1984, this interactive video work has the interactor play a journalist who interviews characters in Colombia, selecting choices from a list. Foreign-language interactive fiction works are particularly well suited to language learning since interactive fiction requires input in the language being learned as well as comprehension of the text that is presented. (If the text isn't really understood, puzzles cannot be solved.) Of course a program that accepts grammatically incorrect input is not as tolerable in a situation like this, since it could reinforce poor usage. Still, interactive fiction has obvious potential in this situation and in many sorts of educational situations related to language and computing. Perhaps it can also help students develop cognitive skills and aid in teaching about other sorts of subject matter that can be simulated in textually presented worlds. These computerized riddles should turn out to be helpful teachers in many new circumstances.

Interactive fiction has influenced the incidents in and the style of at least one important work of hypertext fiction, Stuart Moulthrop's *Victory Garden*. An "interactive dream" sequence in this work—an IF-like experience that is the result of a university research project—is told in the second person, as is typical in interactive fiction. *Adventure* has also been an important part of a play; the 1990 *PICK UP AX* by Anthony Clarvoe is a period piece (set in the frenzied Silicon Valley of the early 1980s) in which one of the programmers, Keith, plays a work of interactive fiction like *Adventure,* complete with dwarves and axes. During the play he learns to turn his thinking about computing and his mastery of the game world into action in dealing with the other characters, suggesting that the experience of interactive fiction can have meaning beyond the computer's screen (Jerz 2000b).

In print fiction, Jayne Loader's 1989 short story "Wild America" twisted the typical text adventure in a different way:

> You are a thirty-year-old *auto* worker in *Detroit, Michigan*. Ten years ago you married a fellow worker. You now have two children. A year ago, your factory closed. Neither you nor your spouse were able to find other employment. Your unemployment insurance has run out. Although your savings are gone, you do not qualify for welfare. You've already sold your lakeside cabin. Now the bank is

threatening to take away your house, the car dealership to repossess your car, and the furniture store to confiscate all your furniture, including the TV set. To top it off, your baby needs an operation!

You may now begin your adventure. I will be your eyes and hands. Direct me with commands of one or two words. If you need help type HELP. To see how you're doing type SCORE.

Although one critic finds that Loader's story is an attack on the lack of interactivity in interactive fiction (Sloane 2000), this reading is at best questionable. The story, presenting a doomed interactor who can do nothing to escape fate, certainly does comment on this lack of freedom, as many interactive fiction works themselves do. As one scholar has written in a note on the Web, "It would almost seem superfluous to point out that Loader is using this image of the illusion of agency in interactive fiction as an allegory for the illusion of freedom offered by capitalist America—an ethical engagement not with a literary form, but with a political system and the ethics of claims of 'equal opportunity' and freedom for all" (Edelmann 2000). Here, then, is another example of how the form of interactive fiction has already been used effectively as a figure outside interactive fiction itself, in a short story.

Interactive fiction's influence is felt in numerous other books. One is the memoir *Extra Life: Coming of Age in Cyberspace* by David Bennahum (1998). That book's chapter 6, "Dungeon," is structured as a commentary on a transcript of interaction with *Zork* (specifically, with the freely available FORTRAN version called *Dungeon*). Bennahum uses that chapter not as a framework for a social commentary unrelated to computing, as Loader did, but to discuss his experience as an interactor and to describe the way the computer created a separate space for him, apart from the outside social world he lived in. The memoir's final chapter is titled "Beyond Zork."

Even more interesting is the way the experience of interactive fiction is woven by Richard Powers into his novel *Plowing the Dark,* which deals with virtual reality as it is being implemented by a sprawling company in a space called the Cavern. There are several allusions and formal connections to interactive fiction, which is important throughout as an early virtual reality development using text and is deeply related to the book's central questions and themes. The form makes its most obvious appearance in chapter

16, which begins with the first diegetic text from *Adventure:* "You are stand-ing at the end of a road before a small brick building." This sentence comes to Jackdaw Acquerelli as a message on his computer. He remembers his first encounter with *Adventure* as an eleven-year-old, having been brought to an office to interact with it (much as Graham Nelson was) and finding himself "at the base camp of pure possibility" (Powers 2001, 105); there, he found *Adventure* to be "nothing less than the transcendental Lego set of the human soul, its pieces infinite in both number and variety" (106). Then came his dis-appointment at how little was actually simulated, although that gave way to "challenge. Another hour, and challenge became obsession" (107). He recalls how his obsession with textual interactive fiction continued, how disap-pointed he was at the arrival of graphical works, and how this passion led him to the work he does now. The grown-up Jackdaw plays *Adventure* with and for a remote audience, but mostly he plays at remembering it with others. Those on the system type fragments back and forth until they confess in a flurry of messages, at the end of the chapter, that none of them ever made it to the end of *Adventure.*

The previous examples should suffice to show that interactive fiction can and already does have some meaning in computer literature and in other literary arts, and that it does not exist apart from our culture as a mere curiosity.

The Future of Interactive Fiction

"We are standing at the beginning of a new fusion of technology and liter-ature" (185), wrote Gary McGath in 1984, continuing with pages of predic-tions about what interactive fiction would be like in years to come—almost all of them wrong. Increased realism, one improvement McGath thought interactors would see, is not a notable feature of later commercial or inde-pendent works; nor has the turn-based system of interaction been discarded as McGath said it might be. In some ways recent efforts have improved upon the simulation of characters and the range of alternatives; interestingly, the best work in these two areas was done after the commercial era ended. A decade later another author naïvely predicted, based on the direction of research at the Oz Project, that interactive fiction would become more "highly interactive," interruptable at any point or else asynchronous and no longer based on turns. This author also mistakenly believed that graphical adventure games might seek ways to integrate the richness of textual communication into the experience. (In fact, such ideas might be borne out in *Façade,* which is in many ways the culmination of the Oz Project.) But given how foolish these particular predictions (Montfort 1995) now look when considering the mass of work that has recently been done in the form, this author is not about to continue in the same vein in this book.

Speculation about what sort of interactive fiction will be created in years to come not only is usually unproductive, but can also be counterproductive. To blithely mention the riddle of a hypothetical IF work effectively ruins the work for any future interactors who read such a prognostication. The supposedly hypothetical work that is so ruined may in fact already be in development, and babbling about what form a future work might take would be the most painful sort of spoiler for an author who is already trying to realize that work. The only real indicators of the future of interactive fiction will be new works from IF authors. Still, there are questions about the future of interactive fiction that are worth pondering. Among them is the matter of whether IF will be seen only as a pleasant and addictive hobby or also as a meaningful art—just "fun" or perhaps "spiritually uplifting" as well, to use Marc Blank's terms (Dyer 1984). There is also the broader question of whether, in the future, the computer will be seen by the general reading populace as a form of potential literature or as one that is capable of providing the sorts of experiences that literary readers value.

WHY CREATE INTERACTIVE FICTION?

Interactive fiction is certainly alive and well, but the reason most interactive fiction is created today can be summed up as *to amuse the initiated.* Looking to the Interactive Fiction Competition as the main context for publication of interactive fiction today, one easily sees that IF works are written for a small group of people already familiar with the form, and the main, if not only, concern is whether that group quickly finds such works enjoyable. Having entered the Interactive Fiction Competition, I do not at all seek to place myself above such a motive. Nor is this motivation somehow an impure or base one. A poet might similarly write an occasional poem to amuse friends or family; this is part of the life of poetry. However, such a purpose hardly defines the limit of poetry.

Ultimately, the most profound impulse to create any art (including interactive fiction) may simply be irrational. It may be a compulsion to decorate the terrifying, as seen in the ornamenting of the destructive machine portrayed in Robert Pinsky's poem "The Figured Wheel." Adam Cadre met the absurdity of the question "Why do you write interactive fiction?" with an amusing answer on rec.arts.int-fiction: "To impress Jodie Foster." Perhaps the desire to write interactive fiction at the turn of the century is, as this reference to John Hinckley's motivation suggests, pathological. The impulse to create interactive fiction already is, and will likely continue to be, as broad and difficult to establish as is the motivation for creating any art, in however usual or unusual a form, however popular or obscure it may be. But certainly it can exceed the narrow type of motivation described earlier. IF works have already shown wonder; in the future they might continue to be created because of metaphysical or political concerns, to explore the relationship between people and computers or between people and texts, to describe utopian as well as dystopian worlds, and to express or challenge cultural notions.

IF BEYOND THE MARKET, BEYOND USENET

Discussion on rec.arts.int-fiction and rec.games.int-fiction sometimes turns to matters of money and to questions of whether or not interactive fiction can be viable in the marketplace again. Few people who consider the topic seriously think that it can be, and there are many people in the IF community who would prefer, regardless of its commercial potential, that the form remain on the margins. Some authors and interactors would rather have interactive fiction be a hobby for a group of enthusiasts. They see that wider popularity and interest from other sectors (commercial or academic) risks dissolving or weakening the current community.

Commercial interactive fiction in the future would have to take a very different shape than it did in the 1980s. If interactive fiction did somehow become more widespread as a result of such a commercial venture, this might change the nature of today's community, since the somewhat esoteric nature of interactive fiction is part of what defines this group. However, the future of interactive fiction in our culture is not limited to only two options—a commercial boom or the continued existence of *only* a single group of fans calling itself "the IF community." There is another possibility for more widespread appreciation of the form, which would neither require a miraculous business breakthrough nor dissipate the group of interactors and authors involved with interactive fiction today. New sorts of interactors might come to appreciate the form and to author works in it through a route other than physical or virtual software stores.

Already, different language communities are creating interactive fiction. There is also a community of blind interactors that is essentially separate from the group calling itself "the IF community" and that has its own online journal. There is another group of people who create and enjoy adult interactive fiction (AIF), which depicts sexual activity. The concept of *the* IF community as it is so often mentioned is in fact a myth; although such a group exists, it is one of several with an interest in interactive fiction. For academics and parties interested in literature to join in appreciating the form, and even authoring works, could easily add to the diversity of interactive fiction works available rather than simply ruining this one existing community.

Despite the fixation on commerce that Americans exhibit, other signs of success besides market share exist, even within our culture. Poetry is a good example of an art that is relevant to the everyday lives of Americans but has never been economically sustaining in this country, even for poets who are highly esteemed. Like poetry, interactive fiction does not need to be lucrative to become a form that helps us gain new realizations about our world, a form that is relevant to our lives. However, interactive fiction can benefit from institutional and cultural respect if it is to be a part of culture in the way that poetry is.

This author is one of several people working to bring legitimacy to the concept of computer literature, also called electronic literature—which includes interactive fiction and other forms based on the computer's ability to present different media according to rules and user input. Today, it is easy to go into many public libraries and use a computer to look up a phone number or consult a street map on the Web. It is also easy to pull a novel off the shelf at such a library, sit down, and start reading it. But many of the places that are most congenial to reading, such as the library, are not well suited for the experience of interactive fiction and other types of computer literature. Nor are librarians or booksellers prepared to advise readers about how to find works of computer literature that they might enjoy. There are other reasons that computer literature is a difficult concept for people to accept. A cultural bias against the computer as a literary medium exists; most people experience the computer as either a workplace fixture or a device for less cerebral entertainment in the form of video games. (Such games have their own interesting textures that are too often dismissed, and the way in which they structure the actions of one or more players is a woefully overlooked topic. Still, it is certainly the case that common preconceptions about what a computer game is and the common way in which such games are dismissed make it harder to accept the idea of computer literature.) Finally, there are a handful of purportedly anti-technology readers and critics who employ the machinery of the manual typewriter to denounce the computer. Such fetishists of gears and rollers can hardly be taken seriously, and the only popular trend they represent is a general fear—not of technology, obviously—but of the replacement of their familiar technologies (books as well as typewriters) with unfamiliar ones. Interactive fiction is hardly out to displace or replace the book in some simplistic way, and arguments assuming that it is will soon be seen as obsolete. What is more troubling is that many people who are capable computer users and who also enjoy literature have never even imagined that something like interactive fiction could be part of their literary and computing life.

The event described at the beginning of this book, the reading called the Boston T1 Party, held at the Boston Public Library, was one attempt to bring computer literature into a context that has traditionally supported literature, and to bring it to the attention of a new group of people. (Interactive fiction was represented along with many other forms at that event; eleven authors participated in reading from eight different works). As is the case for other forms of computer literature, while creative progress in interactive fiction is essential to the future of the form, such progress will be almost impossible, and will be for all practical purposes irrelevant, if the number of people with a deep interest in interactive fiction, worldwide, is only in the hundreds. The true popularity of computer literature—not its mass marketability or brazen promotion, but rather making works in the form available to those outside a narrow academic or newsgroup-based community—is an essential, not incidental, concern for all writers who use the computer as a medium for their work.

People promoting computer literature are not doing so just to show other people what is nice about this unusual literary purpose to which computers can be put, although that is one reason. The very concept of interactive fiction and computer literature more broadly makes the argument that the computer can be a device that challenges and enlarges us, a way of communicating powerful and disturbing and deeply necessary ideas. This argument answers the concept of the computer as a government-regulated entertainment device, a soothing palliative that can only emit family-safe and brand-conscious advertisements for mediocrity. This is the concept that the Disney Corporation and the motion picture industry are spending millions of dollars to promote among lawmakers; this is the very tyranny of thought that is opposed directly by an IF work like *A Mind Forever Voyaging*. It is opposed by the way interactive fiction is now created outside of corporate control by individuals from many different walks of life, worldwide. It is opposed as well by the shattered perceptions of *Suspended* that assert that things can be seen in different ways, and even by the way that product placement is mocked in *Coke Is It!* The trend to complacent entertainment is also challenged by the unanswerable terror beneath the surfaces of *Shade* and *Little Blue Men* and indeed by the very complexity and individuality of vision manifest in almost every large interactive fiction work of the last ten years.

As one of many forms of computer literature, interactive fiction has already offered vital and relevant worlds to fathom, riddles that challenge our assumptions, and machines that accept and produce texts so as to engage us with both their outputs and their workings. Given its history, it would come as no surprise if authors and interactors were to continue to pursue interactive fiction not only for fun but as a form that can offer transforming and profound experiences.

INTERACTIVE FICTION WORKS CITED

Note: Only text-based works of interactive fiction, the main topic of this book, are included in this list. Other digital works, including other sorts of computer games and other forms of electronic literature, can be found in the index or, if I have quoted from or paraphrased them, in the secondary sources bibliography.

The format of this list is based upon that used by Graham Nelson for a similar list in *The Inform Designer's Manual* (2001b). Since interactive fiction is more commonly recognized by title than by author, and since many commercial works were distributed without the authors' names even visible on the outside of the packaging, the title is given first. The date of original publication or distribution follows, or a date range if the work was developed over several years and made available in intermediate versions during that time. The names of the creators are given next. If the work was developed at a company or if it was done in a university context that was particularly significant, that institution is named next. However, the name of a university does not indicate that a work was an official product of the university. With the exception of the Oz Project text worlds, none of these works were. Although most IF works were or are available for a large number of different computers and operating systems, what is listed next is the platform for which a work was originally developed, which may be a single computer and operating system or a single virtual machine. The language in which the work was written is given after a solidus. If there was a publisher or distributor who is separate from the institution that developed the work, that information is given next. In the interest of brevity, this list omits other information that is of interest, such as the details of later ports and versions, the physical media on which some of these works were distributed, the file size, the number of rooms in the simulated space, and the other items (such as booklets and maps) that were packaged with some of these works.

If any functioning version of the work is available for download from the Interactive Fiction Archive as of 2003, "(IF Archive.)" is added at the end of the entry. Source code for platforms not currently in use and other resources may be available at the IF Archive even if this notation is not present, or the work may be available somewhere else online. Searching on Baf's Guide to the Interactive Fiction Archive <http://www.wurb.com/if/> will allow quick access to any of the works that are available there. Since ports of earlier works have been made and common interpreters for interactive fiction are widely available, almost all of the works that can be downloaded will run on any common computer and operating system.

9:05. 1999. Adam Cadre. Z-Machine/Inform. (IF Archive.)

Acheton. 1978-1981. Jon Thackray, David Seal, and Jonathan R. Partington; Cambridge University. IBM 370/Phoenix. Topologika, Acornsoft. (IF Archive.)

Adventure. 1975-1976. Will Crowther and Don Woods. PDP-1/FORTRAN. Numerous publishers; sometimes distributed as *Colossal Cave*. (IF Archive.)

Adventure Quest. Mike Austin, Nick Austin, and Pete Austin; Level 9. A-code. (IF Archive.)

Adventure in the Fifth Dimension. 1983. Brian Moriarty. *ANALOG* #11, November. Atari 400/BASIC.

Adventureland. 1978. Scott Adams; Adventure International. TRS-80/BASIC. (IF Archive.)

Aisle. 1999. Sam Barlow. Z-Machine/Inform. (IF Archive.)

All Roads. 2001. Jon Ingold. Z-Machine/Inform. (IF Archive.)

Amnesia. 1986. Thomas M. Disch, author and Kevin Bentley, programmer; Cognetics Corporation. Electronic Arts. KingEdward.

Arthur: The Quest for Excalibur. 1989. Bob Bates; Challenge, Inc. Z-Machine/ZIL. Infocom.

Avon. [1978?] Jon Thackray and Jonathan R. Partington; Cambridge University. IBM 370/Phoenix. Topologika, Acornsoft. (IF Archive.)

Babel. 1997. Ian Finley. TADS. (IF Archive.)

Bad Machine. 1998. Dan Shiovitz. TADS. (IF Archive.)

Ballyhoo. 1986. Jeff O'Neill; Infocom. Z-Machine/ZIL.

Being Andrew Plotkin. 2000. J. Robinson Wheeler. Z-Machine/Inform. (IF Archive.)

Best of Three. 2001. Emily Short. Glulx/Inform. (IF Archive.)

Beyond Zork: The Coconut of Quendor. 1987. Brian Moriarty; Infocom. Z-Machine/ZIL.

Boggit, The. 1986. Fergus McNeill and Judith Child; Delta 4 Software. The Quill. CRL Group PLC, Zenobi Software. (IF Archive.)

BrandX. 1979. Jonathan Mestel and Peter Killworth; Cambridge University. IBM 370/Phoenix. Distributed by Topologika, Acornsoft as *Philosopher's Quest.* (IF Archive.)

Breakers. 1986. Rod Smith, author, Joe Vierra and William Mataga, programmers; Synapse. BTZ. Brøderbund.

Brimstone: The Dream of Gawain. 1985. James Paul, author, David Bunch, William Mataga, and Bill Darrah, programmers; Synapse. BTZ. Brøderbund.

Bureaucracy. 1987. Douglas Adams; Infocom. Z-Machine/ZIL.

Change in the Weather, A. 1995. Andrew Plotkin. Z-Machine/Inform. (IF Archive.)

Christminster. 1995. Gareth Rees. Z-Machine/Inform. (IF Archive.)

Coke Is It! 1999. Adam Cadre, David Dyte, Michael Fessler, Dan Shiovitz, Lucian P. Smith, Adam Thornton, and J. Robinson Wheeler. Z-Machine/Inform. (IF Archive.)

Colossal Cave. See *Adventure.*

Corruption. 1988. Robert Steggles, Hugh Steers, Alan Hunnisett, and Richard Selby; Magnetic Scrolls. Rainbird.

CosmoServe: An Adventure Game for the BBS-Enslaved. 1991. Judith Pintar. AGT. (IF Archive.)

Crash Dive! 1984. Brian Moriarty. *ANALOG* #18, June. Atari 400/Assembly.

Crobe. 1986. Jonathan R. Partington; Cambridge University. IBM 370/Phoenix. (IF Archive.)

Curses. 1994-1995. Graham Nelson. Z-Machine/Inform. (IF Archive.)

Cutthroats. 1984. Michael Berlyn and Jerry Wolper; Infocom. Z-Machine/ZIL.

Cyborg. 1981. Michael Berlyn; Sentient Software. Apple II.

Deadline. 1982. Marc Blank; Infocom. Z-Machine/ZIL.

Detective. 1993. Matt Barringer. AGT. (IF Archive.)

Dog Star Adventure. 1979. Lance Micklus. TRS-80/BASIC. *Softside*, May. (IF Archive.)

Dr. Dumont's Wild P.A.R.T.I. 1988, 1999. Michael Berlyn and Muffy Berlyn. 1988 in C, 1999 in Z-Machine/Inform. First Row Software, Cascade Mountain Publishing. (IF Archive.)

Dungeon. See *Zork.* (IF Archive.)

Enchanter. 1983. Marc Blank and Dave Lebling; Infocom. Z-Machine/ZIL.

Eric the Unready. 1993. Bob Bates; Legend Entertainment. MS-DOS.

Essex. 1985. Bill Darrah, author and programmer, and William Mataga, programmer; Synapse. BTZ. Brøderbund.

Exhibition. 1999. Ian Finley. TADS. (IF Archive.)

Fahrenheit 451. 1984. Len Neufeld and Byron Preiss; based on the novel by Ray Bradbury; Trillium/Telarium.

FisK. 1982. Authors unknown; Stanford University. DEC-20.

Fish! 1988. John Molloy et al.; Magnetic Scrolls. Rainbird.

For a Change. 1999. Dan Schmidt. Z-Machine/Inform. (IF Archive.)

Frederik Pohl's Gateway. 1992. Mike Verdu, Michael Lindner and Glen Dahlgren; Legend Entertainment. MS-DOS.

Fyleet. 1986. Jonathan R. Partington; Cambridge University. IBM 370/Phoenix. (IF Archive.)

GC: A Thrashing Parity Bit of the Mind. 1993. Carl de Marcken, Dave Baggett, and Pearl Tsai; Massachusetts Institute of Technology. TADS.

Galatea. 2000. Emily Short. Z-Machine/Inform. (IF Archive.)

Gateway II: Homeworld. 1993. Mike Verdu and Glen Dahlgren; Legend Entertainment. MS-DOS.

Gnome Ranger. 1987. Pete Austin and Peter McBride; Level 9. KAOS.

Guild of Thieves, The. 1987. Rob Steggles, author, Ken Gordon, programmer, Geoff Quilley and Tristan Humphries, graphics; Magnetic Scrolls. Rainbird.

Hamil. 1980. Jonathan R. Partington; Cambridge University. IBM 370/Phoenix. Distributed by Topologika, Acornsoft as *Kingdom of Hamil.* (IF Archive.)

Haunt. 1979-1982. John Laird; Carnegie Mellon Univeristy. OPS-4.

Hezarin. 1980. Steve Tinney, Alex Ship, and Jon Thackray; Cambridge University. IBM 370/Phoenix.

Hi-Res Adventure. See *Mystery House.*

Hitchhiker's Guide to the Galaxy, The. 1984. Douglas Adams and Steve Meretzky; Infocom. Z-Machine/ZIL.

Hobbit, The. Veronika Megler and Philip Mitchell, based on the novel by J. R. R. Tolkien; Melbourne House. Inglish. (IF Archive.)

Hollywood Hijinks. 1986. Dave Anderson and Liz Cyr-Jones; Infocom. Z-Machine/ZIL.

Hunter, in Darkness. 1998. Andrew Plotkin. Z-Machine/Inform. (IF Archive.)

I-0 (Interstate Zero). 1997. Adam Cadre. Z-Machine/Inform. (IF Archive.)

Infidel. 1983. Michael Berlyn and Patricia Fogelman; Infocom. Z-Machine/ZIL.

James Clavell's Shogun. 1989. Dave Lebling; Infocom. Z-Machine/ZIL.

Jigsaw. 1995. Graham Nelson. Z-Machine/Inform. (IF Archive.)

John's Fire Witch. 1995. John Baker. TADS. (IF Archive.)

Knight Orc, The. 1987. Pete Austin; Level 9. KAOS.

Lancelot. 1988. Christina Erskin; Level 9. KAOS.

Leather Goddesses of Phobos. 1986. Steve Meretzky; Infocom. Z-Machine/ZIL.

Lists and Lists. 1996. Andrew Plotkin. Z-Machine/Inform. (IF Archive.)

Little Blue Men. 1998. Michael S. Gentry. Z-Machine/Inform. (IF Archive.)

Lord. 1981. Olli J. Paavola. DEC-20.

Lugi. Date unknown. Authors unknown; Stanford University. DEC-20.

Lurking Horror, The. 1987. Dave Lebling; Infocom. Z-Machine/ZIL.

Lyotard. 1992. Scott Neal Reilly and Joseph Bates; Carnegie Mellon University. LISP.

MacWesleyan. 1995. Neil deMause. TADS. (IF Archive.)

Martian Adventure. [1980?] Brad Templeton and Kieran Carroll; University of Waterloo. Honeywell Level 66/F.

Metamorphoses. 2000. Emily Short. Z-Machine/Inform. (IF Archive.)

Meteor, the Stone, and the Long Glass of Sherbert, The. 1996. Graham Nelson. Z-Machine/Inform. (IF Archive.)

Mind Forever Voyaging, A. 1985. Steve Meretzky; Infocom. Z-Machine/ZIL.

Mindwheel. 1984. Robert Pinsky, author, Steve Hales and William Mataga, programmers; Synapse. BTZ. Brøderbund.

Mist, The. 1985. Authors unknown, based on a novella by Stephen King; Angelsoft. ASG.

Moonmist. 1986. Stu Galley and Jim Lawrence; Infocom. Z-Machine/ZIL.

Murdac. Date unknown. Jon Thackray and Jonathan R. Partington; Cambridge University. IBM 370/Phoenix. Topologika, Acornsoft. (IF Archive.)

My Angel. 2000. Jon Ingold. Z-Machine/Inform. (IF Archive.)

Mystery House. 1980. Ken Williams and Roberta Williams. On-Line Systems (Sierra). Originally called *Hi-Res Adventure.* (IF Archive.)

Mystery Mansion. Date unknown. Bill Wolpert. HP–1000/FORTRAN. (IF Archive.)

Mystery Science Theater 3000 Presents "Detective." 1995. C. E. Forman. Z-Machine/Inform. (IF Archive.)

New Adventure. Date unknown. Marc Niemiec; University of Waterloo. Honeywell Level 66/F.

Nidus. 1987. Adam Atkinson; Cambridge University. IBM 370/Phoenix.

Nine Princes in Amber. 1985. Numerous authors; based on novels by Roger Zelazny; Telarium.

Nord and Bert Couldn't Make Head or Tail of It. 1987. Jeff O'Neill; Infocom. Z-Machine/ZIL.

Office Politics. [1994?] Scott Neal Reilly; Carnegie Mellon University. LISP.

Once and Future. 1998. G. Kevin Wilson. TADS. Cascade Mountain Publishing. (IF Archive.)

Oo-topos. 1981. Michael Berlyn and Muffy Berlyn; Sentient Software. Apple II. Penguin/Polarware. (IF Archive.)

Parc. Date unknown. Author unknown; Cambridge University. IBM 370/Phoenix.

Pass the Banana. 1999. Admiral Jota. Z-Machine/Inform.

Pawn, The. 1985. Rob Steggles; Magnetic Scrolls. Rainbird.

Philosopher's Quest. See *BrandX.*

Photopia. 1998. Adam Cadre. Z-Machine/Inform. (IF Archive.)

Pirate Adventure. 1978. Scott Adams and Alexis Adams; Adventure International. TRS-80/BASIC. (IF Archive.)

Planetfall. 1983. Steve Meretzky; Infocom. Z-Machine/ZIL.

Playground, The. [1994?] Scott Neal Reilly; Carnegie Mellon University. LISP.

Plundered Hearts. 1987. Amy Briggs; Infocom. Z-Machine/ZIL.

Pork 1: The Great Underground Sewer System. 1988. Anonymous. AGT. (IF Archive.)

Quondam. 1980. Ron Underwood; Cambridge University. IBM 370/Phoenix.

Rematch. 2000. Andrew D. Pontious. TADS. (IF Archive.)

Rendezvous with Rama. 1984. Ronald Martinez; based on the novel by Arthur C. Clarke; Trillium/Telarium.

Return to Eden. 1984. Nick Austin, Tim Noyce, and Chris Queen; Level 9. A-code.

Revenge of the Killer Surf Nazi Robot Babes from Hell. 1998. David Dyte; TextFire. Z-Machine/Inform. (IF Archive.)

Robbery World. [1994?] Scott Neal Reilly; Carnegie Mellon University. LISP.

Robots of Dawn. 1984. Jon Leupp; based on the novel by Isaac Asimov; Epyx.

Sangraal. 1987. Jonathan R. Partington; Cambridge University. IBM 370/Phoenix. Also called *Quest for the Sangraal.* (IF Archive.)

Save Princeton. 1991. Jacob Weinstein and Karine Schaefer. TADS. (IF Archive.)

Savoir Faire. 2002. Emily Short. Z-Machine/Inform. (IF Archive.)

Scapeghost. 1989. Sandra Sharkey, Pete Gerrard, and Pete Austin; Level 9. KAOS.

Seastalker. 1984. Stu Galley and Jim Lawrence; Infocom. Z-Machine/ZIL.

Shade. 2000. Andrew Plotkin. Z-Machine/Inform. (IF Archive.)

Sherlock: The Riddle of the Crown Jewels. 1987. Bob Bates; Challenge, Inc. Z-Machine/ZIL. Infocom.

Shrapnel. 2000. Adam Cadre. Z–Machine/Inform. (IF Archive.)

Six Micro Stories. 1980. Robert Lafore. TRS-80/BASIC. Adventure International.

Snowball. 1983. Mike Austin, Nick Austin, Pete Austin, and Ian Buxton; Level 9. A-code.

So Far. 1996. Andrew Plotkin. Z–Machine/Inform. (IF Archive.)

Softporn Adventure. 1981. Chuck Benton. Sierra. (IF Archive.)

Sorcerer. 1984. Steve Meretzky; Infocom. Z–Machine/ZIL.

Spellbreaker. 1985. Dave Lebling; Infocom. Z–Machine/ZIL.

Spellcasting 101: Sorcerers Get All the Girls. 1990. Steve Meretzky; Legend Entertainment.

Spellcasting 201: The Sorcerer's Appliance. 1991. Steve Meretzky; Legend Entertainment.

Spellcasting 301: Spring Break. 1992. Steve Meretzky; Legend Entertainment.

Spider and Web. 1998. Andrew Plotkin. Z–Machine/Inform. (IF Archive.)

Spycatcher. Date unknown. Jonathan R. Partington; Cambridge University. IBM 370/Phoenix.

Starcross. 1982. Dave Lebling; Infocom. Z–Machine/ZIL.

Stationfall. 1987. Steve Meretzky; Infocom. Z–Machine/ZIL.

Suspect. 1984. Dave Lebling; Infocom. Z–Machine/ZIL.

Suspended. 1983. Michael Berlyn; Infocom. Z-Machine/ZIL.

Tempest. 1997. Graham Nelson, writing as William Shakespeare. Z-Machine/Inform. (IF Archive.)

TextFire Golf. 1998. Adam Cadre; TextFire. Z-Machine/Inform. (IF Archive.)

Timequest. 1991. Bob Bates; Legend Entertainment. MS-DOS.

Trinity. 1986. Brian Moriarty; Infocom. Z-Machine/ZIL.

Uncle Zebulon's Will. 1995. Magnus Olsson. TADS. (IF Archive.)

Varicella. 1999. Adam Cadre. Z-Machine/Inform. (IF Archive.)

Verb! 1998. Neil deMause; TextFire. TADS. (IF Archive.)

Warp. Date unknown. Author unknown. HP-1000.

Wishbringer. 1985. Brian Moriarty; Infocom. Z-Machine/ZIL.

Witness, The. 1983. Stu Galley; Infocom. Z-Machine/ZIL.

Wonderland. 1990. David Bishop; Magnetic Scrolls. Magnetic Windows.

Worm in Paradise, The. 1985. Mike Austin, Nick Austin, and Pete Austin; Level 9. A-code.

Xeno. Date unknown. Jonathan Mestel; Cambridge University. IBM 370/Phoenix.

Xerb. Date unknown. Andrew Lipson; Cambridge University. IBM 370/Phoenix.

Zork. 1978-1979. Tim Anderson, Marc Blank, Bruce Daniels, and Dave Lebling; Massachusetts Institute of Technology. PDP-10/MDL. A FORTRAN port is called *Dungeon.* (IF Archive.)

Zork I: The Great Underground Empire. 1980. Marc Blank and Dave Lebling; Infocom. Z-Machine/ZIL.

Zork II: The Wizard of Frobozz. 1981. Marc Blank and Dave Lebling; Infocom. Z-Machine/ZIL.

Zork III: The Dungeon Master. 1982. Marc Blank and Dave Lebling; Infocom. Z-Machine/ZIL.

Zork Zero: The Revenge of Megaboz. 1988. Steve Meretzky; Infocom. Z-Machine/ZIL.

Zork: The Undiscovered Underground. 1997. Marc Blank and Michael Berlyn. Z-Machine/Inform. Activision. (IF Archive.)

Zugzwang: The Interactive Life of a Chess Piece. 1998. Magnus Olsson; TextFire. Z-Machine/Inform. (IF Archive.)

SECONDARY SOURCES

Aarseth, Espen. 1997. *Cybertext: Perspectives on Ergodic Literature.* Baltimore, MD: Johns Hopkins University Press.

Abrahams, Roger D. 1980. "Between the Living and the Dead." *Folklore Fellows Communications* 95(2): 224.

Adams, Rick. 2002. "A History of 'Adventure.'" Available online at <http://www.rickadams.org/adventure/a_history.html>.

Addams, Shay. 1984. "The Wizards of Infocom." *Computer Games* (February): 34–37, 52.

Adler, Darin. 1996. "20 Years of Computer Software." Available online at <http://www.spies.com/~darin/monologue.html>.

Agnes, Rogers. 1953. *How Come?* New York: Doubleday.

Amit, Ilan. 1996. "Squaring the Circle." In *Untying the Knot: On Riddles and Other Enigmatic Modes,* ed. Galit Hasan-Rokem and David Shulman, 284–293. New York: Oxford University Press.

Amonlirdviman, Kevin, ed. 1996. *How to Get Around MIT.* 27th ed. June.

Anderson, Tim. 1985a. "The History of Zork—First in a Series." *The New Zork Times* 4(1)(Winter): 6–7, 11. Available online at <http://www.csd.uwo.ca/~pete/Infocom/Articles/NZT/zorkhist.html>.

Anderson, Tim. 1985b. "The History of Zork—Second in a Series." *The New Zork Times* 4(2)(Spring): 3–5. Available online at <http://www.csd.uwo.ca/~pete/Infocom/Articles/NZT/zorkhist.html>.

Anderson, Tim. 2001. Personal interview. January 9. Cambridge, MA.

Apollodorus. 1921. *The Library.* Ed. and trans. Sir James George Frazer. Loeb Classical Library. Cambridge: Harvard University Press. Available online at <http://www.Perseus.tufts.edu/Texts/apollod.summ.html>.

Aristotle. 1961. *Poetics.* Trans. S. H. Butcher. Intro. Francis Fergusson. New York: Hill and Wang. Trans. Available online at <http://classics.mit.edu/Aristotle/poetics.html>.

Atkinson, George W. 1993. *Chess and Machine Intuition.* Norwood, NJ: Ablex.

Bachelard, Gaston. 1994. *The Poetics of Space.* Trans. Maria Jolas. Boston: Beacon Press.

Baggett, David. 1993. "NEW Unnkulian Unventures! Commerical Quality Text Adventures for FTP." Posted on <news://rec.games.int-fiction>. Message-ID 1nhkcpINN4mu @life.ai.mit.edu 9 March.

Baker, John. 1995. "Release of 'John's Fire Witch.'" Posted on <news://rec.arts.int-fiction>. Message-ID 3gi307$i0g@ixnews3.ix.netcom.com 30 January.

Barthes, Roland. 1974. *S/Z.* Trans. Richard Miller. New York: Hill and Wang.

Barthes, Roland. 1974. *The Pleasure of the Text.* Trans. Richard Miller. New York: Hill and Wang.

Baudrillard, Jean. 1983. *The Ecstacy of Communication.* New York: Semiotext[e].

Bennahum, David. 1998. *Extra Life: Coming of Age in Cyberspace.* New York: Basic Books.

Bennett, John M. 1990. "Early Computer Days in Britain and Australia—Some Autobiographical Snippets." *Annals of the History of Computing* 12(4): 281–285.

Berners-Lee, Tim. 1989. "Information Management: A Proposal." March. Available online at <http://www. w3.org/History/1989/proposal.html>.

Bolter, Jay. 2001. *Writing Space: Computers, Hypertext, and The Remediation of Print.* 2d ed. Mahwah, NJ: Lawrence Earlbaum Associates.

Bonner, Anthony. 1997. "What Was Llull Up To?" *Transformation-Based Reactive Systems Development,* 1– 14. 4th International AMAST Workshop on Real-Time Systems and Concurrent and Distributed Software, ARTS '97. Palma, Mallorca, Spain, May 21–23.

Briceño, Hector, Wesley Chao, Andrew Glenn, Stanley Hu, Ashwin Krishnamurthy, and Bruce Tsuchida. "Down from the Top of Its Game: The Story of Infocom, Inc." Available online at <http://web.mit.edu/6.933/www/Fall2000/infocom/infocom-paper.pdf>. December 15.

Britton, Susan. 1998. "The TextFire Hoax." Part of *The World of Interactive Fiction.* Available online at <http://www.igs.net/~tril/if/humor/textfire/>.

Brucker, Roger W., and Richard A. Watson. 1987. *The Longest Cave.* 2d ed. New York: Knopf.

Buckles, Mary Ann. 1985. Interactive Fiction: The Computer Storygame 'Adventure.' Ph.D. diss. University of California at San Diego.

Burroughs, William S. 2003. "The Cut-Up Method of Brion Gysin." In *The New Media Reader,* ed. Noah Wardrip-Fruin and Nick Montfort, 89–91. Cambridge, MA: The MIT Press. Originally published in *The Third Mind,* William S. Burroughs and Brion Gysin, 29–33. New York: Seaver Books, 1978.

Cadre, Adam. 1998. "The Photopia Phaq." Version 1.0. November 18. Available online at <http://adamcadre.ac/content/phaq.txt>.

Cadre, Adam. 2000. "Cascade Mountain Publishing." Calendar entry at adamcadre.ac for April 30. Available online at <http://adamcadre.ac/calendar/09582.html>.

Cadre, Adam. 2001. Personal interview. August 1. Brooklyn, NY.

Cadre, Adam. 2002a. Interview in *L'avventura è L'avventura*. January. Available online at <http://www.avventuretestuali.com/Interviste/Original/adam_cadre.htm>.

Cadre, Adam. 2002b. "Re: Default Parser Responses: How Do They Affect the Gaming/Authorship Experience?" Posted on <news://rec.arts.int-fiction>. Message-ID a11jtp$8kk$1@drizzle.com 3 January.

Campbell, P. Michael. 1987. "Interactive Fiction and Narrative Theory: Towards an Anti-Theory." *New England Journal and Bread Loaf Quarterly* 10: 76–84.

Campbell, Keith. 1988. Review of *Fish! Computer and Video Games*. August. Available online at <http://www.if-legends.org/%7Emsmemorial/legacy/articles.htm/cvg888.htm>.

Carbol, Roger. 2001. "Locational Puzzle Theory." Posted on <news://rec.arts.int-fiction>. Message-ID 82675075. 0110020840.12d1c469@posting.google.com 2 October.

Chatman, Seymour. 1975. "Towards a Theory of Narrative." *New Literary History* 6(2)(Winter): 295-318.

Clarvoe, Anthony. 1991. *PICK UP AX*. New York: Broadway Play Publishing.

Cohen, Shlomith. 1996. "Connecting Through Riddles, or the Riddle of Connecting." In *Untying the Knot: On Riddles and Other Enigmatic Modes,* ed. Galit Hasan-Rokem and David Shulman, 294–315. New York: Oxford University Press.

Cole, James. 1998. "Adam C. Engst on rec.arts.int-fiction." Posted on <news://rec.arts.int-fiction>. Message-ID 3527893f.4724 5355@news.netspace.net.au 5 April.

Cornhill Magazine. 1891. *Cornhill Magazine* 17(101)(July): 512–522. Available online at <http://home.pacific.net.au/~turner23/riddles.html>.

Cree, Graeme. 1995. Reviews of *Stationfall* and *Wishbringer*. *SPAG (Society for the Promotion of Adventure Games)* #5. April 19. Available online at <http://www.sparkynet.com/spag/backissues/SPAG5>.

Cree, Graeme. 2001. "Infonotes: Incredibly Niggling Facts About Infocom Games." November 11. Available online at <http://members.aol.com/graemecree/infobugs/infonote.htm>.

Crossley-Holland, Kevin, trans. 1993. *The Exeter Book Riddles*. Rev. ed. London: Penguin.

Crowe, Malcolm, trans. 1996. "The Verses of Heraclitus of Ephesus." *Systemist* 18: 161–176. Available online at <http://cis.paisley.ac.uk/crow-ci0/Articles/heraclitus.html>.

Crowther, Will. 1994. Interview by Katie Hafner. DJVU format. Available online at <http://ftp.archive.org/arpanet-o300/WC111.djvu>.

Darling, Sharon. 1985. "Inside View: Douglas Adams and Steve Meretzky—Designers Behind *The Hitchhiker's Guide to the Galaxy*." *COMPUTE!'s Gazette*. April. Available online at <http://www.atarimagazines.com/compute/gazette/198504-hitchhiker.html>.

DaCosta, Frank. 1982. *Writing BASIC Adventure Programs for the TRS-80*. Blue Ridge Summit, PA: Tab Books.

de Boer, Jelle Zeilinga, Jeffrey R. Hale, and John Chanton. 2001. "New Evidence of the Geological Origins of the Ancient Delphic Oracle (Greece)." *Geology* 29: 707–710.

de Bono, Edward. 1967. *New Think: The Use of Lateral Thinking in the Generation of New Ideas*. New York: Basic Books.

de Filippis, Michele. 1948. *The Literary Riddle in Italy to the End of the Sixteenth Century*. Berkeley: University of California Press.

de Filippis, Michele. 1953. *The Literary Riddle in Italy in the Seventeenth Century*. Berkeley: University of California Press.

de Filippis, Michele. 1967. *The Literary Riddle in Italy in the Eighteenth Century*. Berkeley: University of California Press.

de Geus, A. F., J. H. Jongean, and A. M. Koelmans. 1985. *Adventure Description Language: A New Way to Generate Adventure Games*. Wilmslow, UK: Sigma Press.

Desilets, Brendan. 1999. "Interactive Fiction vs. the Pause that Distresses: How Computer-Based Literature Interrupts the Reading Process Without Stopping the Fun." *Currents in Electronic Literacy* 1. Available online at <http://www.cwrl.utexas.edu/currents/spr99/desilets.html>.

Dewdney, A. K. 1989. "Turing Machines: The Simplest Computers." In *The Turing Omnibus: 61 Excursions in Computer Science*, 186–194. Rockville, MD: Computer Science Press.

Dickinson, Emily. 1960. *The Complete Poems of Emily Dickinson*, ed. Thomas H. Johnson. Boston: Little, Brown, and Company.

Disch, Thomas. 1990. Interviewed by Larry McCaffrey. In *Across the Wounded Galaxy: Interviews with Contemporary American Science Fiction Writers*, 105–129, ed. Larry McCaffrey. Urbana: University of Illinois Press.

Dornbrook, Mike. 2000. Conversation with author. February 10. MIT, Cambridge, MA.

Dorst, John D. "Neck-Riddle as a Dialogue of Genres: Applying Bakhtin's Genre Theory." *Journal of American Folklore* 96 (October–December): 413–433.

Douglas, J. Yellowlees. 2000. *The End of Books—Or Books Without End?: Reading Interactive Narratives*. Ann Arbor: University of Michigan Press.

Dyer, Richard. 1984. "Masters of the Game." *The Boston Globe Magazine*. May 6. Available online at <http://www.ifarchive.org/if-archive/infocom/articles/Globe84-text>.

Eames, Charles, and Ray Eames. 1973. *A Computer Perspective*. Cambridge: Harvard University Press.

Edelmann, Peter. 2000. Note on *Wild America*. Available online at <http://www.tao.ca/~peter/html/research/loader89_fic.htm>.

Filmore, Thomas. 1980. "The Play's the Thing . . ." In *Best of the Dragon: From The Strategic Review and The Dragon Vols. I & II,* 17. Consists of material first published in 1975–1978. Lake Geneva, WI: TSR Hobbies, Inc.

Fontenrose, Joseph. 1978. *The Delphic Oracle, Its Responses and Operations.* Berkeley: University of California Press.

Foust, John. 2001. "The UCSD P-System Museum." Available online at <http://www.threedee.com/jcm/psystem/>.

Friedland, Nat. 1984. "Coming Adventures: State-of-the-art Interactive Fiction." *Antic* 3(7)(November): 28. Available online at <http://www.atarimagazines.com/v3n7/Coming_Adventures.html>.

Frye, Northrop. 1976. *Spiritus Mundi.* Bloomington: Indiana University Press.

Gaiman, Neil. 1993. *Don't Panic: Douglas Adams & The Hitchhiker's Guide to the Galaxy.* London: Titan Books.

Galley, Stu. 1985. "The History of Zork—The Final(?) Chapter: MIT, MDL, ZIL, ZIP." *The New Zork Times* 4(3)(Summer) [misnumbered as 4(2)]: 4–5. Available online at <http://www.csd.uwo.ca/~pete/Infocom/Articles/NZT/zorkhist.html>.

Garfinkel, Simson. 1999. "Fountain of Ideas." *Technology Review* 102(3)(May/June): 82–85.

Genette, Gérard. 1980. *Narrative Discourse: An Essay in Method.* Trans. Jane E. Lewin. Ithaca, NY: Cornell University Press.

Georges, Robert A., and Alan Dundes. 1963. "Toward a Structural Definition of the Riddle." *Journal of American Folklore* 76(300)(April–June): 111–118.

Gildemeister, David. 1996. Email published in the "Letters" Section. *XYZZYnews* #8. March–April. Available online at <http://www.xyzzynews.com/xyzzy.8c.html>.

Gillies, James, and Robert Cailliau. 2000. *How the Web Was Born.* New York: Oxford University Press.

Glasser, David, maintainer. 2000. "Interactive Fiction Authorship [rec.arts.int-fiction] FAQ." March 27. Available online at <http://www.davidglasser.net/raiffaq/>.

Goetz, Phil. 1994. "Interactive Fiction and Computers." *Interactive Fantasy* 1, 98–115. Crashing Boar Books. Available online at <http://www.mud.co.uk/richard/ifan194.htm>.

Graetz, J. M. 1981. "The Origin of Spacewar." *Creative Computing.* August. Available online at <http://www. zorg.org/spacewar/origins.html>.

Granade, Stephen. 1999a. "History of IF: Scott Adams." *About.com.* June 28. Available online at <http://www. phy.duke.edu/~sgranade/about2/adventuregames.about .com/library/weekly/aa062899.htm>.

Granade, Stephen. 1999b. "History of IF: Level 9." *About.com.* July 19. Available online at <http://www. phy.duke.edu/~sgranade/about2/adventuregames.about. com/library/weekly/aa071999.htm>.

Granade, Stephen. 2001a. "What Killed Cascade Mountain Publishing?" *About.com.* May 8. Available online at <http://www.phy.duke.edu/~sgranade/about2/adventuregames. about.com/library/weekly/aa050800b.htm>.

Granade, Stephen. 2001b. "History of IF: Magnetic Scrolls." *About.com.* July 26. Available online at <http://www. phy.duke.edu/~sgranade/about2/adventuregames .about.com/library/weekly/aa072699.htm>.

Granade, Stephen. 2002. "A Brief History of Interactive Fiction." Poster. Design by Misty Granade. Timeline available online at <http://brasslantern.org/community/ history/timeline.html>.

Graves, David. 1987. "Second Generation Adventure Games." *The Journal of Computer Game Design.* 1(2)(August): 4–7. Available online at <http://www.tela.bc.ca/tads/ authoring/articles/graves1.html>.

Green, Bert F. Jr., Alice K. Wolf, Carol Chomsky, and Kenneth Laughery. 1963. "BASEBALL: An Automatic Question Answerer." In *Computers and Thought,* ed. Edward A. Feigenbaum and Julian Feldman, 207–216. New York: McGraw-Hill.

Greenlee, Steven. 1996. "Where Are They Now?" *Computer Game Review* (April), 82–88. Available online at <http://www.csd.uwo.ca/Infocom/Articles/where.html>.

Greville, Fulke. 2000. "Caelica #100." January. Available online at <http://slate.msn .com/id/68627/>.

Guest, Tim. 2002. "Mortal Kombat and the new narrative architecture." *The Telegraph*. May 18. Available online at <http://www.telegraph.co.uk/arts/main.jhtml?xml= /arts/2002/05/18/bacomp18.xml&sSheet=/arts/2002/05/18/Ixartleft.htm>.

Gutman, Dan. 1984. "Shoot Your Own Men! And Other Weird Ways to Play." *Computer Games*. December/January. Available online at <http://members.tripod.com/ ~gamesmuseum/texts/shootmen.txt>

Guy, Neil K. 2001. "A Brief History of Amateur IF." October 18. Available online at <http://www.tela.bc. ca/tads/authoring/articles/if-history.html>.

Gygax, Gary. 1980. "Gary Gygax on Dungeons & Dragons: Origins of the Game." In *Best of the Dragon: From The Strategic Review and The Dragon Vols. I & II*, 29. Consists of material first published in 1975–1978. Lake Geneva, WI: TSR Hobbies, Inc.

Gysin, Brion. 1982. *Here to Go: Planet R-101. Brion Gysin Interviewed by Terry Wilson*. San Francisco: Re/Search Publications.

Hale-Evans, Ron. 1994. "HELP! Preserve Enormous Interactive Fiction Collection!" Posted on <news://rec.arts.int- fiction>. Message-ID rwheCy5x48.LFI@netcom.com 24 October.

Hartman, Jed. 1993. "rec.puzzles Archive (logic), part 24 of 35." August 17. Available online at <http://www.cs.uu.nl/wais/html/na-dir/puzzles/archive/logic/part3. html>.

Hartman, Jed. 1998. "Lateral Thinking?" August 27. Available online at <http:// www.kith.org/logos/things/sitpuz/lateral.html>.

Hartman, Jed. 1999. "Situation Puzzles List." July 18. Available online at <http:// www.kith.org/logos/things/sitpuz/situations.html>.

Hasan-Rokem, Galit, and David Shulman. 1996. "Introduction," and "Afterword." In *Untying the Knot: On Riddles and Other Enigmatic Modes,* ed. Galit Hasan- Rokem and David Shulman, 3–9, 316–320. New York: Oxford University Press.

Haverson, Ira, and Tiffany Fulton-Pearson, eds. 1996. *"Is This the Way to Baker House?": A Compendium of MIT Hacking Lore.* Cambridge, MA: MIT Museum.

Herz, J. C. 1997. *Joystick Nation: How Videogames Gobbled Our Money, Won Our Hearts and Rewired Our Minds.* London: Abacus.

Hewison, Richard. 1992. "Level 9: Past Masters of the Adventure Game? A Personal Review of Level 9 by Richard Hewison." *Red Herring* 7. October. Available online at <http://www.waddington.fslife.co.uk/level9.htm>.

Howell, Gordon, and Jane Yellowlees Douglas. 1990. "The Evolution of Interactive Fiction." *Computer Assisted Language Learning* 2: 93–109.

Horn, Delton T. 1984. *Golden Flutes and Great Escapes: How to Write Adventure Games.* Beaverton, OR: Dilithium Press.

Infocom, Inc. 1984. "Frank Answers to the Ten Most Frequently Asked Questions." *The New Zork Times.* 3(2)(Spring): 1. Available online at <http://www.csd.uwo.ca/ Infocom/Articles/NZT/Nztspr84.html#frank>.

Infocom, Inc. 1985. "Zork Banned" and "A Mind Forever Voyaging Goes to the Library." *The New Zork Times* 4(4)(Fall): 1, 6. Available online at <http://www.csd. uwo.ca/Infocom/Articles/NZT/Nztfal85.html>.

Infocom, Inc. 1989. *Learning ZIL, or Everything You Always Wanted to Know About Writing Interactive Fiction But Couldn't Find Anyone Still Working Here to Ask.*

Internick, The. 1997. "Interactor's Nightmare." *Suck.* January 27. Available online at <http://www.suck.com/daily/97/01/27/>.

Ingold, Jon. 1999. "My Angel." [Essay on the making of *My Angel.*] Available online at <http://www.ingold.fsnet. co.uk/my_angel.htm>.

Jan, Paulo. 1996. "Greetings from Spain." Posted on <news://rec.arts.int-fiction>. Message-ID DMoJwL.1z0@news.zippo.com 12 February.

Jan, Paulo. 1996. "Greetings from Spain (part 2)." Posted on <news://rec.arts.int-fiction>. Message-ID 4klvke$7jl@comsrv.ddnet.es 12 April.

Jerz, Dennis G. 2000a. "What Is Interactive Fiction?" January 27. Available online at <http://jerz.setonhill.edu/if>.

Jerz, Dennis G. 2000b. Review of PICK UP AX. SPAG (Society for the Promotion of Adventure Games) #22. September 15. Available online at <http://jerz.setonhill.edu/if>.

Jerz, Dennis G. 2001a. "An Annotated Bibliography of Interactive Fiction Scholarship." September 3. Available online at <http://jerz.setonhill.edu/if>.

Jerz, Dennis G. 2001b. "Colossal Cave Adventure (c1975)." December 18. Available online at <http://jerz.setonhill.edu/if>.

Johnston, Moira, ed. 1997. The Walters Art Gallery: Guide to the Collections. Baltimore, MD: Walters Art Gallery.

Joyce, Michael. 1995. Of Two Minds: Hypertext Pedagogy and Poetics. Ann Arbor: University of Michigan Press.

Kantrowitz, Mark. 1990. "Natural Language Text Generation in the Oz Interactive Fiction Project." Technical Report CMU-CS-90-158, School of Computer Science, Carnegie Mellon University, Pittsburgh, PA, July. Available online at <http://www-2.cs.cmu.edu/afs/cs.cmu.edu/project/oz/web/papers/CMU-CS-90-158.ps>.

Katz, Arnie. 1996. Inside Electronic Game Design. Rocklin, CA: Prima Publishing.

Kelso, Margaret Thomas, Peter Weyhrauch, and Joseph Bates. 1992. "Dramatic Presence." Technical Report CMU-CS-92-195, School of Computer Science, Carnegie Mellon University, Pittsburgh, PA, December. Originally appeared in PRESENCE: The Journal *of Teleoperators and Virtual Environments* 2: 1. Available online at <http://www-2.cs. cmu.edu/afs/cs.cmu.edu/project/oz/web/papers/CMU-CS-92-195.ps>/li>.

Kidder, Tracy. 1981. *The Soul of a New Machine.* Boston: Little, Brown, and Company.

Kinzler, Steve, et al. 1989–2002. *The Internet Oracle.* Available online at <http:// cgi.cs.indiana.edu/~oracle/index.cgi>.

Knuth, Donald. 1998. "Adventure." [Notes about the Implemention in CWEB.] September. Available online at <http://www.literateprogramming.com/adventure .pdf>.

Kuntz, Rob. 1980. "Tolkien in Dungeons & Dragons." In *Best of the Dragon: From The Strategic Review and The Dragon Vols. I & II,* 24. Consists of material first published in 1975–1978. Lake Geneva, WI: TSR Hobbies, Inc.

Lafore, Robert. 2002. Interview. *Studio B.* Available online at <http://www. studiob.com/content.asp?cID=183>.

Laird, John. 1997. "John Laird's Computer Games Research: Haunt." Available online at <http://ai.eecs.umich.edu/people/laird/haunt.html>.

Laird, John. 1998. Untitled email. September 28. Excerpted online at <http://www. lysator.liu.se/adventure/Mainframe_adventures.html>.

Laird, John. 2001. "Haunt 2." August 23. Available online at <http://ai.eecs.umich .edu/people/laird/papers/Haunt2.html>.

Landow, George. 1992. *Hypertext: The Convergence of Contemporary Critical Theory and Technology.* Baltimore, MD: Johns Hopkins University Press.

Laurel, Brenda. 1986. Towards the Design of a Computer-based Interactive Fantasy System. Ph.D. diss., Ohio State University.

Laurel, Brenda. 1993. *Computers as Theatre.* Reading, MA: Addison-Wesley.

Lebling, P. David, Marc S. Blank, and Timothy A. Anderson. 1979. "Zork: A Computerized Fantasy Simulation Game." *IEEE Computer* 12(4)(April): 51–59. Available online at <http://www.csd.uwo.ca/~pete/Infocom/Articles/ieee.html>.

Lebling, P. David. 1980. "Zork and the Future of Computerized Fantasy Simulations." *Byte* (December), 172–182. Available online at <http://www.csd.uwo.ca/~pete/Infocom/Articles/byte.html>.

Lebling, P. David. 1988. "Is It GUE Tech or MIT? Dave Lebling Explains It . . ." *The Status Line* (Winter–Spring): 5.

Lebling, P. David. 1996. "Re: Infocom's language?" Posted on <news://rec.arts.int-fiction>. Message-ID 311f5ddc. 5930659@nova.avid.com 12 February.

Lebling, P. David. 1997. "Re: IF History Quiz [possibly off-topic]." Posted on <news://rec.arts.int-fiction> Message-ID 347314AE.426C@avid.com 19 November.

Lebling, P. David. 2002. Email to author. March 5.

Leibowitz, Brian. 1990. *The Journal of the Institute for Hacks, TomFoolery, and Pranks at MIT.* Cambridge: MIT Museum.

Leonard, Andrew. 1998. *Bots: Origin of a New Species.* New York: Penguin.

Lescure, Jean. 1986. "A Brief History of the Oulipo." In *Oulipo: A Primer of Potential Literature,* ed. and trans. Warren F. Motte Jr., 32–39. Lincoln: University of Nebraska Press. Reprinted in *The New Media Reader,* ed. Noah Wardrip-Fruin and Nick Montfort, 172–176. Cambridge, MA: The MIT Press, 2003.

Levy, Steven. 1984. *Hackers: Heroes of the Computer Revolution.* New York: Doubleday.

Lewis, Harry R., and Christos H. Papadimitriou. 1981. *Elements of the Theory of Computation.* Engelwood Cliffs, NJ: Prentice Hall.

Liddil, Bob. 1981. "Interactive Fiction: Six Micro Stories." *Byte* 6(9)(September): 436.

Loader, Jayne. 1989. "Wild America." In *Wild America: Stories.* New York: Grove Press. Available online at <www.publicshelter.com/wench/96/960307.html>.

Looney, Kristin. 1999. "The Space Under the Window." Available online at <http://www.wunderland.com/EBooks/Window/Window.html>.

Lopez, Steve. 1998. "The Silicon Schachmeister: Of Babbages and Kings." *Smart Chess Online.* March–April. Available online at <http://www.smartchess.com/SmartChessOnline/SmartChessOnline/MarApr98/silicon1.htm>.

Lucas, Dolores Dyer. 1969. *Emily Dickinson and Riddle.* DeKalb: Northern Illinois University Press.

Malmberg, David. 1994. "Softworks Announces 'em; the Seventh Annual Contest Winners." April 24. Available online at <ftp://ftp.ifarchive.org/ifarchive/programming/agt/contests/agt7.txt>.

Mangram, Lloyd. 1984. "Hobbit, HURG, and Holmes." *Crash ZX Spectrum* (April): 3. Available online at <http://www. mjwilson.demon.co.uk/crash/03/hobbit.htm>.

Marsh, Steven. 1999. Review of and resources for *Spellcasting 101: Sorcerers Get All the Girls.* Available online at <http://www.waitingforgo.com/legend/s101/>.

Masterson, Sean. 1986. "Four Minds Forever Voyaging." *ZZap!* 64 (May): Part I in 13, 42–44. (June), Part II in 14, 49–51. Available online at <http://www.ifarchive.org/if-archive/infocom/articles/zzap64.txt>.

Mateas, Michael, and Andre Stern. 2001. "Towards Building a Fully-Realized Interactive Drama." Digital Arts and Culture (DAC). April. Available online at <http://www.stg.brown.edu/conferences/DAC/subs_in/Mateas.html>.

Mathews, Harry, and Alastair Brotchie, eds. 1998. *Oulipo Compendium.* London: Atlas Press.

McComb, Gordon. 1990. *WordPerfect 5.1 Macros and Templates.* New York: Bantam Electronic Publishing. Available online at <http://gmccomb.com/wpdos/>.

McGath, Gary. 1984. *Compute!'s Guide to Adventure Games*. Greensboro, NC: Compute! Publications.

Meehan, James. 1980. *The Metanovel: Writing Stories by Computer*. New York: Garland Publishing.

Meier, Stefan, maintainer, and Hans Persson, creator. 2002. *Adventureland*. Founded 1997. Available online at <http://www.if-legends.org/~adventure/>.

Menick, Jim. 1984. *Basic Adventure and Strategy Game Design for the Apple*. New York: Facts on File.

Meretzky, Steven. 2002. Email to author. March 15.

Montfort, Nick. 1995. Interfacing with Computer Narratives: Literary Possibilities for Interactive Fiction. B.A. thesis, University of Texas at Austin. Available online at <http://nickm.com/writing/bathesis/>.

Montfort, Nick. 2000. "Computer Co-Authors for Fiction." Presentation at Computers and Writing, Fort Worth, TX, May 27. Available online at <http://nickm.com/writing/cw2k.txt>.

Montfort, Nick. 2000–2001. "Cybertext Killed the Hypertext Star." *ebr (Electronic Book Review)* 11 (Winter). Available online at <http://www.electronicbookreview.com/ebr11/11mon/index.html>.

Montfort, Nick. 2002a. "How *Zork* Advanced the State of Interactive Fiction's Literary Art." *Text Technology* 11(2)(Winter): 1–17.

Montfort, Nick. 2002b. "Toward a Theory of Interactive Fiction." Version 3. December 29. Available online at <http://nickm.com/if/toward.html>. Final version to appear in *IF Theory*, ed. Emily Short. St. Charles, IL: The Interactive Fiction Library, 2004.

Montfort, Nick. 2003. "Interactive Fiction as 'Story,' 'Game,' 'Storygame,' 'Novel,' 'World,' 'Literature,' 'Puzzle,' 'Problem,' 'Riddle,' and 'Machine.'" In *First Person: New Media as Story, Game, and Performance*. Cambridge, MA: The MIT Press.

Montfort, Nick, and Stuart Moulthrop. 2003. "Face It, Tiger, You Just Hit the Jackpot: Reading and Playing Cadre's *Varicella.*" Paper at Digital Arts and Culture, May 19-24, Melbourne, Australia.

Moriarty, Brian. 1987. "Infocom Online." Transcript of a discussion on a Delphi conference. Available online at <http://www.ifarchive.org/if-archive/infocom/misc/moriarty-online.txt>.

Motte, Warren F. Jr., ed. and trans. 1997. *Oulipo: A Primer of Potential Literature.* 2d ed. Normal, IL: Dalkey Archive Press.

Moulthrop, Stuart. 1991. *Victory Garden.* Watertown, MA: Eastgate Systems.

Moulthrop, Stuart, and Nancy Kaplan. 1991. "Something to Imagine: Literature, Composition, and Interactive Fiction." *Computers and Composition* 9(1): 7–23. Available online at <http://www.cwrl.utexas.edu/~ccjrnl/Archives/v9/9_1_html/9_1_1_Moulthrop.html>.

Moulthrop, Stuart. 1999. "Misadventure: Future Fiction and The New Networks." *Style* 33(2): 184–203. Available online at <http://iat.ubalt.edu/moulthrop/essays/misadventure/>.

Muckenhoupt, Carl. 2002. *Baf's Guide to the Interactive Fiction Archive.* Founded 2000. Available online at <http://www.wurb.com/if/index>.

Murray, Janet. 1995. "The Pedagogy of Cyberfiction: Teaching a Course on Reading and Writing Interactive Narrative." In *Contextual Media: Multimedia and Interpretation,* ed. Edward Barrett and Marie Redmond, 129–162. Cambridge, MA: The MIT Press.

Murray, Janet. 1997. *Hamlet on the Holodeck: The Future of Narrative in Cyberspace.* New York: Free Press.

Murray, Matthew. 1997. "Re: Best Original Infocom Games?" Posted on <news://rec.games.int-fiction> Message-ID Pine.ULT.3.91.970308211625.29045A-100000 @statler. cc.wwu.edu 8 March.

Murray, Matthew. 2001. "Review of *A Mind Forever Voyaging.*" Available online at <http://www.matthewmurray.net/Reviews/ComputerGames/AMFV.html>.

Nelson, Graham. 1993. "A Bill of Player's Rights." Reprinted in "The Craft of Adventure." Posted on <news://rec.arts.int-fiction> Message-ID 1993May18.223852 .18303@infodev.cam.ac.uk 18 May.

Nelson, Graham. 1995a. "The Craft of Adventure: Five Articles on the Design of Adventure Games." January 19. Available online at <http://www.if-archive.org/if-archive/programming/general-discussion/Craft.Of.Adventure.txt>.

Nelson, Graham. 1995b. Interviewed by Eileen Mullin. *XYZZYnews* 1. January/ February. Available online at <http://www.xyzzynews.com/xyzzy.1c.html>.

Nelson, Graham. 1999a. "Re: [ANNOUNCE] Lost Adventures of Topologika" Posted on <news://rec.games.int-fiction>. Message-ID ant180053868M+4%@ gnelson.demon.co.uk 18 July.

Nelson, Graham. 1999b. "Announcement: Three Lost Games Restored: Fyleet, Crobe, Sangraal." August 24. Available online at <http://www.ifarchive.org/if-archive/phoenix/info/Phoenix-games.txt>.

Nelson, Graham. 2001a. "Dr. G.A. Nelson." January 3. Available online at <http://sag.maths.ox.ac.uk/st-annes/people_NG.htm>.

Nelson, Graham. 2001b. *The Inform Designer's Manual.* 4th ed. (1st print ed.) St. Charles, IL: The Interactive Fiction Library. Available online at <http://www.gnelson .demon.co.uk/inform/DM4.pdf>.

Nelson, Graham. 2002. Email to author. June 7.

Nelson, Theodor H. 1981. *Literary Machines.* Sausalito, CA: Mindful Press.

Niesz, Anthony and Norman Holland. 1984. "Interactive Fiction." *Critical Inquiry* 11: 110–129.

Noll, Landon Curt, Simon Cooper, Peter Seebach, and Leonid A. Broukhis. 2002. *The International Obfuscated C Code Contest.* Available online at <http://gmccomb.com/wpdos/>.

Novak, Marcos. 1991. "Liquid Architectures in Cyberspace." In *Cyberspace, First Steps,* ed. Michael Benedikt, 225– 254. Cambridge, MA: The MIT Press.

Oberg, Jonas. *Tixo.org.* 2001. Available online at <http://tixo.org>.

O'Brian, Paul. 1993. "Interactive Fiction and Reader Response Criticism." Paper for Literary Theory, a graduate class at the University of Colorado at Boulder. Available online at <http://ucsu.colorado. edu/~obrian/ifrrc.txt>.

Ohl, Raymond Theodore, ed. and trans. 1928. The Enigmas of Symphosius. Ph.D. thesis, University of Pennsylvania.

Olsson, Magnus. 1997. "What Is a Meta-Command?" Posted on <news://rec.arts .int-fiction>. Message-ID 5g6fqg$5t5@bartlet.df.lth.se 12 March.

Pagis, Dan. 1996. "Toward a Theory of the Literary Riddle." In *Untying the Knot: On Riddles and Other Enigmatic Modes,* ed. Galit Hasan-Rokem and David Shulman, 81–108. New York: Oxford University Press.

Parke, Herbert William. 1939. *A History of the Delphic Oracle.* Oxford: Basil Blackwell.

Pepicello, W. J., and Thomas A. Green. 1984. *The Language of Riddles: New Perspectives.* Columbus: Ohio State University Press.

Perera Domínguez, Manuel. 1997. "Ingenieros ilustres: Leonardo Torres Quevedo." April. Available online at <http://www.cs.us.es/~perer/publicac/ltq/leonardo.html>.

Persson, Hans. 1994. "Adventure Game Creators." May 10. Available online at <http://www.ifarchive.org/if-archive/info/adventure-game-systems>.

Peterson, Dale. 1983. *Genesis II: Creation and Recreation with Computers.* Reston, VA: Reston Publishing Co.

Pinsky, Robert. 1984. *History of My Heart.* New York: Ecco Press.

Pinsky, Robert. "The Poetics of *Zork*." 1995. *The New York Times Book Review,* March 19, 3+.

Pinsky, Robert. 1996. "Nerds, Technocrats, and Enlightened Spirits." *DoubleTake* 2(4)(Fall): 41–46.

Pinsky, Robert. 1997. "Computers and Poetics." MIT Media Lab Colloquium speech. Available online at <http://nickm.com/vox /computers_poetics.html>. February 5.

Pinsky, Robert. 2001. Conversation with author. June 5. Cambridge, MA.

Pinsky, Robert. 2002. Email to author. April 2.

Plotkin, Andrew. 2001. "Interactive Fiction." May 25. Available online at <http:// www.eblong.com/zarf/if.html>.

Powers, Richard. 2001. *Plowing the Dark.* New York: Picador USA.

Prince, Gerald. 1980. "Aspects of a Grammar of Narrative." *Poetics Today* 1(3): 49–63.

Prince, Gerald. 1987. *A Dictionary of Narratology.* Lincoln: University of Nebraska Press.

Randall, Neil. 1988. "Determining Literariness in Interactive Fiction." *Computers and the Humanities* 22: 183–191.

Randell, Brian. 1982. "From Analytical Engine to Electronic Digital Computer: The Contributions of Ludgate, Torres, and Bush." *IEEE Annals of the History of Computing* 4(4)(October): 327–341.

Raphael, B. 1968. "SIR: A Computer Program for Semantic Information Retrieval." In *Semantic Information Processing,* ed. Marvin Minsky, 33–134. Cambridge, MA: The MIT Press.

Rees, Gareth. 1993. "Planetfall Criticism (★spoilers★)." Posted on <news://rec.arts .int-fiction>. Message-ID 1993May7.173439.23535@infodev.cam.ac.uk 7 May.

Rees, Gareth. 1995. "About 'Christminster' . . ." Posted on <news://rec.arts.int-fiction>. Message-ID GDR11.95Aug8160614@stint.cl.cam.ac.uk 8 August.

Rees, Gareth. 2001. "Christminster." Part of www.garethrees.org. December 15. Available online at <http://www.garethrees.org/1995/08/08/christminster/>.

Rees, Gareth. 2002. Email to author. May 30.

Rigby, Paul. 1991. "From here to Trinity . . . and Back Again." *Adventure Probe* 5(5)(May): 15–19. Available online at <http://www.csd.uwo.ca/Infocom/Articles/moriarty.html>.

Robie, Joan Hake. 1991. *The Truth about Dungeons and Dragons.* Starburst Publishers: Lancaster, PA. November.

Rothstein, Edward. 1983. "Reading and Writing: Participatory Novels." *The New York Times Book Review.* May 8. Available online at <http://www.csd.uwo.ca/Infocom/Articles/nyt83.html>.

Rothstein, Edward. 1998. "In a Text Game, No Object Is Superfluous." *The New York Times,* April 6.

Russotto, Matthew T. 2000. "[REVIEW] Acheton." Posted on <news://rec .games.int-fiction>. Message-ID QkWu5.73$Uc.4450@monger.newsread.com 11 September.

Samuel, Arthur L. 1963. "Some Studies in Machine Learning Using the Game of Checkers." In *Computers and Thought,* ed. Edward A. Feigenbaum and Julian Feldman, 71–105. New York: McGraw-Hill.

Scientific American Supplement. 1915. "Torres and His Remarkable Automatic Devices." *Scientific American Supplement* 80(2079)(November): 296–298.

Schevill, Rudolph. 1911. "Some Forms of the Riddle Question and the Exercise of the Wits in Popular Fiction and Formal Literature." *University of California Publications in Modern Philology* 2(3)(November): 183–237.

Schmidt, Miron, and Manuel Schulz. 1999. "The Level 9 Fact Sheet." Available online at <http://www.if-legends.org/~l9memorial/html/l9facts.html>.

Shanken, Edward A. 1998. "The House That Jack Built: Jack Burnham's Concept of "Software" as a Metaphor for Art." *Leonardo Electronic Almanac* 6(November): 10. Available online at <http://www.duke.edu/~giftwrap/House.html>.

Shannon, Claude. 1950. "Programming a Computer for Playing Chess." *Philosophical Magazine* 41: 256–275.

Sherwin, Robb. 1999. Reviews of *Zork* and *The Knight Orc*. *Reviews from Trotting Krips.* August. Available online at <http://host4u.upws.net/bryanb/>.

Short, Emily. 2001. "What's IF?" November 29. Available online at <http://emshort .home.mindspring.com/whatsif.html>.

Short, Emily, ed. 2004. *IF Theory.* St. Charles, IL: The Interactive Fiction Library.

Sloane, Sarah. 2000. *Digital Fictions: Storytelling in a Material World.* Westport, CT: Albex Publishing.

Smith, Jennifer, and Andrew Cowan. 1999. "Frequently Asked Questions: Basic Information about MUDs and MUDding." Part 1 of 4. Available online at <http:// www.mudconnect.com/mudfaq/mudfaq-p1.html>.

Snyder, Ilana. 1996. *Hypertext: The Electronic Labyrinth.* Melbourne: Melbourne University Press.

Solomon, Eric. 1984. *Games Programming.* Cambridge: Cambridge University Press.

Spencer, Donald D. 1968. *Game Playing with Computers.* New York: Spartan Books.

Stevens, Duncan. 1997. Review of *Zork I*. *SPAG (Society for the Promotion of Adventure Games)* #12. December 13. Available online at <http://www.sparkynet.com/spag/backissues/SPAG12>.

Stevens, Duncan. 1998. Reviews of *Beyond Zork* and *Zork Zero*. *SPAG (Society for the Promotion of Adventure Games)* #14. May 17. Available online at <http://www.sparkynet.com/spag/backissues/SPAG14>.

Stevens, Chuck. 1999. "Re: Amusing Source Code Comments (again)." Posted on <news://alt.folklore.computers>. Message-ID 7vskjhgev1@mail.pl.unisys.com 4 November.

Strand, Mark. 1985. "The President's Resignation." In *Mr. and Mrs. Baby and Other Stories*, 31–35. New York: Knopf.

Suplee, Curt. 1983. "Through the Zorking Glass." *The Washington Post*, December 22, C1. Available online at <http://www.ifarchive.org/if-archive/infocom/articles/Post83-text>.

Swenson, May. 1966. *Poems to Solve*. New York: Charles Scribner's Sons.

Swift, Jonathan. 2002. *Travels into Several Remote Nations of the World*. [*Gulliver's Travels*.] Hypertext edition by Lee Jaffe, May 15. Based on Motte ed., 1726, with corrections from Faulkner ed., 1735. Available online at <http://www.jaffebros.com/lee/gulliver/contents.html>.

Taylor, Archer. 1948. *The Literary Riddle Before 1600*. Berkeley: University of California Press.

Tottel, Richard, publisher. 1995. *Songes and Sonettes eritten by the ryght honorable Lorde Henry Haward late Earle of Surrey, and other*. [*Tottel's Miscellany*.] Electronic Text Center, University of Virginia Library. 1557. Electronic version ed. Raymond G. Siemens, Available online at <http://etext.lib.virginia.edu/toc/modeng/public/TotMisc.html>.

Tupper, Frederick, ed. 1910. *The Riddles of the Exeter Book*. New York: Ginn.

Turco, Louis. 1986. *The New Books of Forms: A Handbook of Poetics.* Expanded ed. Hanover, NH: New England University Press.

Turing, Alan. 1950. "Computing Machinery and Intelligence." *Mind: A Quarterly Review of Psychology and Philosophy.* 59(236): 433–460. October. Reprinted in *The New Media Reader,* ed. Noah Wardrip-Fruin and Nick Montfort, 49–64. Cambridge, MA: The MIT Press, 2003.

Turner, William. 1999. "Raymond Lully (Ramon Lull)." *The Catholic Encyclopedia,* Vol. XII. Robert Appleton Company, 1911. Online edition Kevin Knight. Available online at <http://www.newadvent.org/cathen/12670c.htm>

Tyler, Jenny, and Les Howarth. 1983. *Write Your Own Adventure Programs for Your Microcomputer.* London: Usborne Publishing.

Tzara, Tristan. 1951. "Dadaism" from "Dada Manifesto" (1918) and "Lecture on Dada" (1922), trans. Robert Motherwell. In *Dada Painters and Poets,* Robert Motherwell, 78–79, 81, 246–51. New York: George Wittenborn. Available online at <http://www.english. upenn.edu/~jenglish/English104/tzara.html>.

Vile, Richard C. 1984. *Programming Your Own Adventure Games in Pascal.* Blue Ridge Summit, PA: Tab Books.

Wehlau, Ruth. 1997. *The Riddle of Creation: Metaphor Structures in Old English Poetry.* Studies in the Humanities 14. New York: Peter Lang Publishing.

Weiss, Eric A. 1985. "Johnathan Swift's Computing Invention." *Annals of the History of Computing* 7(2)(April): 164–165.

Weizenbaum, Joseph. 1966. "ELIZA—A Computer Program for the Study of Natural Language Communication between Man and Machine." *Communications of the ACM* 9(1) (January): 36–45.

Weizenbaum, Joseph. 1967. "Contextual Understanding by Computers." *Communications of the ACM* 10(8): 474–480. August.

Weizenbaum, Joseph. 1976. *Computer Power and Human Reason: From Judgement to Calculation*. San Francisco: W. H. Freeman and Company.

Welch, Mark. 1997. "The Adventure Game Toolkit (AGT)." May. Available online at <http://www.markwelch.com/agt.htm>.

Weldon, John, and James Bjornstad. 1984. *Playing with Fire*. Chicago: Moody Bible Institute.

Welsh, Andrew. 1978. *Roots of Lyric: Primative Poetry and Modern Poetics*. Princeton, NJ: Princeton University Press.

Wichman, Glenn R. 1997. "A Brief History of 'Rogue.'" Available online at <http://www.wichman.org/roguehistory.html>.

Wilbur, Richard. 1989. "The Persistence of Riddles." *The Yale Review* 78(3): 333–351.

Wilhelm, Richard. 1950. "Introduction." *The I Ching or Book of Changes*. Translator to German, Richard Wilhelm. Translator to English, Cary F. Baynes. Foreword by C. G. Jung. Bollingen Series 19. Pantheon Books: New York.

Wille, Niels Erik. 1999. "The Date of Creation of the First Text Adventure (An Exercise in Source Criticsm)." August. Available online at <http://www.komm.ruc.dk/Personale/new/tekster/adventure.pdf>.

Williams, Thomas G. 1972. "Some Studies in Game Playing with a Digital Computer." Chapter 3 in *Representation and Meaning: Experiments with Information Processing Systems*, ed. Herbert A. Simon and Laurent Siklossy. Englewood Cliffs, NJ: Prentice Hall.

Wilson, Gerry Kevin. 1995. "Re: Inform Competition." Posted on <news://rec.arts.int-fiction>. Message-ID 427d7s$puv@agate.berkeley.edu 18 May.

Winalski, Paul. 1997. "Re: IF history quiz [possibly off- topic]." Posted on <news://rec.arts.int-fiction>. Message-ID 34737C11.A9595E9F@lspace.zko.dec.com 19 November.

Winograd, Terry. 1972. *Understanding Natural Language*. New York: Academic Press.

Winograd, Terry. 1999. "SHRDLU." Available online at <http://hci.stanford.edu/ ~winograd/shrdlu/index.html>.

Wolosenko, Ihor. 1983. "Hanging Ten on the Software Wave." Interviewed by Robert Dewitt. *Antic* 2(1):21. April. Available online at <http://www.atarimagazines.com/ v2n1/interview.html>.

Woods, Don. 2002. Email to author. March 13.

INDEX